SOCIAL HISTORY OF NEPAL

SOCIAL HISTORY OF NEPAL

By

Tulasi Ram Vaidya • Tri Ratna Manandhar
Shankar Lal Joshi

ANMOL PUBLICATIONS PVT. LTD.
NEW DELHI - 110 002 (INDIA)

ANMOL PUBLICATIONS PVT. LTD.
4374/4B, Ansari Road, Daryaganj
New Delhi - 110 002

Social History of Nepal

First Edition, 1993
Reprint 2001
ISBN 81-7041-799-6

PRINTED IN INDIA

Published by J.L. Kumar for Anmol Publications Pvt. Ltd., New Delhi - 110 002 and Printed at Mehra Offset Press, Delhi.

Preface

The present work is the revised version of a project report submitted to the Research Division, Tribhuvan University in 1986. In this book we have tried to analyse the main issues pertaining to Social History of Nepal from earliest times to the 1950 movement, with necessary cross references of the post revolutionary period.

The report is divided into ten chapters, dealing with the different aspects of Nepali social history. The first chapter analyses the socio-anthropological aspects of the Nepali people in historical perspective; and the second chapter presents the changing structure of the Nepali society. Family system is the subject of third chapter, and the fourth chapter gives a vivid picture of habitational sites of Nepal, specially during the ancient and medieval periods. Position of women and the Nepali food habits have been discussed in the fifth and sixth chapters respectively. In the seventh chapter, dress and ornaments of the Nepali people (from royal family to poor peasants) have been analysed in historical perspective. Eighth chapter gives a descriptive account of the social entertainments enjoyed by the Nepali people throughout the pages of history. Nineth chapter deals with the types of the education of Nepal through ages. In the last chapter, we have tried to analyse the changing trend of Nepali society in its historical perspective.

This book is mainly based on documentary sources—published and unpublished. The unpublished documents have been obtained from different archival offices of India and Nepal; and for the published sources we have depended on the writings of contemporary scholars and a few valuable edited works of Nepali scholars. We have suppressed the foot notes and bibliographical accounts, keeping in view the length of the book.

We have received help and co-operation from many persons in completing the book, and it is not possible to mention them all. We are thankful to Dr. Madhav Raj Pande and Sri Dhana Bajra Bajracharya, for their valuable comments and suggestions, and Sri Santa Bahadur Gurung the then Chief, Research Division, T.U. for giving us an opportunity to undertake this research project.

The shortcomings of this book are wholly ours, and we invite healthy criticism and comments to make the work more comprehensive.

Tulasi Ram Vaidya
Tri Ratna Manandhar
Shankar Lal Joshi

Contents

1

People

Introduction

Nepal, although a small country situated between two big powers like China and India, has its own type of social life. There are various ethnic communities with their own cultural background. While studying a particular community one has to believe that each one is entirely different from another. But the pragmatic and mature policy of the rulers of Nepal has made the communities as the members of the same family. We have never seen or experienced any bitter communal clashes or conflicts in Nepal. All the communities have realised that they comprised one nationality *i.e.* the Nepalese nationality. The uniformity in diversity is the basic feature of the Nepalese nationality. Although many of them had been the migrants to Nepal in the days yore, they have ignored their past and have settled here with full loyalty to the country. They have contributed in forming a united Nepalese society with the undithuring feeling of oneness, the result of which due to lapse of time is the composition of the very rich Nepalese socio-cultural heritage in the history of the world.

The present day picture of the Nepalese society comprises many groups. The data gives us the idea of the position of various groups of communities in Nepal. As a student of history we have to trace the origin and development of various groups, only then we can get the exact picture of our cultural heritage. Moreover it will be apt to describe the picture of various groups of the people at various times. It will not be improper here to trace the history of the various groups of people who dwelt in Nepal at different times.

In ancient time the Nepalese society comprised many groups of people some of which are unknown now. The history of Nepal, based on epigraphy, begins only from the 3rd century B.C. and that of Kathmandu from 5th century A.D., whereas the history of Nepal prior to that period is based on the *Vamsavalis*, compiled later on, the literacy accounts like *Mahabharat*, some other Buddhist texts like *Mulasarvastivad Vinaya Sangraha*, compiled by Tinamitra and translated by Itsing in 700 A.D., and many other works like foreigners' (Fahien and Hiuen Tsang) accounts, Indian epigraphic evidences and so on. These various sources give us some hints relating to the various groups of people inhabited in Nepal prior to the historic period.

Gopalas

Gopala was a community which had come to reside in Nepal during the proto-historic period. The paucity of sources comes in the way while dealing with the question how, from where and when did they come to Nepal. According to the *Gopal Vamsavali* (the oldest chronicle of Nepal) a group of cow-herds named *Nepa* was the first group of persons who settled over the Kathmandu Valley. According to another chronicle, the valley was a big lake long days yore. The traditional legend mentions that the water of the dammed lake was let out by Lord Krishna. Another belief was that it was Manjusri who made a gorge to let out the water. It is still shrouded in mystery as to who let the water out. Might be the very changing geological movement of the area or the hydrolic pressure made a way to let the water flow out. Thus the Chobhar gorge was made, and the valley remained swampy area for some period; and later on when it got dried up, many natural vegetations started growing up and it became quite habitable with favourable climate.

At such a time, a group of migratory people along with the cattle who were travelling for food entered the Kathmandu Valley. In the pre or prôto-historic period groups of people with their cattle used to migrate from country to country in search of food and favourable climate. A group of persons named *Nepa* might be one of such migratory people, who entered the valley. When they found the valley rich in green vegetation for cattle, quite suitable for settlement with fertile land and favourable climate they settled over here. As the first settlers over here were the *Nepas*, the name of the area where they settled was called Nepal. Were those Gopalas a group of Dravidans, driven away by the victorous nomadic Aryans tribe ? On the basis of their worshipping the phallus, it can be surmised that they were those Dravidans who were compelled to flee away after being vanquished by the Aryans in ancient India. Thus the first group of the people who settled over the Kathmandu Valley were the *Nepas*. Since they were the cow-herds, the later *Vamsavalis* called them Gopala (cowherds). They seemed to have settled in the Kathmandu Valley in circa 19th or 18th century B.C.

Mahispalas

The next group of the people, according to the *vamsavalis*, to have come to settle in the valley after defeating the Gopalas was the Abhiras or Mahispalas (buffalo-herds). The Mahispalas were in power for about two hundred years. They were also defeated by another group of the people called Kiratas, who must have come from north. The Kiratas might have come to Nepal in about 15th or 14th century B.C. They belonged to non-Hindu community about whom there are references in ancient Hindu texts like *Mahabharat*, *Manusmriti*, *Arthashastra*, etc.

When we think of the Gopalas and Mahispalas they seemed to be the earlier inhabitants of the Kathmandu Valley. No epigraphic evidences of these groups are available so far. Further archaeological activities might reveal some authentic evidences about them; but the presence of some of the cow-herds of Kirtipur, Kilagal and other areas are guessed to have been the descendants of those Gopalas and Mahispalas of those days. K P. Malla opines that the term "Nepalebhya" mentioned in an inscription belonging to Amsuvarma a powerful ruler of ancient Nepal) denoted to those Gapalas of the ancient time. In the absence of the authentic archacological evidences nothing can be said in certainity. However the habitation of some cowherds following their traditional occupation and the mention of the Gopalas and Mahispalas in the *Vamsavalis* make us believe that they were the autochthonous people of Nepal.

Nagas

Nagas can be taken as one of the groups who inhabited in Nepal in those days. Many ancient holy texts have described the Naga community as the snakes or serpants. Ajatasaturu, the king of Magadha and contemporary to Lord Buddha, also belonged to the Naga community. Huien Tsang's account mentions that when Emperor Ashok was about to open the Ramagrama chaitya, situated at Nawalaparasi district of Nepal, a Naga implored the king not to do that. The Chinese pilgrim, here, has described the Naga as a snake. But it is quite probable the Naga referred to by Huien Tsang was no other than a Naga chief or a chief of the area belonging to the Naga community. It seems that after the conquest of the area by Ajatasatru, the people of the Naga tribe might have come to settle over there. Later on when Emperor Ashok tried to open the stupa, those every Nagas might have requested him not to do so in order to maintain its sanctity. In the Kathmandu Valley also there seems to have been the people of Naga tribe, as the story of a farmer and a Naga reveals. In those days the Naga tribe was one of the active tribes in the

Indian subcontinent. Due to the lapse of time the community disappeared. Most probably it was compelled to be merged with some other powerful tribes and was reduced to a lower social status by the victorious tribe, as such incidents occurred very often in history. Many communities which had played very active and important role disappeared in the pages of history.

Kiratas

Prior to historic period of the Kathmandu Valley, the Kiratas had been very active in Nepal Wright's *vamsavali* mentions the Kiratas contemporary to Lord Buddha and Emperor Ashok *Gopal Vamsavali* mentions them as the imme-diate predecessors of the Lichchhavi rulers in Nepal. Here it is ascertained that the Kiratas had ruled Nepal from about fifteenth or fourteenth century B C. to sixth century or fifth century B.C. According to *Gopal Vamsavali* thirty two Kirata kings had ruled over Napal. The long rule of the Kiratas prove that they had been in a large number, strong enough and well organised. The Kiratas had well organised social life, administrative system and economy, as a result of which the Lichchhavis, their successors, had given due importance to their legacy. The Kiratas seemed to have been in existence in various habitational sites not only in the Kathmandu Valley but also outside the valley during the Lichchhavi rule in Nepal.

Kiratus can be taken as the inhabitants of Nepal not only during proto-historic period in Nepal but also cf the historic period. *Gopal Vamsavali* mentions that they were vanquished by the solar race Lichchhavis. Moreover almost all the names of places, rivers, hillocks, canals and four offices of importance of the Lichchhavis were in non-Sanskrit dialect – prerumably the Kirata language. Thus, although the scribe of the *Gopal Vamsavali* mentioned that the Kiratas existed in the Kosi region later on, they lived in the Kathmandu Valley also. Most probably when the war broke out between the Lichchhavies and Kiratas, the ruling Kiratas fled away to the Kosi region whereas the commoners remain unaffected and continued to reside in the valley. A Lichchhavi inscription mentions the employment of a person named Kedumbata who was no other than a Kirat. Another inscription, contemporary to Amsuvarma, also mentions the existence of the Kirat.

Koliyas

Another community which existed first in the western-Tarai and later on in the Kathmandu Valley was the Koliyas. The Koliyas and the Sakyas had ruled in Koligam (or Ramagrama) and Kapilavastu respectively during the days of Lord Buddha. Both of them had familial relations. Lord Buddha's mother Mahamaya and wife Yasodhara were princesses of Koliya ruling family. The Koliyas had taken a share of the ashes of Lord Buddha and built a stupa in his commemoration. But, later on, with the rise of the Magadha there was the fall of various weaker states in the adjoining areas. Koligrama was one of them. Thus being defeated, the Koliyas fled to the safe place *i.e.* Kathmandu Valley for shelter. The presence of the Koliyas it proved by the existence of Koliyagrama and Dakshina Koligrama in the Kathmandu Valley during the Lichchhavi period.

These Koliyas seemed to have resided in two sites of the Kathmandu town. The present Ranipokhari area, Ason, Indrachok constituted Koliya grama and the area in the south of Hanumandhoka was Dakshinakoliyagrama. These Koliyas had played active role in the Kathmandu Valley during the Lichchhavi rule.

Mallas

Mallas constituted another strong community in the then Nepal. While referring to the ancient Indian history the Mallas had small republican principalities at Pava and Kushinara. Buddhist texts mention them along with the Sakyas and Koliyas as active communities with elected kingship. Lord Buddha had expired at Kusinara (Kushinagar), the Malla principality. The Mallas had their fall with rise of Magadha. Having been vanquished by Magadha after the death of Lord Buddha, the Mallas fled to the interior part of Nepal on the other side of river Kali Gandaki. They must have established a small but strong principality called Mallapuri in a safe place of Nepal. Here also they could not remain independent for a long time, as the Lichchhavis of Nepal had made them their vassal. Manadev I had suppressed them after a strong fight and reduced them to a vassal state. Inspite of defeat, the Mallas seemed to have maintained their militant spirit for a long time. That is why the Mallas, mentioned in 464 A.D., could become the rulers of Nepal from 1200 A.D. to 1769 A.D. During the early medieval period also the Mallas were referred at time as the feudatories.

Vajjis

Vajjis constituted another group of the people during the Lichchhavi period. King Narendradev's inscription mentions the existence of the Vajjis in the Kathmandu Valley. The Vajjis constituted one of the republican states during the sixth century B.C. According to Rhys Davids, they were one of the eight confederated class among whom the Lichchhavis and Videhas were the most important. After the rise of Magadh all these clans were vanquished which led to their disperse. As other groups, some of the Vajjis had also entered the Kathmandu Valley for shelter. It seems that their number was quite low, so there is only an isolated mention of them in the Lichchhavi inscriptions.

Lichchhavis

The Lichchhavis occupied the most prominent position during the ancient period in Nepal. The constituted the ruling class in the then Nepalese society. They had also come to Nepal for shelter after being vanquished by Magadh. They had ruled over Vaishali during the life time of Lord Buddha. According to *Manusmriti* they were the Vratya Kshetriya *i.e.*

those Kshetriyas who did not observe the rules prescribed by the Hindu Holy texts. It is mentioned in the Buddhist text that Ajatasatru, the King of Magadh, had tried his best to conquer the Lichchhavi confederacy many times but in vain. At last during the last days of Lord Buddha, Ajatasatru defeated them in a decietful way. After that they must have come in a big group and conquered the auchtothonous ruling people the Kiratas and ruled over Nepal. According to *Gopala Vamsavali*, the first Lichchhavi ruler of Nepal was Supuspa. The Lichchhavi inscription also mentions him as the first ruler of Nepal. But most of the historians of Nepal refer Jayadev I as the founder of the dynasty in the circa first century A.D. But it is more reliable to believe that the Lichchhavis under Supuspa had come to Nepal immediataly after being defeated by Ajatasatru.

Guptas

Another group of people referred by the contemporary Nepalese inscriptions was the Abhir Guptas, who had played very active role during the period. Some of them had become the *defacto* rulers. To think of the active role they played and the position they occupied, it can be guessed that they must have been very influential from the time they came to Nepal. The epigraphic evidences of India mention Samudra Gupta as the *Lichchhavi dohitra* (son of a Lichchhavi princess) because Samudra Gupta's mother was a Lichchhavi princess, possibly a princess of Nepal. Because of the matrimonial alliance, the Guptas might have occupied the influential status in Nepal. Most probably after the fall of the Gupta during the reign of Buddha Gupta in India, some of the Guptas might have come to Nepal. Because of their high position and experiences in India they occupied very significant position in Nepal also.

Sakyas

Sakyas are referred in some of the old texts. They had resided at Kapilvastu (the present Kapilavastu district).

Gautam Buddha was a Sakya prince. According to the Buddhist text Biruddhaka, the Kosala king, had invaded Kapilvastu and slaughtered a large member of the Sakyas to average them the humiliation he had to face from the Sakyas. Being scared by the Kosalan atrocities, a group of the Sakyas fled from Kapilvastu and took shelter in the Kathmandu Valley. According to the *Mulasa rvastivada Vinaya*, Ananda, a disciple of Lord Buddha, had come to meet his and Lord Buddha's relatives at Kathmandu. The Sakyas were very strict in maintaining the purity of their blood. That very event had led to the invasion of Bruddhaka over them. They seem to have been very conserva tive in keeping themselves pure. That is reason why the Sakyas still exist as a community whereas the other communities disappeared as they were mingled together to form a new community in Nepal forgetting their past.

These were some of the communities which resided in the Kathmandu Valley during the ancient period. Outside the Kathmandu Valley also there were people of various communities. The Changu inscription mentions the invasion of Manadev I to the east and the west, which means that those areas were also well inhabited. Similarly *Gopal Vamsavali* mentions the habitation of the Kiratas in the eastern Nepal. Up to the present time, the Kiratas are the main population there. Moreover the documents of modern period also refer to the Kiratas as the major population of the area. Thus it is historically well proved that the Kiratas had been the main population in the eastern Nepal right from their defeat by the Lichchhavis. Hamilton wrote that the Khas and Kiratas were taken as impure infidels.

In the western Nepal, the Lichchhavi had expanded their kingdom to a very far off area. The availability of the two Lichchhavi inscriptions at Gorkha and the terra-cotta Lichchhavi chaitya seals in Jumla also give a solid proof of the habitation of the people in the areas. Manadev's Changu inscription stands as a solid evidence of the Malla's habitation in the other side of river Kali Gandaki. The accounts of

Fahien and Huien Tsang also refer to the habitation in Lumbini and Kapilavastu, although they were in the desolate condition. Both the Chinese travellers do not clearly mention as to who were inhabiting the area. They might be the descendants of those very Shakyas and others who could not or did not run away from the area as the others did. Both the travellers have mentioned the existence of the monks in the area.

The other hilly regions also must have been inhabited. But due to the want of evidence nothing can be said in certainity. There might have been very thin population in those areas. The northern hilly area must have been occupied by the emigres of the North *i.e.* Tibet and China. In those days aggressive rulers like Atilla (?– 453 A.D.) had been marching with their huge army for the conquest of the vast area. Such events led to the fleeing of many people to escape the atrocities committed by those fierce warriors. Sometimes different communities had migrated to the various new region for their better future, like the Kushans. Among those migrated communities those which were well organised and superior in skill of warfare could become the rulers in the new regions like the Kushans in India, but the others who came just as fugitives and weak in organisation resided in the new area just as ordinary refugees. Such refugees had resided at different hilly regions of Nepal. Further research and exploratory works will reveal this pertinent question.

The far western region *i.e.* Karnali basin area was also inhabited most probably by those people who had come to Nepal either from north or from west. After the Lichchhavis had become weak in the Kathmandu Valley the century, we find the rise of two new dynasties rising into power in two directions *i.e.* far-west and south-east of Nepal. Meanwhile the Kathmandu Valley along with some of the areas in the west like Lamjung, Gulmi and in the east Udayapur etc., were ruled by the rulers whose names are similar to the Lichchhavi kings. The end name of the then rulers "Deva" raises a question : were the rulers of the early medieval period the

Lichchhavis ? The end name "Deva" of the rulers show much possibility of these rulers being Lichchhavis, If so, why did not they claim themselves as the "*Lichchhavi. Kulaketu*" as the former Lichchhavi kings did ? Moreover Wright's *vamsavali* mentions them as the Thakuris from Nuwakot, whereas *Gopal Vamsavali* is silent about the name of the dynasty. As to the dynasty they belonged to it is not clear. Most probably they belonged to a group other than Lichchhavis.

Khasas

Meantime in the Karnali region there was a rise of a new dynasty which was mentioned in the *Gopal Vamsavali* as the Khasiya Mallas. The Khasas seem to have come to Nepal from Kashmir, which seems to have been named after the Khasa people. Khasas seemed to have first migrated from central Asia and became the rulers of the Karnali area in due course of time. But we donot exactly know as to when these people came to Nepal. Available evidences give us the information of Nagaraj as the founder of the dynasty in A.D. The Khasas had ruled a vast tract of land from Garhwal to Trisuli river and Manosarowar (Tibet) to the Tarai region. Thus the Khasas were the ruling tribe of the area for about four hundred years. The Khasas were very militant and strong warriors. Because of their militancy and valour, they could rule such a vast tract of rugged mountainous region. They started to spread throughout the whole kingdom. Moreover because of their trade relations with western Tibet, many Tibetans might have entered Nepal.

It is quite possible that during their reign many groups of hard labouring people started inhabitating at different hilly regions. They must have deputed many officers and soldiers at different regions to maintain law and other. Thus the Khasa people started migrating from the western Nepal to the eastern side, that is, from the Karnali region to the hilly region of eastern Nepal. The language spoken by these Khasiyas was called "Khas Kura." Later on they seemed to have constituted a major bulk of the population of the three Malla Kingdoms of the Kathmandu Valley. So the Malla Kings refer Khasas when they issued orders to the people. While issuing an order to the peoples of Dolakha, Jayaprakash Malla referred to Khasas first then only others like Magar, Gurung, Kiratas and others.

Similarly in one treaty signed between Bhupatindra Malla, the King of Bhaktapur, and Bhaskar Malla, the King of Kantipur, dated 1703 A.D., it is mentioned that Rs. 36,000/- were deposited as Caution money. In case any one of the contracting parties would violate the terms of the treaty, the Khasas, Magars, *umreas* (officials) and *Pauchas* were entitled to plunder the property of the violating party. Pratap Malla's Ranipokhari inscription, dated 1670 A.D., mentions Khasas and Magars along with others as witnes. Khasas are also referred to as the followers of Devidas Chikuti, a *chautara* of Kautipur, in a document dated 1687 A.D. They are also discribed to have cut and killed Laxmi Narayan Joshi, a powerful *bhautara*, in 1690 A.D. Thus the khasas seemed to have been very much influential and had been quite active in the Kathmandu Valley also. Jayaprakash Malla had the army of the Khasas and Magars. In this the Khasas were well established not only in the Western Nepal but also in the Kathmandu Valley. They were given priority because of their militant spirit. Malla Kings could not ignore them so they were referred to in the royal orders and edicts.

In one local *Vamsavali* it is mentioned that when a group of Tibetans (Bhotiyas) called Kukus created trouble in the Kingdom, Ratna Malla with the help of Mukunda Sena, the King of Palpa, Duppressed them. Af er that found groups of the Khasas were given Birta and permitted to settle at different places of the Kingdom of Kautipur by Ratna Malla.

Khasas must have impressed the Malla Kings with their Valour. That is why khasas and Magars had much influence in the Court of the Mallas and also had played an active role in the medieval politics.

Khas was a distinct race and the language spoken by them was the "Khas Kura," now well known as the Nepali language. Prithvi Narayan Shah had referred them as fast and smart people.

Meanwhile the establishment and development of the Karnatak rule in Simroangarh led to the influx of many groups of the people in the Kingdom. The *Gopal Vamsavali* refers the people of the Simroangarh as the *Doyas*. Later on Ghiyasuddin Tughluq destroyed the capital Simroangarh in 1326 A.D. As its result, king Harisimha Deva fled to the northern mountainous region with his wife Devaladevi, his son Jagat Simha and followers. The king died on the way and Devaladevi, her son and followers got asylum in the Kathmandu Valley. The devastation of the well established pure Hindu Capital must have resulted in the migration of a huge number of the orthodox Hindus to the Kathmandu Valley to save their life and religion.

Meanwhile India was invaded and much blood was shed by the Muslims. There was a great problem for the orthodox Hindus and Buddhists. These peace-loving people had to run away in search of a safe place to protect their life and religion. So, groups of the people entered Nepal for shelter. Among them the famous groups were the Senas and Shahs who could become the kings of various regions. These emmigres were well received by the aborigines of the area like Magars, Gurungs, Tamangs and others, because of their superiority in wisdom, warfare and noble behaviour. These people were well polished and very social and could adopt themselves in the new environment and with the host communities. Some of those newly migrated communities adjusted themselves by having matrimonal alliances. Some of them maintained their purity of blood and religion. Many hordes of people came to Nepal at different times. The Shahs and Senas were the Rajputs, who had come to Nepal as the refugees being vanquished by the Muslims' atrocities. *Gorkha Vamsavali* has clearly given an account of how did they come to Nepal. These Shahs first entered Nepal via Rupandehi, Palpa and settled at Lashargha, from where they gradually spread to various parts of western Nepal.

Magars

Before the hordes of the refugees entered Nepal, there were already many new groups like Magars, Gurungs and Tamangs. It is very difficult to trace the origin of these communities. Equally difficult question is when did they come to Nepal. These communities are considered to be of Mongolian origin. It is quite possible that these people had come to Nepal from north at different times. The Magars were mentioned as "Mangor" in some of the medieval documents. During the medieval period the whole area from Palpa to Gorkha was called the *Magarat* as the area was inhabited by the Magars. Prithvi Narayan Shah had claimed himself as the king of *Magarat*. The medieval epigraphic evidences have mentioned Mukunda Sena as the Magar King, because he had ruled over the Magar people. Most probably the Magar were the Mongols, who were, later on, called "Mongora," and how "Magar." These Magars seemed to have been very influential people after the fall of the Khasiya Mallas. Most probably there must have been various Magar chieftains at various regions of the western Nepal. Later on these Magar chieftains were replaced by the Rajput refugees—the Senas and Shahs. They had been very powerful and influential people in the Kathmandu Valley also. So Magars are referred now and then in the Malla documents. One inscription dated 1641 A D. mentions Khasas and Magra (Magars) as heitness. Jayaprakash Malla's document mentions them as Magarat. Jagajjaya Malla's copper plate dated 1729 A D. mentions Magars along with others.

Gurungs

Gurungs comprised another community of the Nepalese society. They also belonged to the Mongoliod group. Like the Magars, the Gurungs were also divided into many sub-castes. Both of these communities were the high-landers. One document of Jayaprakash Malla (dated between 1751 and 1754 A.D.) mentions "Gurun" (Gurung) along with other subjects residing at Dolakha. They reside in the high mountains and are hard people. Because of their honesty, courage, bravery and dedication, they were preferred in the British Gorkha army.

During the days of Prithvinarayan Shah, Nepal was inhabitated by various groups of the people. In one of his letters, he had mentioned various groups like Majhis, Thami, Kumala, Danuwar, Daraye, Tharu, Pahari, Kushahari, Hayu, Sunuwar, Chewang, Jolaha, Kushalya and Newars. These various communities resided in various parts of Nepal. Many of them are the aborigines. About them Landor has mentioned,

> "Perhaps among the most prominent aboriginal tribes we should mention the Magars, Gurungs, Newars, Sunwars, the Khambas or Khambu, and Yakshas (the later two closely resemble Rais), and Yakkhumbas, Murmis, and Lepchas. Then in the forests of the western Nepal we find to this day wild tribes of Chepang and Kusundas. In the Tarai district live the Tarus (Tharus) a servile and illshaped people of no great strength of character...,"

The Magars, Gurungs, Yakthumbas, Lapchas, Khampas, Tamangs resided in the hilly regions, Newars in the Kathmandu Valley and the Tharus in the Tarai plains.

Tharus

The Tharus constituted one of the tribes of the whole Tarai areas. They are one of the aborigines. Dr. Iswor Baral is of opinion that they were the descendants of the Rajput women who were sent to Nepal by their husbands for safety. When their husbands did not join them, as they perished fighting with the Muslims, these women took their servants as husbands. The offsprings of such union are called Tharus. The Tharus are divided intc many sub-divisions. They resided both in the west and the East. But tradition of the Tharus the west differ from those of the East. According to their tradition, the Tharu family of western Nepal look down upon their husbands whereas in the east there is no such tradition.

Chepangs and Kusundas

Chepangs and Kusundas are still the backward communities in Nepal. Hodgson has given an account of them which is as follows :

> They toil not, neither do they spin, they pay not taxes, acknowledge no allegiance, but, living entirely upon wild fruits and the produce of the cultivated country as they are of the unredeemed waste.

Although Hodgson has mentioned the Chepangs as the backward people residing almost in the state of nature, a letter of Prithvinarayan Shah mentioned the Chewangs (Chepang) as the tax-payers. In this way it can be said that not all the Chepangs were as backward as Hodgson mentioned. Some of them had cultivated land, and they having land property, were levied tax during the days of Prithvinarayan Shah. According to a legend Lahavi (Lava) and Kushahari (Kusha) were the ancestors of Chepang and Kusunda. But this legend cannot be accepted *in toto*. Had they been the descendants of Lava and Kusha, they should have been Aryan in race and well developed. But up to present time, they, are not so well advanced as others. They are at present found in some areas of Dhading, Gorkha, Makwanpur, and Chitwan.

Darai

Darai is another autochthonous group of Nepal. They are still timid and reside at a separate place. They live on hand to mouth condition because they do not have much land to cultivate. They catch fish for their nutritious food and also eat the yeild of their chase. They are found in Chitwan now. Similar other aborigines were Danuwars, Majhis, and Kumalas. They have striking cultural and physical similarities with the Tharus.

Newars

The Newars of the Kathmandu Valley constitute an entirely self-dependent community. About their origin there is much constroversy. Gopal Singh Nepali is of opinion that they were the Nayars of South India, as he noticed cultural similarities between the two. The identical terms "Nepal" and "Newar" make a scholar to think about the relations between the two. The interchange of 'p' and 'l' respectively with 'w' and 'r' made one call "Nepal" as "Newar." Dealing with the matter is a subject of further research. T.R. Vaidya is of the opinion that :

> The Newars are not an ethnic group but a mixed community absorbing all the people entering the Kathmandu Valley by its rich culture. The Newars are drawn from the Gopalas, Abhirs, Guptas, Koliyas, Sakyas, Kiratas, Lichchhavis, Thakuris, Karnatakas, Mallas, even the Kanya Kubja Brahmins. Thus the Newar is a complex of many communal groups having a common language, customs, tradition and culture.

One interesting feature is that, so long the Mallas were ruling over the Kathmandu Valley, they did not call themselves as Newars. Only the subjects residing in the Kathmandu Valley were called Newars and the Mallas called themselves as the Rajputs. Once the Mallas were defeated, they were reduoed to Newars.

Inspite of such thing the Newar community is self-dependent.......Within the community there are people of the four *varnas* and different professional castes. Jayasthiti Malla (1390 – 1395 A.D.) had elassified the community on different professional castes which still exist. Within the community there are people of various professional castes right from the Brahmin on the apex to the Sudras on the lowest. No other community in Nepal is so well organised as the Newars she interesting characteristic of the community is that it is the only community which worships the King as a thing God.

Muslims

Besides these above mentioned communities there are many other communities also. Muslims were specially linked with trade of bangles, embriodery etc. These Muslims were allotted a separate place for habitation. According to a chronicle, the Muslims had entered the Kathmandu Valley during the reign of Ratna Malla. Later on they had a mart of their own which is known as *Raqi* (Iraqui) bazar in the heart of Kathmandu. Some documents are now being revealed which prove the facilities given to the Persians, Iraqis and other Muslims to promote trade in Kathmandu Valley. In other kingdoms of the medieval period Muslims had been allowed to reside for the promotion of the trade.

Tamangs

One interesting thing is that the Gurungs and Tamangs were not mentioned in the early medieval documents, whereas the Magars were mentioned from the beginning of the twelveth century A.D. The occasional references to the Magaras in the medieval period prove, as already mentioned, that the Gandaki region was called as Magarat area. But the Tamangs and Gurungs are not mentioned. There are references to the *Sayen i.e.* the Tibetans or people with the Tibetan culture. In these days the *Sayen* might have comprised the Tibetans, Tamangs, Gurungs and others who had come from Tibet. Prithvinarayan Shah had mentioned the Gurungs as lethargic.

In the modern period also the same communities resided in Nepal. But due to lapse of time many communities disappeared as they were absorbed in the bigger and influential communities, for example, various groups in the Kathmandu Valley were merged in the Newar society. Some of the ruling families also disappeared, for example, the Senas and others. Some of the ruling Thakuri families of the *Baisis* and *Chaubisis* exist even now as the common people. These various communities have their own identity which is reflected by their own customs, traditions, culture and even own dialects. It is most likely that many of the communities which had a settled life were turned into momads, as Bahadurshah had taken a very harsh step against those who had resisted very stubboruly. His order was, "The entire enemy male population in areas where the war is fought shall be slaughtered" Another order mentions to do away with all the males aging above twelves years who had entired the jungle and rehabilate the females and children. It was issued to Subha Bhakta Thapa, an affair of Jumla. Thus Nepalese society is a conglomoration of diverse groups of people with their own customs, traditions, culture and dialects or language.

2

Social Structure

The present constitution declares Nepal a Hindu Kingdom, the only Hindu Kingdom in the world. Hinduism implies the implementation of the traditional Hindu rules, *i.e.* the existence of the *varna* system. We still take pride in mentioning the Nepalese society as the garden of the *Char Varna Chhatis Jat*, which was mentioned in the *Dibya Upadesh* of Prithvinarayan Shah. Moreover at the eoronation ceremony of a king the presence of the representatives of the four *varnas* i e. Brahman, Kshetriya, Vaisya and Sudra is required. But the *Muluki Ain* of 1963 declares the equality of all castes before law. In consideration with changing situation this revolutionary *Ain* was promulgated by king Mahendra. The Brahmins are no more *Avadhya.* They suffer the same punishment (for a crime) which a Sudra suffers now.

Nature of the Nepalese Society

The Nepalese society, as we have observed, is a composition of various groups some of which were non-Hindus. The Kirata, Magar, Gurung, Tamang and many other communities did not come in the Hindu-fold They could be taken as non-Hind communities with entirely different religious tradition and culture. When we unfold the pages of history we will be well acquainted with the changing pattern of the social structure of the Nepalese society at different phases of history.

Before we discuss the subject in detail, it will not be improper here to mention that Nepal had never suffered the yoke of foreign rule unlike the case of India. As such, the Nepalese society did not face the problem of the pressure of any foreign anti-Hindu religious feeling. In India when the Muslims ruled for centuries, they tried their best to convert the Hindus into Islam and those who did not accept it had to suffer. Many of them were put to death, while others had to pay the religious tax *i.e.*, the *Jizia* tax and some of them had to flee to a safe place were they could follow their religion undisturbed. The last group came to Nepal. The pressure from the ruling group had certain positive and negative effects on the Hindu society of India. Those, who could venture to do something, started bringing about the reformation in India to cope with the situation like Bhakti movement and others. Later on during the British rule attempts were made by great men to safeguard the Hinduism. Some attempted to save their tradition by forming a society which adopted the half-way policy like Ram Mohan Roy's Brahmo Samaj, while others took the firm stand based on Vedas like Dayananda Saraswati's Arya Samaj. Thus the scholars had tried their best to retain their religion, as attempts were made to destory Hinduism. Moreover the struggles to safeguard the religion produced many great reformers right from the Muslim to British period. Mass awakening could take place. Many evils which had crept in the Hinduism were brushed away. Hindu renaissance took place during the 19th century India.

On the other hand since Nepal did not have to cope with such situation the Hinduism flourished undisturbed. Since there was no such challange to it, on reforms were felt necessary. Many evil practices crept in, which we will discuss in due place.

We do not exactly know the exact type of social structure of Nepal prior to the historic period. Whether the Gopalas,

Mahisapalas, and Kiratas can be taken as Hindus is a subject of controversy. It is said that since they were the phallus worshippers, they were the Hindus. But the cult of phallus worship existed even among many communities before the idea of Hindusim developed. The people of Mohenjadaro and Harappa had also the cult of phallus worship. But we do not take them as Hindus. The Vedas also have mentioned the *Anaryas* (non-Aryans) worshipping the phallus. If we follow it, those Gopalas, Mahisapalas and Kiratas were not Hindus. Later Hindus treatises have mentioned the Kiratas as the savagious low grade people. The Kiratas were not considered as the Hindus. So the social structure of the then Nepal was not based on Hinduism and they must have their own way of structure, might be they were divided into ruler and ruled classes.

Introduction of the Varna System

According to the available source of the Nepalese history Supuspa was the first Lichchhavi ruler to introduce the *Varna Vyavastha* in Nepal in circa fifth century. B.C. *Gopal Vamsavali* mentions "*Raja Sri Supuspa deva Varsa 76, Tena his Nepala bhumischaturyarna Krita.*" Further it is mentioned that King Supuspa is credited to have beautified the town *i.e.* capital, organised the whole kingdom and ruled the people in a justful way. The original line is "*Tata Sundaranirmmita Nagaram Sakalarajyamarjjada Kritya Nyayena Praja Samasta Pratipalitani.*" Thus Supuspa is credited to have classified the people into four *Varnas* and they were ruled in a justful way according the *Marjjada* which means *Aryamarayada.* We have seen the rise of Magadh in India leading to the fall of many principalities. Consequently many of the vanquished people (followers of Hinduism) entered Nepal mostly in the Kathmandu Valley. Lichchhavis, one of the migrated groups, could become the rulers of Nepal. After that Supuspa, the Lichchhavi ruler, paid attention in ruling the people according to the principles of Hinduism. Many of the emigres who entered the Kathmandu Valley were the Hindus, whereas the host area was inhabitated by the non-Hindus. So to safeguard their religion, Supuspa, a Hindu King introduced the *Varna Vyavastha* in Nepal But it is not clear what status was given to the non-Hindu subjects. In can not be assumed that the non-Hindu subjects might have been compelled to adopt Hinduism in the initial phase by the Lichchhavi rulers. They must have been treated well although they were not included into *Varna Vyavastha* which was meant only for those Hindu emigres.

When the Lichchhavis became powerful enough and were well established, they gave more and more emphasis on the Hinduism. The Lichchhavi rulers, later on, took pride in their successful implemention of the *Arya Maryada*. Amsuvarma had issued a decree which mentioned that if there was a case relating to *Dharmashankar*, let it be dealt with by the palace king itself. Moreover on other inscription mentions Amsuvarma as abiding by the *Aryamaryada*. Shivadeva II had mentioned with pride from the Kailashakut Bhavan (royal palace) that the *Varnashram Vyavastha* was strongly adhered to.

The Lichhavis were staunch supporters of the Hinduism and the *Varna Vyavastha*. In order toretain the system Amsu Varma established an office called *Bhattadhikarna*. According to Dhana Vajra vajracharya the main function of the office was to keep an eye on the people as to whether they had observed the rules and regulations of the *Varna Vyavastha*. "No violation of the *Varna Vyavastha* (*i.e. Dharmashankar*)" was the motto of the Lichchhavi period.

Such accounts give us full proof that the Lichchhavis had laid much emphasis on the *Varna Vyavastha* which was alsocalled *Aryamaryada*. In fact Arya, is one sense, meant a group of tribe in an ancient world. When they enteredIndia, they found other tribes already in existence. They were fair in complex, quite handsome, well behaved and good mannered people according to their own texts, whereas the autochthonous people of India were described as dark complexed, ill-mannered and brutish. These aborigines are described as *Anarya*, who were reduced to slaves. The term Arya also denotes the people of noble character, gentle and well mannered. *Anarya* meant ill mannered, uncivilised and inferior quality people. These Aryas in course of time in India developed a social system to have a well organised and disciplined society as well as to accommodate the aborigines in their social structure. The system *i.e. Aryamaryada* became the main crux of the social structure among them *i.e.* the Hindus.

Brahmins

According to that system the Brahmins were placed on the apex of the Hindu social hierarchy, whose functions were to read and teach, perform and make others perform the *Yajnas*, to donate and to accept donations. The duty of a Kshetriya was to read, perform *Yajna*, donate, to maintain life by the use of weapons and protect the living beings. Vaisya, third in status, was to read, perform *Yajna*, donate, and engage in agriculture and trade and commerce and rear animals. The Sudra, lowest in status, was to serve, cultivate land, rear animals, engage in handicraft and to sing and dance. These Aryas accommodated the other aborigines in the social hierarchy most probably in the lower status according to the latter's capability. One who would observe the system was called a pure Hindu. The staunch Hindu rulers strictly followed this principle. The famous Hindu law-givers like Manu, Yajnavalkya, Brihaspati, Narad and others started framing laws protecting the privileges of the higher status people. The system was strictly followed by the staunch Hindu rulers of India like the Sungas, Guptas and others.

In Nepal the Lichchhavis, who were also the staunch Hindus, followed the same practice. It is vary difficult to point out which groups of the people were placed in which social strata due to the paucity of the sufficient material. The mention of the term 'Aryamaryada, gives us sufficient ground to believe the existence of the *Varna* system. So here the classification of the people is made on the traditional basis *i.e.* on the ground of functions. The Brahmins were given much importance and donated by the kings. Manadev I had donated a lot of property after his successful military campaign in the west and the east. The Lichchhavis of Nepal were contemporary to the Nauryas, Sungas, Guptas and others in India.

The Gupta period was considered as the period of revival of Hinduism in India, which had been overshadowed by the Buddhism temporarily. The Brahmin scholars were quite active under the royal patronage of the Guptas. Specially the Gupta period was the glorious period of the Hinduism in India. There were the Hindu renaissance and revival of Brahminism during the period The Brahmins enjoyed most facilities and privileges. It had its impact in Nepal also. The Lichchhavis had given much importance to the Hinduism. Brahmins in Nepal also were the most privileged group. In one way they were much donated, on the other hand the people of the lowest social strata who used to eat the uneatable things (according to the Hindu rules) like pork, onion, garlic etc. had to pay the taxs like *Sukar Kara*, *Palandu kara*, *Lasuna kara* etc. Thus on the basis of the available evidences the Brahmins had enjoyed the highest status in the society. They were given special patronage. King Shivadeva's decree granted twenty *manikas* (40 maunds) of paddy to the *Bhagavan Vasudev Brahmana Gosthi* (a trustee of the Vaisnavite Brahmins), ten *manikas* to the *Brahmanashanatthya Gosthi.* All those *three* Gosthis were of the Lembati Drang (the present Lele). Thus it is evident that the Brahmins were well organised and had enjoyed special patronage. Another inscription mentions the Brahmins first while referring the people of a certain area. Thus the Brahmins were at the apex of the social heirarchy of the then society. According to the Hindu laws they must have enjoyed the status of *Avadhya* (not to be killed for any crime).

Kshetriyas

Next to the Brahmins were the Kshestriyas according to the *Aryamaryada.* The position of the Kshitriyas must have been enjoyed by the Lichchhavis, the then ruling class. Although the Manusmriti mentions the Lichchhavis as the Vratya Kshetriyas *i.e.* Kshetriyas of inferior type as they did not abide by the regulations prescribed by the Dharmashastras, it seems that the status of the Lichchhavis as the Kshetriya could not be challanged by others since they were the then rulers of Nepal. The inscriptions mention one caste gomi both as Kshetriya and Brahmin. Punya Gomi was a Brahmin, whereas Bhogavarma Gomi was the Kshetriya. About the Gomi it seems that those with the end name "Varma" were the Kshetriyas like Bhoga Varma Gomi, Desha Varma Gomi and others. Varma, also called Varmmana, was the Kshetriya, most probably the Thakuris. The tratition of mentioning the rulers as Varmana continued up to the Malla period in Nepal. The 'Rajputra' mentioned in the inscriptions might be the Kshetriyas of the time, for example, Vikrama Sena, Vajraratha and others. Amsuvarma was mentioned as a Kshetriya by the Chinese travellar, Huien Tsang also. Only the Kshetriyas occupying higher administrative posts are referred in the inscriptions. There might be many others not mentioned in the inscriptions.

But it is not known, on the basis of the inscriptions, how the Lichchhavis had taken the Kshetriyas of other groups like the Koliyas, Sakyas, Mallas and others. Most probably the Kshetriyas of those groups were not given due status in the society. The refugees who had fled to Nepal were mostly from the ruling group *i e.* the Kshetriyas. But they did not seem to have been taken as the Kshetriyas in the then Nepalese society. Only the Lichchhavis and their near relatives were counted as the Kshetriyas ingnoring others. The system continued in the history of Nepal up to the modern period. It seemed that the rulers had effective role in determining the social status of the people.

Vaisyas

We have already pointed out that the epigraphic evidences prove the existence of the Brahmins and Kshetriyas in ancient Nepal. Regarding the Vaisyas, the third group of the Varna system, it has to be worked out on the basis of the assumption. The ground of the assumption is based on the profession *i.e.* those who were engaged on trade and commerce, agriculture and the like business are referred here as the Vaisyas. Thus when we think of the people engaged on business, Huien Tsang had mentioned that the traders outnumbered the cultivators. Thus the large number of the traders and cultivators are mentioned here as the Vaisyas, according to the Manusmriti. The Lichchhavi inscriptions here and there mention the existence of the *Sarthavahu* which means the leader of the traders. Ratna Sangha, mentioned as the *Sarthavahu*, was a very rich businessman whose two inscriptions are available. He had erected temples of Ratneswor Shiva and Prabhukeswor. He had also consecreted a vast tract of land to both temples. Guhamitra was another rich businessman contemporary to Manadev I. He is also mentioned as *Sarthavahu.* The later inscriptions do not mention the *Sarthavahus* but there is the mention of the flourishing trade, commerce, and industries. The mention of *Apanakara* denotes the existence of the shops and the tax on the shops. Moreover *Adhikamasa tula danda* is also an evidence of the system of fine for misuse of the weights. Thus there was a large number of businessmen throughout the Lichchhavi period. They were the Vaisyas of the time, who were the backbone of the society from economic point of view.

Sudras

The Sudras constituted the lowest strata of the society. Due to the paucity of abundant sources it is quite difficult to pinpoint which community or group of the people was to be called the Sudras. Whether the autochthnous people, whom the Lichchhavis had conquered were reduced to Sudra or some other group of the people ? The evidences do not give clear idea about it. Only one inscription mentions the existence of the Chandalas. There was a tradition of reducing the vanquished ruling family to Sudra. If the people of the higher Varnas including Brahmins, committed heinous crime, they were also out-casted and reduced to Sudra. The Lichchhavi inscriptions clearly mention the enslavement of all the members of the family if anybody in the family committed the *Panchaparadha*. Such enslaved people can also be considered as the Sudras. In the inscriptions there were references to the *Sukarakara, Matsyakara, Palandukara*, and *Lasunakara.* To explain them we have to refer the food habit of the then India. The orthodox Hindus did not take the pork, fish, onion and garlic. Only the people of lower Varṇa *i.e.*, the Sudras used to take them. These objects were the "Nishedha" (prohibited objects) for the high caste people. The high caste people were not allowed even to touch the swine, chicken, onion etc., who might be the people that used to rear the swine, chicken and fish ? Such job was done even today in orthodox Hindu society only by the low caste people *i.e.*, the Sudras. So in those days also those Sudras used to rear the swine, chicken, and fish and cultivate the onion and garlic. The Lichchhavis in their initial stage of rule were so orthodox that they levied taxes on those Sudras who were engaged in the farmings of those things. It seems that major number of the people *i.e.*, the autochthonous people took those *Nishedha* objects. The Lichchhavis had economically exploited them by imposing those above mentioned taxes on the food habit of the non-Hindus and the Sudras.

A Lichchhavi inscription mentioned the eighteen groups of people including Brahmins, the original version being "*Brahmnapradhana Sastadashaprakritaya.*" We also notice the word "*Brahmanapurassaran....*" Thus it is quite evident that the Brahmins were at the apex in the social heirarchy and there were eighteen communitites including the Brahmins in those days. The eighteen communities might be Brahmins. Kshetriyas, Vaisyas, Sudras, Koliyas, Shakyas, Kiratas, Khasas (?), Guptas, Mallas, and others. The inscription of Vasantadev mentions Branhum, Salahmu, Tepul as the names of the communitites but just the reference to these name in an isolated inscription does not make their identity clear. The practice of referring to the *Astadasha Prakriti* continued up to the early medieval period in Nepal. Dhanavajra Vajracharya in context to the reference of the terminology in the inscription raises a question : Whether it was the terminology to refer all the subjects of a kingdom just like "*Char Varna Chhatis Jat*" during the latter medeival period in Nepal ? Even then there must be some logic behind it as to why and how did the concept of the *Astadashaprakriti* come into existence. Until further evidences are available nothing definite can be said about it. On such condition we can say this much that in order to adjust all the communities - Hindus and non-Hindu aborigines the term *Astadasaaprakriti* was mentioned. It is not clear in which *varna* the Shakyas, Koliyas, Mallas, Guptas, Kiratas were included. In general it is mentioned that the Lichchhavi rulers were particular of *Aryamaryada*.

Moreover during the period we see some sort of differences between Hinduism and Buddhism. The powerful Anuparama had used untoward words against the Buddhists. Aparently these two seets have entirely different way of social life. Hinduism prompts the classification of the society in four *varnas* whereas the Buddhism abhors to any classifications, because everyone is equal in that sect. In the minds of staunch Hindus the Buddhists were the athiests. Might be with that feeling Anapuram, a staunch Hindu, used words of hate against the Buddhists. The Lichchhavi rulers up to Amsuvarma seemed to be staunch Hindus with the attitude of looking down upon or exploiting the autochthonous groups of people or the Sudras. But from the time of Amsuvarma the policy gradually changed. The people who were engaged in breeding the swine, fishes, chicken, and cultivating the onion and garlics were gradually released of the taxes like the *Sukar Kara*, *Matsya Kara*, *Lasuna Kara*, *Palandu Kara*, though in certain areas only. Moreover Amsuvarma is being mentioned as the ornament of the Buddhist monasteries. He had shown much favour to the sect. It does not mean that all his predecessors were opposed to Buddhism. The Lichchhavi kings like Manadev I and Shivadev I had constructed the Buddhist monasteries. For some time the Abhir Gomis had behaved with prejudice against the Buddhists. But the far-sighted rulers like Amsuvarma and his successors had shown equal favour to the Buddhists also, although the *Arya Maryada* was the state-recognised policy. Under such circumstance a question arises *i.e.*, in which *varna* the Buddhists were adjusted. We do not exactly know the social position of the Buddhists at that time.

Social Change during the Medieval Period

As already mentioned, the concept of the *Astadasha Prakriti* continued in the early medieval period. The history of Nepal for about a century during the early medieval period *i.e.*, after 879 A.D. was shrouded in mystery. After that period we have the epigraphic evidences, during which period many rulers with the end name "Deva" like the Lichchhavis ruled up to the ascendancy of the Mallas. But the history during the period was a disturbed on from the political point of view.

Although the earlier *Vamsavalis* like *Gopal Vamsavali* and *Vamsavali* of Kaisar Library mention the rulers of the period as belonging to solar race without any name of the dynasty, the latter *Vamsavalis* refer them as the rulers of the Thakuri dynasty. Believing the version of the latter *Vamsavalis* we take them as the Thakuris. In that case the Thakuris appeared as the Kshetriyas, which group had not appeared as a prominent group of Kshetriyas during the Lichchhavi period. Amsuvarma and his family were called the Thakuris during that period. Now the Thakuris came to the prominent position. Moreover during the period, if we believe the wright's chronicle, there were some social disturbances. The Buddhists, who had to lead the life of austerity, indulged in the licentuous life. Similarly the Hindus also were occupied in the corrupt life. Shankaracharya seemed to have come to Nepal twice in the beginning of 12th century. With his help King Shivadeva III seemed to have introduced some reforms. The corrupt Buddhists monks and nuns were expelled from the monasteries and made them lead the family life. But Wright's *Vamsavali*, a Buddhist *Vamsavali*, writes "...the Baudhamargis were soon defeated (in the discussion with Shankaracharya). Some of them fled, and some were put to death. Some, who would not allow that they were defeated, were also killed. The nuns (corrupt) were compelled to marry". Although the chronicler, a Buddhist had exaggerated the account, it seems that the irregularities in the name of religion was put to stop. But the chronicler writes that the Buddhists nurtured the feeling of vengeance; and when a suitable opportunity availed a group of about one thousand *Banras*, the Buddhists, murdered seven hundred Brahmins. The whole account is given in the most confused way without any historical link. So, nothing definite can be said about it. The main question before us is how the Buddhists were adjusted in the *Varna Vyavastha.*

From religious point of view there seems to have developed a synthetic approach between the Hinduism and Buddhism. The Vaisnavite Hindus took Lord Buddha as one of the incarnations of Lord Vishnu and the Saivites had also come closure to the Buddhists, so did the Buddhists. Lord Pashupati is still worshipped as Lord Buddha on the *Mukhastami*, so do the Hindus worship Rato Matchhindra Nath as an incarnation of Lord Shiva on 1st Magha. Guheswori is worshipped as the Goddess Shakti by the Shakta Hindus whereas the Buddhists worship it as Arya Tara. The image of Manjusri at Swayambhu is still worshipped as Goddess Saraswati by the Hindus on Sri Panchami every year. Thus gradually the Hindus and the Buddhists started living in coordination and harmony; and that is the speciality of the Nepalese cultural life.

Social Structure in the Khasiya Malla Kingdom

Meantime a new community started ruling in the far western Nepal *i.e.*, Karnali region, that community was called Khas in the history. The Khas rulers had adopted Buddhism as the state religion. In the initial stage they ruled over only the western part of Nepal. But due to their superior militancy and the weakness in the central government of Kathmandu the Khas rulers started expanding their territory towards the eastern side of their state *i.e.* the Gandaki region. They did not seem to have adopted the Hindu system of *Aryamaryada*, although the Brahmins (the learned people) were well respected. The latter inscriptions of those Khasiya Malla kings refer to the Hindu deities like Brahma, Vishnu and Maheswor. But the society in that state was not classified as in the Hindu Kingdom. There were many communities like the Magars, Gurung, Tamangs, Hindus, and others. They enjoyed full freedom to lead their own way of life. Their society can be classified as such *i.e.* the intellectuals, the scholars of both Hindu and Buddhists, technicians, the ruling family, the courtiers, the military personels, traders and common mass. The Hindu system of classification of society on the basis of *varna vyavastha* did not exist.

Aryamaryada of the Simroangarh Kingdom

On the contrary there emerged another strong state in the south eastern side of Nepal *i.e.* Simroangarh. The kingdom of Simroangarh extended up to Bodhagaya in the south and the whole of Mithila was under the kingdom. The rulers of the Karnatak dynasty were orthodox Hindus and the Hindu renaissance took place in the kingdom when the major position of northern India was under the strict rule of the Muslims. The *Aryamaryada* was strictly observed there and the rulers there were proud of it.

Communities in the Hilly Region

Meantime almost all the hilly regions were peopled by hard labouring people like Magars, Gurungs, Tamangs, Kiratas, Bhotiyas and many other aborigines who were basically non-Hindus. In the Tarai regions the Tharus and other communities resided. The Khasiya Mallas had contributed one language *i.e.* the *Khasa Kura*, later on called *Nepali Bhasa* and militant spirit to these people. Upto the early medieval period these communities had continued on adopting their own traditional religious faith. The concept of Hinduism did not have much impact on them.

Changes in the Medieval Society

Later on, there was an influx of many Hindus including Rajputs from India to save their life and religion. These groups of Hindus came like the waves out of the fear of the Muslim ravages. This sort of waves of migration of orthodox Hindus had its impact in the social structure of the hilly regions also. The strong Khasiya Malla kingdom faced its fall in the last decade of the 14th century. The Malla kingdom of the Kathmandu valley made its last effort to have an extensive kingdom under Yakshya Mall (1428-82 A.D.) That attempt did not last long. For some time the aboriginal tribal chiefs ruled in various regions. The Hindu migrants who had taken shelter in the hilly region were found superior intellect and military skills to the autochthonous communities. Consequently, these local chiefs were gradually replaced by these Hindu migrants. The gradual success of these Hindu groups had brought about a revolutionary change in the social system of Nepal. Those groups who had come as the helpless refugees became the rulers; and they started ruling on the basis of the Hindu concept. The rise of those groups helped in the formation of the Baisi and Chaubisi states. Now these people got full freedom to lead their life in their own way *i.e.* Hinduism. Thus the waves of migration of the Hindus and their success in becoming rulers helped in Hinduising many of those aborigine non-Hindu communities. Sanskritisation became the most-up-to-date fashion of the time. The well versed persons in the Hindu holy texts and Sanskrit literature became privileged elite group supported by the administration. The Hindu rulers gradually started implementing the rules and regulations based on the Hindu scriptures. The process of Hinduisation in the hilly area was a prolonged and gradual one. When these rulers felt themselves strong enough and well established, the *Aryamaryada* was introduced. Further the Hindu religion became the state religion. The local autochthonous people were gradually treated as the inferior ones. Since these aborigines constituted the bulk of the subjects, their importance also could not be ignored, as such give-and-take policy was adopted; classical example of the policy can be cited in Gorkha.

Before the Shah family conquered Gorkha, it was ruled by the tribal groups like Khadkas and Ghales, both aborigines. The Hindu subjects, being ill-treated by these aboriginal rulers, and some dissatisfied aboriginal subjects invited Drabya Shah, a Hindu prince of Lamjung. Drabya Shah invaded and conquered Gorkha; hence-after the Hindu royal family ruled over there. But the far-sighted statesmen as they were, the Shah kings of Gorkha made the Magars the priest of main deiteis like Manakamana; and thus the aborigine people were appeased.

Process of Hinduisation

As a whole what we see in those hilly area is that there was a process of Hinduisation. But due to complexity of the social problem it was very difficult to pinpoint which community was to be adjusted in which *Varna*. Even those aboriginal communities which adopted Hinduism could not be well adjusted in any of the *Varna*. It was a complex problem. So the then rulers maintained the rules and regulations of Hinduism among the Hindus and the aborigines were permitted to continue their traditional culture provided that would not go against the very principles of the Hinduism. The aborigines were not permitted to slaughter a cow. There were many communities which used to take beef and slaughter cow specially in the northern area. The Hinduism does not permit the slaughther of a cow, which was considered both a crime and a sin. *Gohatva* was one of the greatest sins. But the communities of Tibetan origin ate beef. As such the Hindu rulers gradually put a restriction on it. Later on very severe punishment like confiscation of property and enslavement was given to the cow-slaughterers irrespective of the community they belonged to as cited in a document found in Dolakha.

The Malla kings of Kathmandu had recognised the various ethnic groups like Khasas, Magars, Gurung, Kiratas, Majhi and Gagona having their own cultural heritage. The only regulations binding to such communities were that they should not go against the very basic principles of the Hinduism like the cow-slaughter, otherwise they led their own way of life. But they were considered as the people of inferior communities, whereas the Hindus were the superior people. The Brahmins were the most respected group of the people in the society. Moreover they were considered as the *Avadhya*, as such the highest punishment given to them was degradation from social status, banishment and shaving of head and make them eat uneatables (which also means the degradation from social status) as prescribed by the Hindu Shastras.

Changing attitude in the Social Structure

During medieval period there was another wave of a new feeling in the society, according to which every ruling family started claming themselves of Rajput origin. About this Hamilton has written.

"Rajputs were considered as the most respected people in the society specially among the ruling families. In the medieval India the Rajputs of Rajasthan had shown their valour and sacrifice for the sake of their state against the Muslims. Even the Rajput Jaimal, Patta, Maharana Pratap and so many other Rajputs were taken as the ideal heroes among the Hindus. Their bravery was much appreciated; and many of the Hindu rulers felt themselves glorified in showing their familial link with the Rajputs."

These rulers started claiming their origin with the Rajputs. The Mallas of the Kathmandu Valley can be cited as an example in the case.

We have already seen how the Mallas of Pava and Kusinara had entered Nepal for asylum. Later on they settled at Mallapuri in the western bank of Kali Gandaki. Might be these Mallas were further scattered. One group of them went to the western Nepal and another group settled some where near the Kathmandu Valley. These very Mallas, when they got an apportunity, became the rulers of the Kathmandu Valley. Thus the Malla rulers had nothing to do with those brave warrior Rajputs of Rajasthan. Such Mallas also started claiming themselves as of the Rajput origin. In the history of Nepal the Lichchhavis, although of Vaisali origin, never showed any hint of their original place. Once they became the rulers of Nepal they behaved as the Nepalese like the Mughals of India. But the Mallas felt themselves proud of claiming themselves as the Rajputs. Moreover they felt themselves superior to the other Kshetriyas. They became the Thakuris *i.e.*, the superior Kshetriyas whereas the other Kshetriyas were looked down upon. During medieval period in the Kathmandu Valley there were Thakuri Vaisyas also. They might be superior Vaisyas as compared to other Vaisyas.

In the Kathmandu Valley different groups of Brahmins were enjoying the highest position in the society. Some of them were from Kanyakubja, India, and some from South India. When Jayasthiti Malla reorganised the social structure, the Brahmins were divided broadly in Pancha Gauda and Pancha Dravida. The Gauda Brahmins (Brahmins from Bengal ?) were subdivided into five groups, similar was the case of Dravida Brahmins. What it seems is that there was a dearth of well-versed Brahmins; as its consequence the Brahminical rituals could not be performed smoothly. The very foundation of Hinduism was facing a great problem. So Jayasthiti reorganised the whole social structure on the basis of *Shastras* as well as the tradition, which also could not be ignored. The advisory committee consisted of the Kanyakubja, Maithali and Bhatta Brahmins. Wright's Vamsavali mentions "Such laws were formerly in existence, but having fallen in disuse through the lapse of time, they were again compiled from Shastras and brought into use."

The social institutions were in existence during the Lichchhavi period when there was political stability. But, later on, as there was political chaos so many anomalies appeared in the society. As such many of the texts written by the ancient Hindu law-givers were translated in the then Newari script and language. The society was reorganised on the basis of these very laws but due importance was given to the traditional values.

Reorganisation in the Social Structure

According to the reorganisation the *varna vyavastha* was revitalised. The people were reclassified. The Brahmins were also regrouped as the Gauda and Dravida fractions. The Gauda (Bengali ?) Brahmins were divided into five subgroups, similarly the Dravida (South India ?) Brahmins were also classified into five fractions as already mentioned. Those very Brahmins, who adopted the local traditions in due course, were later on called *Rajopadhyaya* in Sanskrit and *Deubhaju* in local version. Up to the present time they are called *Deubhaju* (divinely person). These *Deubhaju* or Rajopadhyaya Brahmins were also treated as Brahmins during the Rana period though they did not enjoy the same stauts as the Brahmins from the hilly region who enjoyed the highest social status as *Rajaguru*, *Rajapurohit* and *Dharmadhikar*. The Rajopadhyaya Brahmins were consulted in case of any matter relating to the Newar tradition. Chanderi, Subedi, Bhandari, Acharya and Daivajna were considered as the Brahmins. Although the document mentions Chanderi, Bhandari and Subedi as the Brahmins in Jayasthiti Malla's reforms, they must have been the Brahmins of the Parbatiya subjects of the Malla kings, as the Newar tradition does not have these people in their community. They were the state recognised Brahmins. The Rajapadhyaya, Daivajna and Acharya were the traditional Brahmins among the Newars.

The then Kshetriya group must have consisted of the ruling Mallas, Shrestha (which consisted of 6 sub-castes) and other courtiers. The Shresthas had been the courtiers and had enjoyed higher status not only in the court of the Kathmandu Valley but also in the court of the Khasiya Mallas. The Shresthas of the Kathmandu Valley consisted of two groups *i.e.* *Tagadhari* (sacred thread wearers) and *Matawali* (alchohol drinkers) The former were considered superior to the latter.

The lower caste people, including the untouchable, were taken as the Sudras. The Sudras comprised Kasai, Kusale, Charmakar, Pode, Kulu, Kapali and others. The other groups of the Newar community constituted the Vaisyas

Besides the Hindu subjects in the Malla period there were a major number of Buddhist subjects It seems that the Buddhists were treated according to their own traditional values. Among the Buddhists also the rules and regulations were framed. *Banras* were taken as the priestly class. Buddhist society also had its own social order.

Besides the Buddhist Newars, there were many other communities like Magars, Khasas, Tamangs, Lamas, Bhotiyas residing in the hilly areas. The people seemed to have been treated as inferior in the society. They were allowed to run their traditional rituals provided these tradition would not go against the basic principles of the Hinduism. These people also, whether in the Malla Kingdoms or in the Chaubisis or Baisis, were gradually influenced by the Hinduism, as already mentioned Attempts were made to bring about harmany and uniformity but without making any effort to antagonise their traditional values. For example, they had their own priests, rituals, and way of life. But since the rulers were the Hindus, there was a tendency of making them participate in the Hindu customs, fairs and festivals. Social pressure made them feel inferior to the Hindus. They were socially, economically and political suppressed people.

Due to lapse of time many complexities developed in the society. There seems to have been struggle within the society to occupy better social status in every strata of the society. This struggle or under current activities continued up to the dawn of democracy in Nepal in 1951 A.D.

The struggle was also supported by the administration. Some times it is quite visible how the rulers with the support of the state priest and preceptors played role in determining the social status of the various groups. When the law could degrade any person from higher caste to lower caste on charge of crime, the rulers suppported by the Brahmins could change the status of people in group not only in the medieval period but also in the modern period prior to 1951 A.D. In this social upheavel, every caste or *Varna* faced the same problem due to self interest. Even among the Brahmins, those Brahmins occupying higher posts like *Rajaguru*, *Raj purohit*, the most honoured people, felt themselves superior to other Brahmins. These Brahmins who were enjoying higher status started running only after acquiring more and more facilities without much interest on enlightening themselves by higher studies. Consequently they became not so perfect in their religious activities Meantime the coming of Maithili Brahmins, Bhatta Brahmins and others from India and settling in Nepal brought about certain clashes. The older or local Brahmins had the ego of self superiority whereas more learned new Brahmins made their (former's) position shaky. In due course of time there appeared conflict between themselves. The local Brahmins claimed themselves superior whereas the other Brahmins started challenging them in knowledge. The traditional local Brahmin and other Brahmins did not pull on well between themselves. In this conflict those who could win over the favour of the rulers enjoyed better status like Nanda Misra in Gorkha, Lambakarna Bhatta, Kirtinath Upadhyaya Kanyakubja, Raghu Nath Jha, Srinatha Bhatta, Mahinath Bhatta, Rananath Jha and others in the Kathmandu Valley. One group used to blame others as inferior. But the priest class of the Buddhists might not have occupied that elevated status, as the other priests among the Hindus; same might be the fate of the priests of other communities.

The Malla kings considered themselves superior to the people. The rules framed by Jayasthiti Malla were meant for Newar subjects. They claimed themselves as Thakura or *Thakuri*. They constituted the highest status in the society. So did the other ruling families.

Jayasthiti Malla had appropriately declared the *Char Varna Chhatisha Jat i.e.* four *varnas* and thirty six communities. The communities were thus recognised and adjusted in the social system. The hilly areas were inhabited by these various communities, as we have seen the habitations of Kiratas, Magras, Gurungs, Bhotiyas, Lepchas and others in Dolakha during the days of Jayaprakash Malla. Similarly such people had resided in Rasuwa, Nuwakot and other hilly areas.

With the rise of house of Gorkha we see again the gradual change in the social hierarchy in Nepal. Nepal was unified under the auspicy of the Shah Kings and many of the petty states were merged to form a unified and bigger Nepal.

Dharma Shastras as a Guiding Spirit during the modern period

Nepal, in the modern period, was governed according to the Hindu Shastras. Every attempt was made to protect the system of *Varna Vyavastha*. Prithvinarayan Shah had the feeling of making Nepal a centre of Hinduism; so did his successors. Later on the *defacto* rulers like Bhimasena Thapa and the Ranas had also given full patronage to Hinduim. As such the *Hindu Varna Vyavastha* was fully implemented. Any violation to that was severely punished. Nepal under the Ranas had followed the traditional Hinduism; as such when pioneer reformers like Madhav Raj Joshi and his son Sukraraj Shastri propagated the doctrines of Arya Samaj, they were severely punished. Thus Hindu Dharma Shastras remained the guideline to the framers of the codes of Nepal. The *Varna Vyavastha* was vigorously maintained.

The society continued to consist of four *Varnas*. The only question was as to who was to be included in which *Varna* The emergence of a new dynasty in the whole of Nepal also necessitated in bringing about and maintaining unity among the various ethnic groups with various cultures, languages and religion. Local system of the petty states gave way to the central system of whole Nepal As such inter-communication and exchange of views were bound to take place. New group of courtiers sought to fulfil their interest While doing so sometimes impositions were laid down in the name of unity.

Brahmins

The Brahmins continued to enjoy the highest status in the society. Among Brahmins also there were various groups which are now identified by their castes. Among them the struggle for obtaining favour and higher ranks continued. Latter on during the Rana period the prominent Brahmins in power were divided mainly in two groups, *i.e.* Kumai and Purbiya. The Kumai Brahmins were said to have come from Kumaon. They were also the migrants since days yore. The Purbiya Brahmins were those who resided in the eastern Nepal. These tow groups of Brahmins still have the marital relations. Inspite of that they had the internal strife for superiority. Purbiya Brahmins still claim themselves superior to the Kumai Brahmins, whereas the latter claim themselves superior.

After the rise of Jang Bahadur, *Vijaya Raj Pandit, a Kumai Brahmin,* was awarded the post of *Rajaguru* for his cooperation in the rise of the Ranas. Since then Vijaya Raj and his family members and his descendants were appointed as the *Rajaguru* and *Rajapurohit* of Nepal. The Kumai Brahmins enjoyed the much coveted posts along with the post of *Dharmadhikar*. Might be this monopoly of that group of the Brahmins provoked jealousy of other groups of Brahmins. Moreover that group of Brahmins started looking down upon the other groups of Brahmins, which had also aggravated others' jealousy. So the other Brahmins also behaved them likewise in social gathering where the political power did not interfere. The Deubhajus or Rajopadhyayas although treated as Brahmins, were looked down upon by the other Brahmins. They could not enjoy that elevated status which they enjoyed during the Malla period

That group of Brahmins, who enjoyed the highest ranks of *Dharmadhikar*, *Rajaguru* and *Rajapurohit*, were just like the higher clergies of pre-Revolutionary France. They lived in palace-like buildings, equipped with all available facilities, enjoying the grace of the Ranas. Lavish donations, *Bakas* and presents from the Ranas enriched them to enjoy the princely life. *Dharmadhikar* was given special privileges and income. The other Brahmins had to seek the mercy of the *Dharmadhikar* (also *Rajaguru*) and *Rajapurohit* for their prospect and career building. These high ranking Brahmins had to seek mercy of the Ranas and on the other hand they were the source of mercy to the other Brahmins. The other Brahmins who had not enjoyed any blessing from either the Ranas or the *Rajaguru* and *Rajapurohit* had to pass very pitiable life although they enjoyed the highest social status. The Brahmins not only led the social life but also were the influential advisors to the Ranas The Brahmins did not permit any non-Brahmins even to study Sanskirt in the *Tin Dhara Pakasala*, a learnnig centre. Now also the non-Brahmins are not allowed to study there (an educational institute meant for Sanskrit education established by Ranauddip Singh). But interestingly the *Tin Dhara Pakshala* had become a boarding for the Brahmin youths to study western education also.

Kshetriyas

Next to the Brahmins were the Kshetriyas. In the Kshetriya group also we see the tremendous change that was brought about. The ruling families constituted the highest status for being the Thakuri and Rajput. All the vanquished rulers of the *Baisis* and *Chaubisis* were also called the Thakuris, as such they also `enjoyed the highest position among the Kshetriyas. Hamilton has written :

> "The Rajputs that are, or that even pretend to be, descended of the colony which came from Chitaur, are very few in number, but the families of the mountain chiefs, who have adopted the Hindus rules of purity, and even some who have neglected to do so, are now universally admitted to be Rajputs."

There is much truth in this version. He has classified the Rajputs of Nepal into three groups. First, real Rajputs who had migrated to Nepal for shelter, second group consisted of those aboriginal rulers who had adopted the Hinduism and took the title of Rajputs; and third group of Rajputs were those who claimed the title just because they were the rulers. There were real Rajputs also who had come to Nepal and became the rulers as already mentioned. The fashion of claiming of being Rajputs by every ruling families caused some confusion.

The social legacy of the medieval period continued in the modern period. As already seen, the influx of the Hindus and the inter-mixture of many castes resulted in the emergence of new group which became the castes later on. The matrimony of the Brahmin with the widow of the same caste led to origin of Jaisi, and Khatri Chetriya was the issue of Brahmin and lower caste (touchable) woman. In this way many new castes emerged.

An order issued during the period of Bhimsena Thapa gives some hint of how the different groups of people were grouped. The Rajputs were considered as equal to Kshetriyas. Thus at that time many castes like Rajputs, Thakuris, Pande, Basnet, Bista, Thapa, Kunwar and others were the well know Kshetriyas. One interesting thing is that the Newars were mentioned at par with the Sudras in a document. Even the Mallas, who claimnel themselves as the Thakuris and Rajputs during their rule in the Kathmandu Valley, were reduced to Newar and the Newar as seen early were considered as the Sudras. It is equally interesting to find why the vanquished Mallas only were reduced to lower social strata whereas the other vanquished rulers of *Chaubisis* and *Baisis* were taken as Thakuri and Rajputs.

Emergence of the Ranas

Later on with rise of Jung Bahadur Kunwar once more there was another read justment in the Kshetriyas group. Kunwars were and are considered to be Kshetriyas. But after the rise of Jang Bahadur Kunwar as the Prime Minister at the time of the Bhandarkhal Parva, he aspired to raise his status from Kunwar to Rana to prove his family of being Rajput origin. So long Jang Bahadur had not attained the high status, he remained satisfied of being an humble Kshetriya. Now he was not satisfied with that. He took the title of Rajput "Rana' by compelling the king, Surendra, to give him a *Lal Mohar*, which narrates the story how a Rajput came to hilly-region of Nepal. That Rajput Ahiram Kunwar was the fore-father of Jang Bahadur. The *Vamsavali*, prepared during the life time of Jang Bahadur, also traces the history of the geneaology of his family. It links the geneaology with the Rajputs of Chittor. Thus Jang Bahadur now became "Kunwar Rana" and later on gave the original surename "Kunwar" and became "Rana" *i.e.* the Rajputs of Chittor.

To think of this incident one can derive the conclusion that any one, who could capture power, could elevate his social status to any status except the Brahmin status. The other Kunwars still are called the Kshetriyas, whereas the Ranas became the Rajput on the basis of power. But the other Kunwars do not take the Ranas as Rajput and count them as upstarts.

Jang Bahadur was not satisfied with the *Lal Mohar* only. He wanted to have social recognition which could be achieved by having marital relations. Kshetriyas were treated inferior to Rajput Thakuris. So Jang Bahadur, for the social recognition, bargained with Guru Pd. Shah, a *Chautaria*, related to the royal family to give his sister in marriage with him (Jang). The Chautaria, who had taken asylum in India after Kot Massacre, was permitted to come back to Nepal and given land as *Birta*. Thus Jang's social status was raised. Moreover he gave his three daughters in marriage with Trailokya Vikram Shah, the then Crown Prince and had his sons married with the daughters of King Surendra. Thus Jang elevated his social status (of the Kunwar Kshetriyas) to the position of the Rajput. This is how the people of lower social status could rise into higher status. It is one of the classical examples in the history of Nepal. Had not Jang Bahadur become the Prime Minister, his family, could never have become the "Rana" or Rajput. So long he was a *Kazi* he did not feel necessity of showing the link of the Kunwar family with the Rajput of Chittor. Had Bhimasena Thapa the brain of Jang, the Thapas of Nepal would have also become the Rajputs. Jang Bahadur made new social heirarchy among the Kshetriyas, according to which the Rajputs were placed on the apex among the Kshetriyas, follwed by the Thakuris and the Kshetriyas in the lowest strata.

Moreover the Ranas had become so absolute that they, with the help of *Dharmadhikar*, could place any group of the people to any social status. Sometimes they did it on their own also. Bir Shamsher had made a beautiful eunuch, belonging to Nakarmi, a low caste Newar, his *Bada Maharani*. (Chief Queen). The other Ranas had to please her to have her favour thence that of Bir Shamsher. Later on, Bir Shamsher had his two daughters (from the *Bada Maharani*) married with King Prithvi Bir Vikram Shah with the expectation of having his grandson (from them) to be the future king of Nepal. King Prithvi had no option but to marry them as he was virtually a figure head of the state. But it is said king Prithvi did not like them because of two reasons, firstly, they were the illegitimate issues that also from a low caste (above mentioned) woman and secondly, they were proud enough for being the daughters of Sri 3 Maharaj. We can now imagine how much the Ranas had arbitrarily ruled over the country. They did not even lag behind in compelling the king to accept such illegitimate daughters of a Prime Minister. Had anyone of them given birth to a son, the baby would have become the king of Nepal. The very luck went against the well planned design of Bir Shamsher as neither of them could give birth to a son.

Within the Rana family also, the social structure underwent changes at the whim of the Prime Ministers. There was not much distinction between the legitimate and illegitimate members of the family in the beginning of the ascendancy of Shamshers. The seventeen brothers sons of Dhir Shamsher, well known in the Nepalese history as *Satrabhai*, were born from different mothers of different castes. Bir Shamsher had included his illegitimate sons in the roll of succession to the Prime Ministership, whereas he dropped his illegitimate brothers from the roll. This sort of thing happened later on also. Later on, when Chandra became Prime Minister, he classified the Ranas into three groups *i.e.* A, B, and C. A class Ranas meant the legitimate issues of the *Satrabhai* B class included those who were legitimate but whose mothers were not pure Kshetriyas, and C class denoted the illigitimate Ranas. Chandra Shamsher had many legitimate sons whereas his brothers, Bhim and Juddha, had a large number of illegitimate issues. Hence to limit the Prime Ministership in his own family Chandra made a rule debarring B and C Ranas from the succession to ***the Prime Ministership.*** But, possibly to avoil direct clash, the Prime Minister did not exclude those B and C Ranas, who had already been included in the roll of succession. The situation worsened when his successor, Bhim Shamsher, in the interest of his favourite illegitimate sons, modified the system and included them in the roll of succession. Bhim's successor, Juddha, acted violently by banishing all C Ranas from the capital having dropped them from the roll of succession. Thereafter, only the A Ranas were entitled to be the Prime Ministers of Nepal. Thus the social structure of the Ranas consisted of three classes *i.e.* A, B and C.

Besides the Rajputs and Thakuris, there were other Kshetriyas, many of whom were geniune Kshetriyas, whereas a new group of Kshetriyas also emerged as the legacy of the medeival period. We have seen the intermixture of various different caste or *Varna* groups. The offsprings of the Brahmin and other caste groups were counted as the Kshetriyas like Pandeys, Panths, Adhikaris Bistas, and others. The children of a Brahmin from a Brahmin widow were also taken as a Jaisi Brahmin in the medieval period but later on they were degraded and not allowed to perform the Brahmin rituals by the way of punishment. The Jaisis emerged as a separate caste group. Similarly so many other caste groups emerged due to lapse of time. Thus to make a water-tight compartment in the social structure is very difficult.

The 1854 Code

According to the 1854 code the people were classified as following :

1. *Tagadharis* : were the sacred thread-bearers. In this group come the Upadhyaya Brahmins, Rajputs, Jaisis, Indian Brahmins like Guzrati, Maharastriya, Dravid etc., Kshetriyas, Deobhajus, and some high caste Newars. Generally the *Tagadharis* were not supposed to drink alchohol. They occupied higher social status.

2. *Matawalis* were those who used to drink wine. This group was subdivided into two groups-*viz. Namashinya*, one who would not lose his social status and *Mashinya*, one who would lose his social status. Some of the Newars, Magars and Gurungs were categorised as the *Namashinya Matawalis*. Bhotiyas (Sherpa and other communities residing in the high mountains), Limbus, Kiratis, Sunuwars, Chepangs, Mayas, Majhis, Danuwars, Darai and others were the Mashinya Matawalis.

3. *Pani Nacholne Choye Chhito Halnu Naparne Jat.* The terminology can be divided into two *i.e.*, *Pane Nachalne* denotes the caste which was not entitled to serve water to high caste people and *Chhove Chhito Halnu Naparne Jat* means the caste whose contamination did not defile the higher caste people. This group included the Muslims, Dhobis (washermen), Kulus, Telis of the Tarai area, Kasais (butchers), Mlechhas (the Europeans), Kusales and some others.

4. *Chhove Chhito Halnu Parne Jat* means those castes whose contamination would defile the higher caste people. If the higher caste people are touched by the people of the castes, they had to purify themselves by sprin kling holy water. People of this caste group were *Sarkis* (cobblers), *Kamis* (iron smiths), Chamars, Hurkyas, Damais, Gaines, wadi Bhada, Podes and Chyamhakhalaks.

These were the general classification of the society. These very groups were also classified on the basis of the *Varna Vayavastha*, according to which the Brahmins and the Kshetriyas come in the Tagadharis. There was no explicit group of the Vaisyas. The *Namashinya* and *Mashinya* groups fall in Sudra Varna. *Chhoye Chhito Halnu Na Parne* and *Chhoye Chitto Halnu Parne* were the water unacceptable and untouchables, respectively who were lower in status than the Sudras. This classification had arbitrarily reduced some communities to Sudras. Although Jang's Code did not mention clearly as to who were the Vaisyas, later on the Newars were taken as the Vaisyas. We have already observed that the Newars constituted the fully contented society in which there are the people of all *varnas*. We have also seen that the Malla rulers, who took themselves as Rajputs and Thakuris were also reduced to the Newars. Jang's code had classified the Newars into mainly three groups : Brahmins, Kshetriyas and Sudras. But many aboriginal communities which had their own priests and culture were arbitrarily reduced to Sudra. Thus the *Varna Vyavastha* was implemented uniformly irrespective of the difference of caste and creed and culture. The Ranas spared no one to upgrade their status, for example, the Kunwars were upgraded to Rajput and developed the matrimonial alliances with the royal family. The other communities, having their own identity, were reduced to the Sudras and Vaishyas.

As a whole, what we see is that in one way during the period of our survey the *varna* system was very strongly implemented but on the other hand the *varna* system was handled arbitrarily at the mere whim of the Ranas. They could upgrade or reduce any one from one *varna* to another. By their order one would be reduced to the Vaisya or Sudra or one would be upgraded to higher status. Only on one thing they sticked *i.e.* the Brahmins were not to be put to death. Might be because of that reason the members of Praja Parishad a political party organised against the Ranas, made a Brahmin their President.

Thus, the *varna* system and professional caste had contributed a lot to maintain the social system intact among the Hindus.

3

Family System

Joint Family System

The institution of family has played a very important role not only in Nepal but throughout the world. It is in this very institution the citizens of a country get the proper training. In Nepal also we have a very strong feeling of loyalty and attachment to the family. We have the joint family system from the very ancient time or dawn of the history, as in India or China. Under the same roof the people of many generations lived together where the system of collectivism worked very smoothly. Whatever earned was shared among the members of the family system. The head of the family was all powerful and it was he who maintained the family intact. The joint family system was cherished politically, culturally and economically.

If any member of a family committed any crime the whole members of the family suffered punishment during the Lichchhavi period. We have found edicts issued by the Lichchhavi kings which mention the special favour granted to some localities. The special favour was that the king being much pleased with the people by their rendering certain services had declared that only the culprit in that area would be punished. The system of giving punishment to the offender alone was the effect of special favour by the king, otherwise the members of the whole family were given the punishment. The system is a proof of the joint family system. The then Chinese and Indians had also adopted the same system.

The system of counting family as a unit existed in Nepal up to the very recent past. Up to the early modern period the population of a state was counted on the basis of homestead or family. Gorkha had twelve thousand families; similarly Kantipur, Bhaktapur, Lalitpur the Chaubisi and Baisi states were counted on family basis. An individual was not counted, he was counted just as a member of the family, although the later codes made a reform in punishing only the individual not the family like Rama Shah's code. But in some heinous crimes all the members of the family were punished. Thus the joint family system as a unit of the state was deep-rooted in the Nepalese society for many centuries. Later on, the system gradually weakened due to social, political and economic reasons. The gradual social influence of the Westerners specially the British had also led to the break-up of the system. Moreover the transfer of the capital from Gorkha to Nuwakot and finally to Kathmandu necessitated the migration of many officials leaving their original houses Moreover posting of the officials at diffirent places also helped in the break-down of the joint family system. Among the ruling family like the Ranas the individual family system was appreciated because of the harems and privacy and impact of westerners and economic prosperity. The Ranas built separate palaces for their sons. There was a proverd for the Ranas that so long the children were in infancy, there was a fear of mortality and when they grew up there was the fear that they might kill the father.

But among the people there was a strong feeling of maintaining the joint family system. To have a big family was a prestige in the society, hence many generations lived together. The agro-economy had its major role in maintaining joint family system intact.

Patriarchal Family

As the family system was governed by the male, the patriarchal family system existed in Nepal. The head of the family was the senior-most male member of the family. He enjoyed the commanding position in the family. Although there is a reference to the matriarchical family system in ancient time, in the Himanchal Pradesh, India, we do not exactly know the existence of the matriarchal family system in a clear-cut way. But the very existence of the polyandary and the female playing dominant role in some communities in Nepal gives us some hint that the matriarchal system prevailed in those days in some of the communities of Nepal, otherwise in general we had the patriarchal family system. Moreover as the religious feeling was quite dominating in the society, the *Hindu Shastras*, a guiding spirit, had laid emphasis on the continuity of the family by having a son. It was considered infilial not to have a son. So in many cases a man married many wives with the expectation of having a son who was necessary for the ancestoral worship as well as the attainment of the heaven. It is mentioned in the Hindu Holy texts that no one would be allowed to enter Heaven after death without having a son.

The *Diwali Puja*, worship of family god, is also an evidence of the patriarchial system. In the main shrine the females were not allowed to participate in general cases. *Si Kaye Bhove*, a feast in which the various parts of the head of the sacrificed animal are offered to the male members of the family on the basis of seniority, is another evidence of the patriarchal social system among the Newars. This sort of feast is a classical system among the Newars only.

Polygamy

Polygamy was another common feature of the family system. A man used to have many wives. When we think of ancient period we have evidences of the Lichchhavi King Mandev I having three queens, among them Bhogini was the

Chief Queen. The general tradition was that one of the queens used to be chief queen. The Malla kings also had many wives. There was also a tradition of having concubines, who used to have lower status. The Shah kings also had many wives. Generally the status of chief queen was enjoyed not on the basls of either seniority or social status but mainly on the basis of the favour of the king. For example, Narendra Laxmi was the second queen of Prithvinarayan Shah but since she was the most favourite one, she enjoyed the status of chief queen. Sometimes illegitimate wives also enjoyed full power which is evidenced by the case of Manju Rani. During the Rana period many of the illegitimate wives of the Ranas became *Badamaharanis* on the basis of the favour they won from their husbands.

Not only among the ruling families but also among the common mass, the people used to have many wives. There were various reasons of the polygamy in Nepal. First reason was the necessity of having a son for the continuity of the family. Secondly, the agro economy of the country also encouraged to have more wives and family members. There is still the practice of having many wives who are deputed various functions. For example, one will look after the cattle, other t e agriculture, third one the domestic affairs and one, generally most beautiful and youngest, fulfills the lust of the husband. Thirdly, it was considered a prestige to have many wives of a man. There was a traditional feeling that the polygamy was the birth right of a man. Up to some year back a service-holder having an additional wife in every step of promotion was a common practice. Fourthly, the transfer of a man to some other places made him have a new wife also. In the patriarchal society a male dominated female and most arbitrarily used to take his wife more a play-mate or means to satisfy his lust. Moreover those male had also framed rules and regulations to safeguard their devilish sex desire with the least consideration of the interest of a female.

But the polygamy and concubinage system had made the domestic life more annoying, and had also caused many unhappy incidents. The family life turned into hell instead of being a heaven. In case of the common people there had been many litigations and quarrels. Generally the favourite wife used to become the target of the discarded wives. In the case of the ruling families such system had affected much. Some times the clashes among the queens had much effect in the politics of the country also. We have seen many such incidents in the history of Nepal *i.e.* clashes between the two queens of Pratap Simha Shah, queens of Rana Bahadur Shah, and the queens of Rajendra Bikram Shah.

Besides these common features of the family life, we can cite some of the interesting characteristics of some groups of the people. The Tharus of Nepalgung, one of the aboriginal communities, had a peculiar system in their family. The Tharu females of the area used to behave their husbands as inferior in social status. So the males were not allowed to enter the kitchen and when the food was served to them the females used to push the tray by their feet. The traditional legend marrates that the ancestors of those Tharus were the Rajputs who had fled to save themselves from the Muslims. The Rajputs, when invaded, first sent their wives escorted by the servants to a safe place to Nepal and went to fight with the Muslims. But they were slain in the battle. Unknown of what had befallen to their husbands, they waited quite some time, but their husbands did not join them. Then these Rajput females took their servants as the husbands. Thus as the servants were made husbands by their mistresses, they used to look down upon their husbands. Although it was a popular version among them it is very difficult to believe the story. There must have been some thing else behind the tradition. It is quite possible that that group of Tharus had carried the tradition since days yore without knowing the past event. Most probably they might have been the descondants of the people who had matricarchal system of family in the days yore.

Right to Ancestoral Property

About the ancestoral property among the common mass, every member of the family had the equal right to property. But among the ruling family specially the Ranas the law provided the legitimate issues six times more than that of the illegitimate sons. Suppose a legitimate son got six rupees the illegitimate son only one rupee.

Rana Family System

The family system of the Ranas was much sophisticated and a bit different from that of the common mass. In case of common mass the issues from the lower class women were given the caste of mother. Such issues were considered lower in status and were not permitted to dine together. But in the case of the Ranas, the descendants were taken as Ranas and considered belonging to higher class. Even the C class Ranas were considered higher than the other ordinary Kshetriyas. These C class Ranas were not allowed to dine together with their mothers as the latter were considered lower in social status than their issues. The Ranas used to have concubines of various ethnic groups whom they considered belonging to lower social status. Their issues were considered higher in status, so the issues were not allowed to dine together with their mothers. It is very interesting system to note down.

Another interesting characteristic of the Rana family was that there was no strong family attachment among the members. They had maintained very strict discipline; and much formalities were observed in the family relation which affected much in family affection and attachment. The young babies were separated from their mother and maid-servants were employed for breast feeding. In those days it was believed that the breast feeding would affect the beauty of the mother. Moreover the Ranas might have also felt that the presence of the babies on the wives' laps was a burdle for their lusty life. These babies were bred up by the maid-servants. When the babies grew up as the young boys and girls they were taken to their parents twice a days *i e.* in the dawn and dusk to make them bow to their parents. That was the only meeting between the parents and the children. As already mentioned the Ranas were classified in three classes A, B and C. The A class Ranas were the most privileged group. They were in the roll of succession to the Sri 3 Maharaj and Prime Minister. There were many strict family rules which had to be observed so as to maintain the discipline in the family. They framed rules and regulations only to serve their own family purposes. Sometimes very narrow regulations were also framed, for example, after the successful coup of 1885, Bir Shamsher framed a rule that no illegitimate members of their family *i.e.* his brothers like Dambar Shamsher, Sher Shamsher and some other should become Prime Minister. Thus the illegitimate brothers were debarred from becoming Prime Minister. Later on Bir Shamsher herself made his younger brothers recognise his illegitimate wife belonging to a lower caste *i.e.* Nakarmi as *Bada Mahkrani.* As already mentioned Bir's brothers used to go on *chakari* to the *Bada Maharani* in order to win her blessings and thence that of their brother Bir. Moreover Bir included his sons through her in the roll of succession of Prime Minister whereas his half-brothers were deprived of the privilege as already mentioned. The arbitrary decision of the Rana Prime Minister was one of the main features in their family life. Later on Bhim Shamsher also made the same arbitrary decision in including his illegitimate sons in the roll of succession of Prime Minister. In 1934 A.D. Prime Minister Juddha took a stern step and ousted the C class Ranas from the roll of succession. Many Ranas were expelled from Kathmandu to implement the decision.

Moreover many new family rules were made. The C class Ranas, however senior in age, had to pay due respect to the A class Ranas. Further, rules were made that only the A class Ranas could become the Prime Minister, whereas the

B class Ranas were to get the post of Commanding Colonel only at the top, and the C class Ranas got the post of full Major. Not only among themselves but also among the mass an impression was given that the A class Ranas were the most superior Ranas. Distinction among them was not only made in social and administrative status but also in religious and domestic life.

At the time of the *Diwali Puja* (worship of the family God) the A and B class Ranas only were allowed to enter the temple and worship the god, while the C class Ranas were not permitted to do so. Moreover the A class Ranas were to sacrifice one goat each from among every male member of the family whereas only one goat was to be sacrificed from the whole family of the C class Ranas. Regarding the law of right to ancestoral property also A class Ranas were entitled six times more than the C class Ranas. Thus if an A class Rana got Rs. 6/- as the inheritance, a C class was entitled only one rupee. But in practice the favourite issues and wives got more than the legitimate sons. Moreover the distinction in A and C class was made even in the food provisions. Sri 3 Maharaj and *Badamaharani* were served in the gold plates whereas other Ranas in silver plates and others in ordinary plates. They had quota system in food provision also for the family members also. The cooks were to serve according to the social status among the members of the same family. Such distinction was made in dress which we will discuss later on. The C class Ranas in many cases were ignored. The Ranas used to bred up their illegitimate issues outside their palaces. We have an interesting case of Man Shamsher, the son of Juddha Shamsher. Man Shamsher was named as Man Bahadur before Juddha Shamsher became Prime Minister. Later, when Juddha became Prime Minister then only Man Bahadur was made Man Shamsher. Another interesting feature of the Rana family system was that the children of a Rana was put under the guardianship of another Rana. An argument in favour of it was that they wanted to have an inter-relation among all the members of the Ranas. Another argument that the system developed out of mutual suspicion also cannot be ignored. The sons of Keshar Shamsher were under the guardianship of Mohan Shamsher and Mohan Shamsher's sons were under the guardian of some other senior Rana. Can it not be taken as a hostage system as we see among the Mughals in India ?

To conclude about the family system among the Ranas, it can be said that the family attachment among them was more formal. The result of which was that there was a least sense of love, affection and closeness among them. The luxury made them lead the debaucherous life. The harem, they maintained, caused clashes among the male members of the family even between father and sons. Such type of loose family system errupted when the people revolted against the Ranas in 1950-51. The C class Ranas who had suffered the social humiliation for a long time revolted against their own brethren and joined with the rebellians just like the lower nobles during the French Revolution. Sex, wine, debauchery and luxury spoilt the Ranas.

Family System Among the Mass

Among the Brahmins, as already mentioned, there were mainly two prominent groups *i e.* Kumai and the Purbiyas. The Kumais, because of the power they enjoyed, used to feel themselves superior. They had also maintained very strict family tradition. They wanted to have the brides from the Purbiya Brahmins for their social recognition. The poor and helpless Purbiyas used to give their daughter in marriage with the Kumais. But once the daughter was married with Kumai Brahmins, she was not allowed to enter the kitchen in her parents' house.

Among the common mass the family system ran in their traditional way. Since many of the regulations were based on *Hindus Shastras* the society remained almost stagnant among the common mass. Later on, although the Ranas adopted western system in many aspects, they wished the people to follow the Hindu laws. With the change of social life in the neighbouring countries some reforms were introduced like abolition of *Jar Katne* (to kill the adulterer by the aggrieved husband), abolition of *Sati* and others. The rulers wished and supported to have a stagnant society, out of which pyramidical set-up, the administrators and the vested interest groups had enjoyed much privileges. For the protection of their special interest also the stagnant society was much emphasised inspite of many changes in the social system in India.

Impact of Joint Family System

The joint family system seemed to have an impact on political system of the country also. During the Lichchhavi period it did not have its effect in the politics. But from the early medieval period the impact of joint family system became obvious among the rulers also. Almost all the brothers of the kings were mentioned as the kings of the country, about which a historian calls it joint rule system. Whether the joint rule system can be justified or not is not the subject to be discussed here, but we have references to many brothers, even nephews mentioned as the *Jaju* (king) in the colophons or inscriptions. Colophon of Shivadharma Shastia mentions the rule of the three brothers, the original line of which runs "*tasmin samaye Sri Rajadhiraja jesthah joraya Dharmmadeva madhya Sri Jayajyotimalladevah Kamestha Jayakirtimalladevah traya Sammate rajye Kratam.*" Besides this colophon, there are many inscriptions and colophons which refer the three brothers as the co-rulers, after the death of Jayasthiti Malla. Later on many other rulers had shared the administration with his brothers. Yakshya Mall (1328-82 A.D.) had also reigned his kingdom along with his younger brother Jiva Mall. Such type of sharing the rule with brothers had both advantages and disadvantages. The advantage was that all the brothers jointly ran administration. The elder brother *i.e.* the king was helped by his brothers to run the administration smoothly.

Sometimes such system led to bitter clashes among the brothers which also led to the division of the kingdom. After Yaksya Malla, all his sons and his grandson through his daughter jointly ruled the kingdom for some years. But some of the princes were ambitions which led to the division of the Kathmandu valley. Same was the case with the Sena Kingdom of Palpa. It is said that Mukunda Sena had divided his kingdom among his sons. But it cannot be accepted as the Sena kingdom was divided only after the death of Mukunda Sena. His sons were highly ambitious as such the junior sons declared themselves independent rulers of the areas where they were ruling as governors. The system of co-rulers was in existence up to the seventeenth century. Jitamitra Malla shared his rule with his younger brother Ugra Mall. This system was much in practice among the Mallas and some other ruling families.

But the Shahs, the ruling family of Gorkha, developed another system, according to which the eldest son became the king and the second son became Chautara, as Rama Shah had promulgated the rule to that effect. Later on many of the king's brothers were made Chautaras and Kazis. Accommodation was thus given to the younger brothers in administration not as the co-rulers but as subordinates or assistants in Gorkha. This system had also its own type of advantages. The Shah rulers did not give any opportunity to the younger brothers to be the co-rulers. Later on when the younger brothers requested Prithvinarayan Shah to share the conqured area among themselves the king refused. The Shah kings never encouraged the co-rulership. They had the rules of taking the king as the most respected and honoured person, whereas the Mallas had the system of joint responsibility. The common mass had maintained the joint family system throughout the extent of present Nepal.

Marriage system

Certain communities in Nepal had some interesting family traditions. Indogamy was the traditional system in the communities like the Magars, Gurungs, Tamangs and some others. The members of the communities married among their own near relations. There is still the popular local version *i.e. Mamacheli Phuphuchela* that means sister's son would be married to the brothers's daughter. It is still a tradition among the communities like Magars, Gurungs and Tamangs that the daughter of father's sister is the birth right of the male. So long he wishes to marry his materenal uncle's daughter, the latter can not marry anyone else. The system *Mamacheli Phuphuchela* was adopted even among the ruling families *i.e.* Shahs and Ranas. What it seems is that the system was not in common practice in early days. Later on during the modern period *i.e.* the Rana period the system became quite popular among the ruling family. The Ranas seemed to have encouraged it and they seemed to have adopted in from the aborigines.

Indogamy was also known in ancient world. The extreme type of indogamy existed in ancient Egypt among the Pharoahs. The Pharoahs used to marry their own sisters as far as possible; if their sisters were not available, they used to marry the cousin sisters. The rulers of Burma, up to its merge with the British empire, also used to marry their own sisters. The reasons, argued in favour of the indogamy, were that these families wanted to maintain purity of blood, as they believed that there should not be mixed blood in the ruling families. Another strong reasoning was that the palace-secrecy would not be exposed to any other family. In those days the medical science was not so much developed to prove defects in genetic in case of the near indogamy. The marriage of the cousins was also in vogue among the Koliyas and Sakyas in the 6th century B.C. in Kapilavastu and Ramagrama.

The indogamy was considered as an incest among the Hindus according to the Hindu Shastras. The Hindus law-givers had laid down very strict rules against the incest. The sexual relations with the teacher's wife was considered as the most heinous incest. Narad has pointed out the near relatives who were :

> "Mothers, mother's sister, mother-in-law, maternal uncle's wife, father's sister, the wife of the paternal uncle, or a friend or a preceptor's wife, a woman of his own Gortra come (to him) for protection, the queen, a female ascetic, a nurse, a virtuous woman, and a woman of the highest class. When a man carnally knows any one out of these women, he is said to have committed the offence of violating the led of a preceptor. For such a crime no other punishment is ordined than the excision of the organ."

Manu writes that the sexual relation with his sister by the sama mother, with the wife of a friend or of a son, with the duaghter of the father's sister and with the mother's sister's daughter or mother's brother's daughter is equal to the violation of teacher's bed. Manu had prescribed a very severe type of punishments like lying on the red hot iron bed or embracing the red-hot image of a female having his organ and testicles cut and putting them on his hand he should walk until he would fall down dead. Thus the Hindu law-givers had very strictly prohibited the incest. But the Nepalese Hindu society was not so strict in this respect. The very thing declared incest by the Hindu law-givers was a common practice even right from Brahmin to Sudras. Why did the Hindus adopt the system in Nepal, which the non-Hindus of Nepal had? For a Hindu, the indogamy as a recognised social practice is very surprising thing in the Nepalese social history. Why did the practice of *Mamacheli Phuphuchelo* come into existence? Was it the effect of the dire necessity of maintenance of the purity of blood among the people who took asylum in Nepal? Even if it is so, had they ignored the Hindu laws regarding the incest in Nepal? Or was it the impcat of the local autochthonous non-Hindu people?

Not only that, there was also a tradition of taking elder brother's wife as one's own wife. Another tradition was to make *Sant Ama* (step-mother) one's wife up to the 19th century in Nepal. General Bhimsena Thapa's order mentions that the tradition of taking the elder brother's wife as one's own wife which existed among the *Char Varna Chhattsh Jat* was a great sin. So in 1836 A.D. it was prohibited on legal basis making it liable to punishment among the people of the aforesaid *Varna* and *Jat* except among the Kiratas, the Limbus, the Lepchas, and the inhabitants of Jumla. Thus prior to that, the elder brother's wife was married with the younger brother after the death of the elder brother. It was only in 1836 the practice was declared as an incest among all the communities except the Kiratas, the Limbus, the Lepchas, and the inhabitants of Jumla.

If any one would ignore the regulation he would be punished as following: if an Upadhyaya Brahmin would marry his elder brother's wife (widous), he would be socially degraded and expelled from the country after having his head shaved; in case of a Kshetriya he would also be expelled from the country after being socially degraded; if a Kshetriya Rajput committed incest, his organ would be cut off; the Khasas, the Vaisyas, the Magars, the Gurung, the Ghales and the Newars would also suffer the same punishment as prescribed to Rajputs. Various other communities like Sunuwars, Danuwars, Valami, Majhis and others were also prohtbited the practice. The Jaisi Brahmins of Pancha Thapaula had the practice of marrying the meternal-uncle's daughter. It was only at the times of Bhimsena Thapa it was prohibited. Similarly there was another system according to which the people of certain communities used to marry the step-mother after the death of the father.

The reasons of such odd family system might be both economic and social. Economically the ancestoral property of a family would be shared by the widows and would go into the hands of other people if the widows were not married by the other male members of the same family. Thus such marriage system saved the ancestoral propery from being lost and fragmented. Socially the system was an impact of the aborigines of Nepal. It was only among the Hindus of India that there were various taboos in the marriage relations among the different level members of the family. But Nepalese society was more pragmatic in approach. It looks something like non-Hinduist but those Hindus who had come to live with the aborigines had adopted the local indigenous system. Whatever might be the causes, up to that time the widow remarriage, although limited within certain members of family, was an accepted system socially as well as legrally. It was only after the edict of Bhimsena Thapa many females had to pass the miserable life of a widow. From the present day point of view the system of widow remarriage was very good and the then Nepalese society was more advance than the present one. The then Hindu rulers deserve such appreciation for accepting the widow remarriage even among the Brahmins. The time when India was having great reformers like Raja Mohan Roy and others who championed the cause of the widow remarriage, Nepal had on the reverse prohibited the widow remarriage which was in existance since centuries. Thus the then Nepalese society was more pragmatic and advance than the then Indian society. The steps taken by Bhimsen Thapa pushed the Nepalese society many centuries back. It was a set-back in the social history as compared to the trend of the history of the neighbouring countries, Bhimsena Thapa's step can be said as an imposition of a stauuch Hindu system on the traditional Nepalese way. When Chandra Gupta II, one of the champions to revive and strengthen the Hinduism in India, had married his brother's wife, the widow remarriage was not an anti-Hindu system. Howover, later on the widow remarriage had crept in the Hindu society of India and it was considered as one of the social evils. It that way the Nepalese society was better than the then Indian society.

The widow remarriage and divorce system were in vogue in certain communities even later on. Many autochthonous societies continued the system of widow remarriage. Divorce system was in vogue in Newar community. The females could have divorced then husbands even among high caste Newars, although it was not much appreciated. There was also a system of chopping off of the head of the wife's paramour by the aggrieved husband up to 1970. The aggrieved husband could kill the seducer of his wife anywhere and any time he wished. It was legally permitted. Thus the husbands used to safeguard their wives from the elopers. But the system was practised only by certain caste groups not by all.

On the whole we can surmise that the Nepalese family system was well managed with the pragmatic approach. The family system was well knitted together culturally, socially, economically and politically. It had developed its own specialities in its own way.

4

Habitational Sites

Introduction

The study on the habitational sites of Nepal through ages is quite interesting. Location and type of the habitational sites in Nepal where determined by many factors, as elsewhere in the world. When we think of the location of the habitational sites of the ancient world three main things *i.e.* water, fertile land and availability of housing materials were taken into consideration. The people resided in those areas where these objects were available. Among those objects also the then people emphasised more on water and fertile land for the settled life. The ancient well known civilizations developed on the banks of rivers like Mesopotamian civilization, Egyptian civilization, Indus valley civilization, Chinese civilization etc. Thus various civilizations of ancient world developed on the plain areas besides the rivers.

Ancient habitational sites

When we talk of the habitational sites of Nepal we have to think of the geo-physical condition of the country. Nepal is an elongated rugged mountainous country. The high current rivers flowing from north to south have partitioned the high mountains at different parts. Valleys at different parts are useful for habitation. The transport and communication from one part to another of the country are still very difficult. Most of the mountains are still barren and rocky without many trees but with only bushes and shrubs. The northern high mountains covered with perenial snow was and is not habitable. The only habitable areas are the middle belt of the mountainous region with sub-tropical climate and the plains in the south with tropical climate. The valleys made by the rivers are quite fertile for the production of food crops. The forest of the sub-tropical and tropical areas provided the wood to be used for the construction material and fuel. The rocks available in abundance could be used for the construction of the houses. The habitational sites developed in different areas of Nepal due to political, economic and social reasons. Let us now deal with some of the habitational sites right from the ancient time.

Videha

According to *Ramayan*, Videha was one of the flourishing states in those days. During the 6th century B.C. it was one of the Ganas of the Vajji Confederacy. The northern part of Videha state was situated in the present Nepal. The capital town of the state extended up to the Janakpur district of Nepal. It was a well planned town with all the facilities required in the ancient world. More details will be revealed only after the archaeological activities in the site.

Kapilavastu

Another developed habitational site was the Kapilavastu town, the home town of Gautam Buddha. The existence of three pillars of Emperor Ashok in Lumbini, Niglihawa and Gotihawa and some archaeological activities in Tilaurakot have revealed the existence of the habitational sites in these areas up to the Mauryan period and after that also. The present Kapilavastu and Nawal Parashi districts were inhabited by the Shakyas and Koliyas respectively during the sixth century B.C. The existence of so many unexplored maunds in these areas is the potential evidence of the well habitated town in those days. According to the Buddhist texts, the main Kapilavastu citadel was a well fortified area surrounded by huge wall and moat, which is also proved by the archaeological evidences.

Kapilavastu, the capital of the Shakyas, was a well developed town. The palace area was well protected by the huge wall and moat. It is described in the Buddhist texts that the huge and attractive buildings were constructed in the town, which was also called *Negama.* In the ancient world Kapilavastu was situated on the high way. So from the commercial point of view it was one of the very busy towns during the sixth century B.C. In the town, Siddharatha Gautam had passed his early twenty nine years. The town was well flourished until it was devastated by Viruddhaka, the King of Kosala. The Kosala king had invaded, massacred a large number of Shakyas and burnt the town. Since after that Kapilavastu could not develop well. A large number of the Shakyas were slaughtered, many fled away helter and skelter and only a few were left in Kapilavastu. The time Fahien visited the town, it was waste and deserted area. There were only a few monks and lay-attendants who clung to the place for its sanctity and devotion. In about 639 A.D. when Huien Tsang visited Kapilavastu he also found it a desolate place. Huien Tsang's account runs :

> "This country is about 4000 li in circuit. There are some ten desert cities in this country wholly desolate and ruined. The capital is overthrown and in ruins. Its circuit cannot be accurately measured. The royal precincts with the city measure some 14 or 15 li round. They were all built of brick. The foundation walls are still strong and high. It has been long deserted. The people of villages are few and waste. ...There are 1000 or more ruined Sangharamas remaining; by the side of the royal precincts there is still a Sangharama with about 3000 (read 30) followers in it...."

Later Kapilavastu area was visited by Emperor Ashok two or three times. In circa 255 B.C. Emperor Ashok visited Niglihawa and erected a pillar in commemoration of Kanakamuni Buddha and had also extended the Chaitya as the inscription of the pillar reads. Again after six years Emperor Ashok visited the famous Lumbini garden, well famed as the birthplace of Lord Shakyamuni Buddha. He had erected a pillar in memory of Lord Buddha there. The third pillar was erected at Gotihawa, the birth-place of Kakruchhanda Buddha. But as the upper portion of the pillar with the inscription is missing we do not know what was inscribed in it.

Thus Kapilavastu was one of the important areas in the history of Nepal as three human Buddha were born in the area. So we find ruins of many monasteries constructed during Maurya, Sunga and Kushan period around the area. Inspite of this, Kapilavastu could not restore its past active, lively and busy life. It was a flourshing state for about two or three centuries and had its fall after the deadly blow it faced from Kosala. So the Chinese pilgrims found it a deserted and desolate area during their visits.

Ramagrama

Another equally well developed and flourished area was Ramagrama which was situated in the present Nawalaparasi district of Nepal. It is described that there were small principalities of the Koliyas knitted together as a loose confederacy. The Koliyas had the matrimonial alliances with the Sakyas; for example, both the mother and wife of Sakya Muni Bundha belonged to Koliya community. The Koliyas had well built state in the area. They constituted one of the active peoples up to the time of the death of Lord Buddha. They had taken a share of the relies of Lord Buddha after his death and constructed a stupa ...relic inside. Although Kapilavastu was destroyed during the life time of Lord Buddha by the Kosalan King the Koliya confederacy was in existence quite later on also. Only after the rise of Magadha, Ramagrama lost its independence and became a part of the Magadhan empire.

Emperor Ashok is described to have visited the Ramagrama stupa in his mission to collect the relics of Lord Buddha to construct many stupas throughout India. Huien Tsang further wrote that the Naga chief of the area pleaded the Mauryan emperor not to open the stupa to collect the relics of Lord Buddha which they had cherished so much. Emperor Ashok was much impressed by the request and left the stupa untouched after paying his homage. Thus up to that time the area was well inhabitated. The people had constructed a monastery not far from the neighbourhood of the Stupa.

But later on the area was deserted due to unknown reason. Huien Tsang's account on the area runs,

> "The kingdom of Lanmo has been waste and desolate for many years. There is no account of its extent. The towns were decayed and the inhabitants few."

What it seems is that up to the time of Emperor Ashok's visit to the area, there was habitation, but, later on, these Koliyas might have faced problems *i.e.* invasions or some other reasons and left their original area and took shelter in Kathmandu, where they built two *gramas i.e. Koliyagrama* and *Dakshina Koliyagrama*.

Lumbini

Lumbini was the garden well maintained both by the Shakyas and Koliyas. It is described as a very pleasant spot covered by *Sal* trees and other varieties of trees. There was a pond watered by a rivulet flowing near by. The Lumbini garden was just like a picnic spot for both Koliyas and Shakyas. Gautam Buddha was born in this very garden, as such this place became one of the four holy places of the Buddhists. Emperor Ashok had visited the spot to pay homage to the Buddhists holy shrine and erected a stone piliar with the figure of a horse on the top as the capital to commemorate the birth of Lord Buddha, as already mentioned. The time Emperor Ashok visited there, it was inhabited by the people as is evidenced by his order of releasing the local people from the tax. The account is well inscribed on the pillar. Later on many stupas and monasteries were constructed there in Lumbini at different times from the Mauryan to the Gupta period, as is proved by the archaeological evidences. The excavations have also revealed the habitational sites nearby the Nativity site. But in those days the area was inhabited by the monks, nuns and other villagers.

The present jungle area in the east of the Rohini area was a well habitated area of the days gone by. When we go to the jungle area we still find a vast area with the debris. The site makes us feel that it was once a well inhabited area. Up to this time when we dig even in the cultivated area around there we find the foundation of many houses lying under the earth. The excavation in the area if undertaken scientifically might reveal the extension of the site. At present we can say this much that once upon a time the whole area was well inhabitated.

Kathmandu Valley

Kathmandu Valley is also an old habitated area. Due to the want of the extensive and scientific archaeological activities we have not got clear-cut picture of the ancient habitational sites of the valley. Lack of historical sense had also destroyed many of the historically important sites even up to the present time, in the Kathmandu Valley, for example, the water conduits constructed from the time of the Lichchhavis are either buried or misused *e.g.* the Bhotahiti, a water conduit situated neardey Asontol and another recently exposed conduit belonging to the period of Amsuvarma, were buried during the days of Ranauddip Simha. Unknown to us many such important sites must have remained buried in various parts of the valley.

The sites of the ancient important numents like Mangriha, Kailashakut Bhavan, and Bhadradhivas Bhavan (the royal palaces of the Lichchhavi period) are yet to be located. According to the *Vamsavalis* and historical records, Nepal had suffered severe earthquakes many times. The latest one in the Kathmandu Valley had occurred in 1934 A.D. and in the far western region a few years back. Thus the present shape of the habitational site of the Kathmandu Valley was the effect of many changes. Juddha Shamsher had reshaped Kathmandu town after 1934 A.D. Moreover, the epidemic diseases that had occurred very often might have also affected in the habitational sites of the area.

Now let us examine the habitational sites of the valley through ages. As already mentioned, in the absence of the scientific and extensive archaeological excavation nothing can be said definitely about the places where the people had resided before the historic period began. If we are to believe the *Vamsavalis*, the earliest habitational sites were located at the Kirtipur and Matatirtha areas. *Gopal Vamsavali* is silent about the habitational site of the Gopalas and Abhirs, the earliest rulers, but the later *Vamsavali* mentions, "These men settled down at Padma Kasthagiri, and built cowsheds", but the palace of the ruler was situated at Matatirtha. The royal precinet was shifted from place to place prior to the historic period in the Kathmandu Valley. It is mentioned that sometimes it was at Matatirtha and at the other time it was at Godavari. Later on from there also it was shifted to Baneswor. Haridatta Varma is described to have built four Narayan temples at Changu, Ichangu, Sekha Narayan and Bisankhu. All these places might have been habitated by the then people.

To begin with the historic period of the Kathmandu Valley we have to consider the habitational sites mentioned in the Lichchhavi inscriptions, which mentioned more than a hundred habitational sites scattered within and outside the valley. There are certain characteristics of the Lichchhavi habitational sites. First of all, the sites were scattered in the various parts of the Kathmandu Valley and outside. Secondly, we have two types of the names of the sites; one was in Sanskrit and the other in the aboriginal language most probably in Kirat language. Those areas, inhabitated by the people, like the Sakyas, the Koliyas, Mallas and others who had migrated later on and were well acquainted with Sanskrit, were named in Sanskrit language like *Yupa Grama*, *Koligrama*, *Dakshina Koligrama*, *Hanshagriha Dranga*, *Vaidyagrama*, *Sambapur* etc. Only a few of the habitational sites were named in Sanskrit, whereas most of the names were in non-Sanskrit. Thus it is proved that before the Lichchhavis, non-Sanskrit language speaking people had inhabited the Kathmandu Valley and outside. On the basis of the list of names of the habitational sites, it is guessed that terms used in naming the places were the then Kirat language. Thirdly, the habitational sites were gradual developing. Those very sites which were termed simply as *grama* gradually developed into *Gulma*, the *Gulma* into *Tala*; and *Dranga* was the most developed habitational site at that time. On our observation it has become evident that there were *Drangas* either in the centre or en route to the districts outside the valley. In the then system *Pradesh* was a bit more developed than the *Grama*. Sometimes the same area was called both *grama* and *Pradesh* like *Yupagrama pradesh*, *Dunlung grama pradesh*, whereas some of the sites were called simply Pradesh like *Vilibikshya Pradesh*, *Khainaspu Pradesh*, *Vagvatipara Pradesh*, *Maishingh Pradesh* etc.

The gradual development of a village Grama into a *Gulma*, *Tala* and *Dranga* can be cited in many cases. Sitati area was first referred to as *Gulma*. Later on it was mentioned as the *Tala*. At last it was referred as the *Dranga*. Thus many of the areas were gradually developing with the growth and development of trade and commerce and population. But most of the areas were in the form of villages called *grama*. The present town of Kathmandu was not so developed in those days. It consisted of scattered villages like *Dakshina Koli grama* and *Koli grama*.

Besides many habitational sites in the Kathmandu Valley there were many such areas outside also. The provinces were called *Janapadas*; the headquarters of which must have been well habitated. The inscription of Shivadeva II, situated at Gorkha, refers to the word *Janapada*. The area around the place with the inscription must have been a habitational site. Similarly, Kurpasi, Tistung, Banepa, Bhatuwal, Dumja, Chitlang, Kewalpur, and others were the habitational areas during the Lichchhavi period. We do not have archaeological evidence of the habitational sites beyond these areas, as no much archaeological explorations have been undertaken there.

During medieval period there was a tremendous change in the habitational sites as the available sources give us a lot of information. We have much information about the early medieval period. On the bais of *Gopataraja Vamsavali*, there were many habitational sites in the valley each under a feudal lord. Some of the sites can not be located now due to the change in the names of those sites. But the *Vamsavali* mentions scores of the place-names, most of which were in the form of forts. Later on when the Malla kingdom was divided into three principalities, the capitals were well fortified. Dr. Old field had found the recius of the fortified wall. According to him :

> "During the time of the Niwar Rajahs each city was surrounded by a high wall, in different parts of which were large gateways, which generally remained open, but in times of danger or disturbance could be closed and depended.
>
> Since the Gorkha Conquest of the valley the walls have been allowed to decay, and have now nearly disappeared, while many of the gateways are in ruins. The limits of each city are, however, still strictly marked along the line where the ancient walls stood, and no

Hindus but those of good caste are allowed to dwell within its precincts."

It is now proper to deal with the growth of the main towns of Nepal.

Bhaktapur

Bhaktapur, also known as Khopa in Newari language, was a small habitational site during the early period of the Lichchhavis In 477 A.D. it has called *Khopring grama.* At that time it was just a village. Another inscription dated 594 A.D. mentions the area as *Khripung grama.* An inscription, situated at Golamadhitole, Bhaktapur, dated 594 A.D. mentions *Makhoprimasataludranga.* Vajracharya opines that Khopring was the old non-Sanskrit name. He further mentions that Khripung and Makhoprim were two separate habitational sites. Makhoprim was a new site which had developed into the status of *Dranga* (a well developed trade centre), whereas khripung, an old site, did not develop and remained just a *grama.* The present Newari term Khopa is derived from khopring.

Bhaktapur became the capital of Nepal after Anandadev had made it capital having constructed Tripura palace king Anandadev was coronated in 1147 A.D. Hence after it developed fastas the capital of Nepal. Up to the first half of the fifteenth century, the capital was not fortified, as it was not felt necessary. The repeated invasions of the new rising houses like Khasiya Mallas, Karnata rulers of Nepal and the Nawab of Bengal made the ruler of the Kathmandu Valley feel the necessity of fortifying the capital town. The rise of a strong and stable government also made the fortification of the capital possible. In India also the capital towns were surrounded by huge wall and moat. In the night the doors were closed and in the day these doors wers opened. In the same way Yakshya Malla (1428-82 A.D.) fortified Bhaktapur in 1453 A.D , whereas the two other towns like Kantipur, and Lalitpur were not fortified up that time. Bhaktapur, which consisted of two habitational sites called Khopring, and Makhopring developed fastly, as it became the capital of the then *Nepal Mandala* (the Kingdom of Nepal). It was the political centre from the early medieval period, as is evident from the contemporary epigraphic evidences. After Yakshya Malla, the division of the Kathmandu Valley took place which led to the deterioration of its importance to a large extent. Now it became the capital of only one of the three kingdoms of the Kathmandu Valley. But the continous attempts of the then Malla rulers resulted in the beautification of the fortified town.

The royal palace was very much extensive in size, as the chronicles mention that there were ninety-nine courtyards within the palace. The Malla kings used to have the temple of their family Goddess Tulaja Bhavani within the palace. The artistic masterpieces of stone and wooden sculpture have enriched and enhanced the beauty of the palace. Almost every Malla king had contributed in the beautification of not only the palace but also the whole town. The well known kings in this respect were Yakshya Malla, Naresh Malla, Jitamitra Malla, Bhupatindra Malla and others. Bhupatindra Malla was given credit to have extended the palace. He constructed a special palace with fifty five windows, one of which had the glass window pane, erected his gold gilted fine status, constructed the *Nyatapola* (five storyed) temple and many others.

Bhaktapur, the capital, had twenty-four localities, as described by the *Vamsavalis*, and twelve thousand homesteads. Thus the habitational sites wnich remained just in form of two villages gradually extended and developed into a town. Although the division of the Kathmandu Valley deteriorated the importance of the town of Bhaktapur to a large extent. yet the town started growing with the lapse of time up to its conquest by the Gorkha king Prithvinarayan Shah, after which the town of Bhaktapur did not enjoy any political importance. Bhaktapur which was once a *Nagar* or *Pura* was once again ignored and was called a *Goan* (named it Bhatgaon), yet it was not so small in form as it was in the ancient. The growth of many big towns in Nepal had only deteriorated its importance and it was called a *Gaon*, otherwise there was growth of population and expansion of its area. She area of the town extended outside the wall and moat of the medieval period during the modern period. Now there are no remnants of the fortified area of the town. Even Daniel Wright, a Resident physician during the days of Jang Bahadur, did not find the ruins of the walls and moats constructed by Yakshya Malla. He had described Bhaktaput in this way :

> "Its shape is said to be that of *Damaru* of Mahadeo. It is built on high ground, streching from east to west, and most of the side streets run down a steep incline towards the bank of a small stream on the southern side, which afterwards join the Bagmati. Bhagaon has much wider, better paved, and cleaner streets than either of the other towns. Its houses too seem in better repair, and it strikes a stranger as being altogether in a more flourishing condition. The population is estimated at about 3000."

The condition of the houses and streets seemed better in Bhaktapur, might, be, because the town was well repaired after the Gorkhalis had burnt major part or the town during their invasion over the town in 1769. During the invasion, the Gorkhalis had burnt more than five hundred houses, which were later on repaired, as such the houses seemed well repaired and streets also well paved and better off.

But, later on, Bhaktapur lagged far behind in its expansion and development as compared to Kantipur. Moreover the construction of Kodari proved to be a further below on Bhaktapur, as prior to it the town was the trade-mark of the eastern Nepal.

Kantipur

Kantipur also knomn as *yan* was one of the three Malla kingdoms. Ratna Malla, an ambitions son of king Yakshya

Malla, had established a separate kingdom of Kantipur in 1484 A.D. hence after it became an independent kingdom. The proper town of Kantipur became the capital of the newly founded kingdom. The later kings like Mahendra Malla, Pratap Malla and Jayaprakash Malla had contributed a lot in the expansion and beautification of the town. After of the conquest, the Shah Kings Prithvi Narayan Shah, Rana Bahadur Shah, and the Prime Ministers Bhimasena Thapa, Jang Bahadur, Ranauddip Singh, Bir Shamsher, Chandra Shamsher, and Juddha Shamsher can be credited to have contributed to the expansion and beautification of the tomn. Kantipur was developed specially after the unification of Nepal as it was made the capital of the unified Nepal. It became not only the political centre but also the centre of the big kingdom in cultural, economic, social, and educational aspects.

Present Kantipur town had mainly two small villages *i.e Dakshin Koligrama* and *Koligrama* during the ancient time After Lichchhavi period the Kantipur town was comprised of *yangala* and *yambec* areas. The terms *Dakshina Koligrama* and *Koligrama* were replaced by *yangal* and *yambec yangal* comprised of the area. Tebahal in the east, Bhimsen than in the west, Makhan Tole in the north and Lagan area in the South. Similarly *yambec* covered the area north of Makhan to Thalieti tole. During the early medieval period, the area was expanded; thus the two scattered villages were joined together. The town of Kantipur was dividedl into two parts *i.e Thatlesl* and *Kodesh* (upper and lower areas) during early modern period. Later on it seem that the proper town of Kantipur was divided into three parts *viz Thane* (upper part), *Kwone* (lower part) and *Dahu Twa* (central area) The northern part of the town is still called tae *Thane* in Newari. The *Tnane* areas comprised of the localities like Thahiti, Nagha, Thaemaru, Ashan etc. *Koane* consisted of the localities like Lagan Tole, Jaisidewal, Brahmatole, Bhimasenathan etc. The *Dathu Twa* comprised of the area from Asan to Makhan, where we find two images of lion. This sort of the division of proper town of Kantipur is evident from the chariot festival of Goddess Kumari on *Bhadra Shukla Chaturadashi* When the chariot was taken around *kwone* area *i.e.* Chikanmugal, Jaisidewal, Lagan, Brahmatole, Bhimasena than. On *Bhdra Sukla Purnima* it was carried around the *Thane* and *Dathu* areas *i.e.* Naradevi, Nhyakha, Bangemuda, Nhyakantala, Asan, Balakumari, Kelatole, Indrachowk and Makhan Another festival *i.e.* the *Gaijatra* also makes the extension of the town area of Kantipur clear. The participants of the festival also go around the town area of the medieval period. We have another festival called *Upaku*, in which people go around peripherial area of the town offering oil lamps in the name of the deceased members of the family on *Bhadra Sukla Dwadashi* every year. Thus the traditional festivals of the area make us clear about the inner and peripherial area of the town. The territorial extension beyond the area around which such festivals take place was the later expansion. Although we do not know the exact date of the beginning of those festivals, yet it can be said that all of them were introduced during the medieval period. Such festivals are the main evidences of the territorial extension of the three towns *i.e.* Kantipur Bhaktapur and Lalitpur. Specially the *Gaijatra* denotes the extension of the main town area of the three main capitals of the medieval period.

During the days of Mahendra Malla the town of Kantipur consisted of twenty-four localities called *Toles.* The central part of the town was the royal palace which was called Hanumandhoka from the time of Pratap Malla (1641-74 A.D.), as he placed the image of Hanuman just besides the main gate of the palace. The royal palace was gradually extended at different times by different rulers. Mahendra Malla constructed a very big temple of Goddess Taleju, the family deity of the Mallas on the northern side of the palace. Pratap Malla is credited to have beautified and extended the palace to a large extent. Manavajra Vajracharya has described that the palace area extended up to the Super Market area,

Nepal Bank Central Office, New Road and Jhochchen Tole during the medieval period. Prithvinarayan Shah had also contributed by constructing a very beautiful, artistic and palatial building in the Hanumandhoka palace area. The artists and masons of Kirtipur, Kantipur, Lalitpur and Bhaktapur were employed to construct the four corners of the palace. The courtyard of the palace well paved as those of the Malla buildings. The structs of the palace were carved with fine artistic masterpieces of erotic scenes and others.

Dhanavajra Vajracharya mentions that the town of Kantipur was a fortified one with walls and moat, but up to 1707 A.D. it was not a fortified one as a contemporary account mentions that there were neither walls nor doors. Desideri has written about Kantipur : The city of Kathmandu, situated on a plain, is large and it contains many hundred thousand inhabitants and has a few handsome buildings." During the medieval period the town was described to have been neat and clean. The road was well paved and drainage system was also well maintained. Many temples were constructed by the kings, members of the royal family, courtiers and the common people also. Pratap Malla had enhanced the beauty of the town by constructing the Ranipokhari just outside the town. The road from Bhotahiti, Asan, Indrachowk, Makhan, the Hanumandhoka palace square, Maru, Chikanmugal, Jaisidewal, Lagan, Brahmantole, Bhimasenthan etc., was also in existence in those days. Oldfield has written, "In Kathmandu alone there a street leading to the darbar along which a four wheeled carriage can be driven. In the other cities, and through the greater extent of Kathmandu itself, the streets leading to the darbar, as well as those which traverse the towns in all directions are mere lanes, adapted only for foot passengers, horses and elephants."

But the condition of Kantipur seems to have detoriorated later on. D. Wright writes about Kantipur in the following words :

> "It is situated at the junction of the Bagmati and Visnumati rivers, but lies closer to the latter, extending along its eastern bank for about a mile. When seen from above, its shape is very irregular, but it is said by the natives to resemble the Khora or Sword of Devi.... The town is built on no regular plan; but the main street may be said to run nearly north and south, and it is crossed at various angles by several others, while between these is a network of narrow dark lanes....In the centre of the town stands the Maharaja's palace, which is a huge, rambling, ungainly building part of it is very old, built in pagoda fashion and covered with elaborate and grotesque carvings. Other parts of it, such as the Durbar room, have been built within the last ten years and possess glass windows which are rare in Nepal being found only in the houses of the wealthiest."

Thus wright writes that Jang Bahadur had extended and built a new part of the palace in a new design. Up to this time that part of palace is standing in the southern and western parts of the Durbar square. This account gives us the information that the glasses were sill a rare object in Nepal, hence no surprise when Bhupatindra Malla fixed glass panes in his palace more than hundred years ago, he felt very proud of it.

Wright, further giving an account of the condition of the roads and the town of Kantipur as a whole, writes :

> "The streets of Kathmandu are very narrow, mere lanes in fact; and the whole town is very dirty. In every lane there is a stagnant ditch, full of putrid mud, and no attempt is ever made to clean these thoroughly. The streets, it is true, are swept in the centre, and part of filth is carried off by the sellers of manure, but to clean the drains would now be impossible without knocking down the entire city, as the whole ground is saturated with filth. ..In short, from the sanitary point of view,

Kathmandu may be said to be built on a dunghill in the middle of latrines."

Oldfield, another writer of the Same time and a medical doctor of the British Resident, described about the horrible condition of the drainage system of the Kathmandu Valley in this wage;

> "There is an ulterabsence in all the cities of any system of drainage; nearly stagnant guthers on each side of the street, running immediately below the house-prouts, do the duty of Sewers, and into them most of the fifth and refuge of the adjecent buildings find their way."

The poor condition of the town from hygein ic point of view is evident from this account. There was a little sense among the people to keep the area neat and clean, as its result almost every year in the summer a large member of people used to die of epidemic diseasses like cholera, small-pox, diarrhoea and typhoid. Even in case of spread of such diseases people felt that it was the result of wrath of the Gods and Goddesses, not because of the unhygienic way of life.

In 1880 A.D. Kantipur had between Sixty thousand and eighty thousand population according to Oldfield.

Jang Bahadur can be credited to have extended the town of Kathmandu constructing his palace at Thapathali, which was situated in the outskirt of the town. There were three gates to enter the palace area. The first gate was situated at Tripureswor, where there was watch-house (*Chowki*); the second gate was just at the entrance of the Thapathali area and the third gate was the main entrance of the palace. The palace of Jang Bahadur was worth seen as mentioned by Wright, who describes about it as follows:

> "Thapathali consists of a succession of square of gigantic houses, four or five stories in height which are occupied by Sir Jung Bahadur, his sons, and their numerous families,

> The buildings and grounds are kept in good order, the place is well worth visiting, especially as the owner most obligingly allows strangers to inspect the public rooms, and the grounds, with all curiousities contained in them. The four public rooms are large lofty, and ornamented with pictures and carvings. They are full of curiosities of Nepalese, Chinese and English manufacture. Of the last it is difficult to say what there is not...."

Thus we get two entirely different pictures about the town of Kantipur. One was the most unhygienic clusters of the houses built on the dunghill in the middle of the latrines occupied by the common mass, in the centre of the clusters the royal family resided. On the other hand there was the new developed area of Thapathali, the seat of the newly emerged Rana Prime Minister. The palace of the Rana Prime Minister as described by Wright consisted of all the most attractive objects of the world. At that we can raise a question : whether the then Nepalese economy permitted that sort of well equipped palace ? From that time onwards the Ranas showed their self centred attitude ignoring the interest of the mass or the welfare of the common mass. There were two worlds in the town of Kantipur *i.e.* the wretched slumps at the very heart of the capital and the most attractive and well decorated palace of the Rana Prime Minister at the distance of about a mile.

The rise of the Ranas led to further widening the gap between the rubrs and the ruled. Their exposure to the western world made them more and more avaricious in leading the most luxurious life at the cost of the welfare of the whole nation in totality. Those the Ranas, who lived in Thapathali, started constructing separate palaces of their own. This sort of tendency led to the construction of so many palaces in the Kathmandu Valley at the cost of the common mass. Thousands of *ropanis* of lands were acquired to construct every new palace for a Rana. The owners of land which was acquired by the Ranas were given meagre or nominal compensation. The Ranas had their own world within the palaces, which were decorated with all the western luxurious objects of the world, whereas the people had to be satisfied with the minimum of their requirements.

In one way the construction of such palatial and spacious buildings resulted in having many well decorated palaces in Kantipur, but, on the other hand, it checked the expansion of the town for the common mass, who had to remain satisfied with the minimum space for their shelter. The whole attention was given in the maintenance of the palaces, whereas the habitational sites of the common mass remained ignored. The most decorated and furnished palace of the Rana period was the palace of Bir Shamsher which was believed to have been envied by almost all the Ranas including the other Prime Ministers later on.

Bir Shamsher Shamsher's palace complex consisted of many palaces which were called the *Phohara Durbar* (palace with fountains), *Lal Durbar* (red palace), *Seto Durbar* (white palace) etc. The halls of the Durbar, specially one, were the most lavishly furnished and decorated. The Durbar was his personal palace constructed out of state exchequer. Not only the Prime Minister, the other Ranas also started constructing big buildings.

Bal Krishna Shama, a Rana, has discribed about his grandfather Damber Shamsher's palace in this way:

> "We had a palatial palace with big halls, which were equipped with chandeliers, big urns, looking glasses or mirror (made in Belgium) big paintings, tables, chairs, carpets, Sofa sets, etc. There were many gardens, tanks with gold and silver fishes and rotus flowers etc. Forty gardeners, looked after the garden, sixty staff served in different capacities, thirty body guards and the maid-servants numbered a hundred. There were six carriages, twenty horses, fifty milking cows and a hundred pigeons."

Later on, Chandra Shamsher constructed a very big palace called *Singh Durbar*. The compound of the palace occupied thousands of ropanies of land. The main palace consisted of hundreds of rooms with well furnished and decorated halls. The palace was made the Prime Minister's residence. Thus many palaces were constructed at the cost of state exchequer and tears and toils of the common mass.

The great earthquake of 1934 caused a great havoc in the central parts of Nepal Thousands of the hovels of the Kathmandu Valley collapsed. Inspite of its disasterous effect, it provided an opportunity to build a new town in Kantipur. Juddha Shamsher, the then Rana Prime Minister, felt the necessity of having a market place worth to be exhibited to the foreigners. The present New Road area was then constructed in a planned way. A park called Bhugol Park was also made. Thus new spacious roads right from the Tundikhel to Hanumandhoka (east & west) and Nagar Palika area to Indrachowk (South & North) were made. In the area well plastered houses were ordered to be constructed. Thus that area became worth exhibiting to the foreigners. In those days such a meagre work was also considered a great grace and blessing of the most gracious and benevolent Rana Prime Minister. The people were much obliged that such a big and benevolent act was achieved by the Prime Minister.

Kantipur was thus extended and beautified step by step. It developed because it was the capital of Nepal, where the foreigners (specially the British) frequented and most of the Ranas constructed their palaces over here. During the period the town area of proper Kantipur also extended in the north and south as well. The Thamel area which was called as *Mughalan* became an intregal part of the Kantipur town by 1951 A.D.

Patan

The third town of the Kathmandu Valley is patan, which was the capital of the Kingdom of Lalitpur under the Mallas. in shape the wheel or chakra of Buddha. Its ancient walls

Patan is derived from the word *Pattan* which meant a town. Although a *Vamsavali* mentions that it was called Lalitpattan or Lalitpur made by a farmer called Lalit by the order of King Birdeva. It is not yet clear as the exact reason for calling the town Lalitpur *i.e.* whether it was named after Lalit the farmer (architect) or because it was a fine town (*Lalit* also means fine) Lalitpur is called *yala* in Newari.

During the Lichchhavi period the present Patan town was not so much developed, as the Lichchhavi inscription mentions only the existence of Yupagrama area only. The Yupagrama also seems to have been developed only after the Sanskrit language-speaking people starting inhabiting in the area, because, during the Kirat period there seems to have not developed the habitational sites in the area. The Kirat habitational sites were called in non-Sanskrit term. In the present Lalitpur district there were many other well developed habitational sites like Lembati dranga, Gundule, Loogayoomi grama, and many others during the Lichchhavi period. The main site Yupagrama which was just a village in S.S. 492 (570 A.D.) developed into a *Dranga* in 643 A D. Around the Yupagrama many new habitational sites developed. Vajracharya is of the opinion that *Yupagrama dranga* was one of the highly developed area around which many *talas* and *gramas* emerged.

During the early medieval period many *Vihras* (monasteries) were built in the proper Patan town, as the major number of population were Buddhists. The area of the Patan town was divided into seven administrative units, as the *Sapta Kutumbajas* (seven families) ruled over there during the early medieval period. Each area was divided on the basis of the localities influenced by the monasteries. This sort of the division of the Patan town continued for some centuries. After the emergence of Lalitpur as an independent kingdom the Mangal Bazar area became the Durbar Square and the Patan town became the capital of Lalitpur kingdom.

During the reign of Srinivas Malla (1661 – 1684 A.D.) the town had 24 localities. Kunu Sharma has described that Lalitpur town was well developed; the roads in the town were well paved; the whole town was surrounded by huge walls and moat. Thus the town was well protected. Giusseppe writes that Lalitpur was an independent kingdom, its capital Patan was well decorated and maintained, as all the Malla kings of the three kingdoms had developed a feeling of competition among themselves in the beautification of their respective capitals. The various Malla kings had constructed many temples, extended their palace camp; and stone water conduits were made to supply drinking water and drainage system was also well maintained in their respective capitals. But after the conquest of all the Malla kingdoms by the Shah kings, we see the gradual decline of the two capitals *i.e.*, Bhaktapur and Patan. According to oldfield, Patan, previous to the Gorkla conquest, was a wealthy, powerful and impartant city (largest city in the Kathmandu Valley). But after the Surrender of Patan to Prithvi Narayan Shah in 1768 the city was given up to plunder, the mobility and principal men were murdered, and the greatest barbarities were practised on the unfortunate inhabitants, who, being mostly Buddhists, recieved but little nurey at the hands of their Hindu Conquerors. The royal palace was dismantled; the dwethings of the wealthy citizens were robhed of every thing valuable that they Contained, and even the temples were not spared. As its result old field found the town in such condition :

"The city books much two large for its inhabitants; its streets as well as its buildings appear to be half empty; there is none of the bustle and activity and palpable prosperity which are visible throughout Kathmandu and Bhatgaon. Rieined buildings and deserted shrines, broken arch ways and mutilated sculptures, meet the eye at every turn; and while these runains are evidences of its former grandeur, they still painfully proclaim the melancholy fact that Patan's "glory has deported" The city is of circular form, and is said to resemble and gateways in most places are ruinous, and in many have quite disappeared".

Patan town was connected with Kantipur by a route through Tekudobhan, Confluence of Bagmati and vishnumati upto the time of Bhimsen Thapa. Bhimsen Thapa constructed a bridge connecting Patan and Kantipur at Thapathali. So it led to the development of two areas called Tripures was at Kantipur and Kopundol at Patan.

Patan became one of the towns under the Shah kings. Later on it became the administrative centre of the district. The condition of Patan was almost worse at the time of Jang Bahadur. Wright describes about Patan in this way :

> "The town of Patan stands on a rising ground, a short distance from the southern bank of the Bagmati, and about two miles south-east of Kathmandu ...It is an older town than Kathmandu. ... The streets are as narrow and dirty, the gutters as offensive, and the temples even more numerous; but it appears much more dilapidated than Kathmandu, many of the houses and temples being in ruins. The main square, however, in the centre of the town, is very handsome. ...The population of the town is said to be about 30,003."

The famous *Gaijatra* festival gives us an idea about the main area of the town during the medieval period, whereas the *Mataya* festival is very much linked with the Buddhist shrine of the town. Some of the Ranas constructed their palaces at Patan. Juddha Shawsher, as he had palace at Patan, constructed a Zoo at Jawalakhel near his palace The presence of so many monasteries and *chaityas* revels the fact that Patan is mainly inhabitated by the Buddhist people.

Kirtipur

Besides the main three towns, there were many other habitational sites of importance in the Kathmandu valley and outside. Kirtipur, a sub-town in Kathmandu Valley, was under the kingdom of Lalitpur during the medieval period. It was a fortified area surrounded by walls, moat and the military check-posts, and one of the *Vanadurgas* (forts in the forest). Although the later *Vamsavali* like Wright's *vamsavali* mentions that it was inhabitated by the *Gopalas* long ago, the archaeological and literary evidences prove its development at the time of Shivadeva III. The old name of the area situated on the hillock was Padmakasthagiri. The area had occupied a very strategic position from the military point of view, as such Prithvinarayan Shah had to fight severe battles at a very heavy cost to conguer it. The brave people of Kirtipur showed their full determination in the battles against the Gorkhas. They surrendered only when they suffered a lot under the duress of the Gorkhalis's blockade of the whole Kirtipur for months together. Up to the present time we see the town of Kirtipur maintaining its medieval feature intact. The town of Kirtipur had occupied the stratigic position from where all the three towns of the Kathmandu Valley are visible and the military operation could be under taken. It did not enjoy any commercial importance as Nuwakot did.

Nuwakot

Nuwakot, situated to the west of the Kathmandu Valley at a distance of a full day's walking for the hill people, was the western gate-way of the kingdom of Kantipur. We do not exactly know about the sub-town during the ancient time. But from the early medieval period we have some references of the town. From that time it was one of the very strong forts. *Gopal Vamsavali* mentions a lot about the active role of the town which was under a feudal chief. It is also mentioned in the *Vamsavalis* that during the early medieval period Vaisya Thakuris, who ruled over Nuwakot became the rulers of Kathmandu. Thus it is evident that Nuwakot had developed as an important town from the early medieval period. Anyway Nuwakot had already developed as one of the active towns and was considered as the western gateway of the Kathmandu Valley. During the period when the Khasiya Mallas invaded the Kathmandu Valley they were first resisted in the Nuwakot area. The then rulers of the Kathmandu Valley had to pay much attention in strengthening the strategic position of the area, as the Khasiya Mallas of Jumla had extended their territory up to Trisuli. Not only the area was developed as a fort for defence, but also the other strategic hill-tops of the region were converted as the *Vanadurgas*. Later on, it seemed that the political chaos in Kathmandu led to the independence of the area. Nuwakot had to be captured by king Ratna Malla in 1491 A.D.

Before the trade route to Kerong was formally opened the area of Nuwakot was considered valuable for its agricultural outputs and strategic position. Later or when the kingdom of Kathmandu enjoyed the trade privileges in Tibet via Kerong, Nuwakot developed as a trade centre. The traders started swarming over the area and as its result it developed as a trade centre. Custom office was established; the lucrative trade with Tibet was the main reason for the development of the area.

During the Malla period the area became famous as *Navakawatha i.e.* the centre of the nine forts around it. The main administrative officer of the area resided there. Later on during the first half of eighteenth century the kingdom of Gorkha under the Shah dynastyl ooked it with covetious eyes. The first two invasions of Gorkha *i.e.* in 1737 and 1743 A.D. were utter failure. But Nuwakot fell in the hands of the Gorkhas in 1744 A.D. After that Prithvinarayan Shah, who was expanding Gorkha, made Nuwakot his capital. Hence after for many years Nuwakot was the main seat, from where the Gorkha king conducted his military activities. The Gorkha conquest changed the nature of Nuwakot from being a trade centre and western gateway to the capital town of Prithvinarayan Shah.

Many of the Gorkha courtiers started building their residential houses at Nuwakot. Prithvinarayan Shah himself constructed a fort like palace in the town. The Malla palaces were also used by the Gorkhalis. The Gorkha king had passed most of his life in Nuwakot after its conquest, as such it was natural that the town flourished from political point of view. Formerly it was much frequented by the businessmen but now it was frequented by the Gorkha courteirs and military personnels. The trade to Kerong came to an end after the Gorkha conquest. Formerly due to the lucrative trade with Kerong, the town of Nuwakot was much busy with the traders. The Malla kings had constructed temples and buildings. So long Prithvinarayan Shah was alive he stayed in Nuwakot most of the time. After him, Pratap Simha Shah resided in the Hanumandhoka Durbar complex at Kathmandu. Thus there was a gradual wane in the importance of Nuwakot. The Gorkhali courtiers had to shift their residence from Nuwakot to Kathmandu.

Thus Nuwakot as a town could not flourish hence after. Only during the political clash between the courtiers and Rana Bahadur Shah the minor king Girbanayuddha was taken to Nuwakot, from where they (the courtiers) ruled over Nepal. For some years the town served as the winter resort of the Gorkha kings. Later on it started losing its importance as the later Shah kings did not go there. Thus the area lost both the economic and political importance. It turned into a mere village. During the Rana period the town of Nuwakot was made the district headquarter. But the shifting of the district quarter from Nuwakot to Bidur proved the last heavy blow on Nuwakot, which is now standing like a deserted village with its past glorious memories represented by the debris of the historical monuments. The routes to the town are now covered with shrubs and bushes. The main road in the town is now mostly covered with mosses Thus Nuwakot is one of the glaring example of the cycle of rise and fall of the towns with the change of time and situation.

Kirkpatrick, the first political agent of the English E st India Company, had met the than Gorkha king Rana Bahadur

Shah in 1792-93 A.D. He had written a lot about the economic and politicali importance of Nuwakot.

Gorkha

Gorkha was the name of the principality and the capital during the medieval period. Although we have not found any epigraphic evidence, it can be guessed that it was named after a sage named Gorkhanath. The Gorkha town also seems to have been inhabited during the Lichchhavi period, as the existence of the two Lichchhavi inscriptions reveal. But due to the broken condition of the inscription we do not exactly know its name during the Lichchhavi period, although at that time it was a *janapada i.e* a district. The *Gorkha Vamsavali* mentioned that sage Gorkhanath had blessed prince Drabya Shah that the latter would be king of Gorkha. On the basis of tradition, almost all areas of the present western region was called *Magarat*, which denotes the area inhabitated by the Magars. Gorkha town is situated on the top of the mountainous region with meagre economy. Prior to the conquest of the area by Drabya Shah, there were petty chieftains who ruled small areas with a few hamlets. These chieftains belonged to Khadka and Ghale communities-both non-Hindus. The present proper Gorkha town was also divided into Upallakot and Tallokot which were ruled by Ghale and Khadka chiefs. After the conquest of both of them by Shah family, Gorkha developed into a town which became the nucleus of the unification of Nepal. The town was gradually expanded and developed by the successive Shah kings. Rama Shah (1609-36 A.D.) had beautified the town by constructing a beautiful palace full of artistic designs and wooden and stone Sculptures with the help of the craftsman and technicians of Lalitpur. Moreover to strengthen the economy and develop the market in the capital, the businessmen from Lalitpur were invited to carry on business in Gorkha. Thus Gorkha started developing. Market place was called *Hathiyathok* in Gorkha. The royal palace was constructed on the top of the mountain from the strategic point of view. The royal palace and the houses of the big nobles only were constructed by the bricks, whereas the houses of the common people were made of boulders and stone-slabs with the thatch roofs. The streets in the town were paved with stone slabs, as in the Kathmandu Valley. Vaidya write about the palace of Gorkha :

> "The palace of the king which exists even today is made of polished fine bricks, most probably imported from Patan, and constructed by Rama Shah. The whole architecture and sculpture are a copy of the Malla style."

About a few hundred feet below, there were the houses of the courtiers. The beauty of the town further enhanced by Prithvipati Shah who, having seen the town planning of Kathmandu, had constructed more temples, a tank and also erected his statue, *cast in Kathmandu.*

Moreover the farsighted and benevolent policy of the Shah rulers made Gorkha centre of attraction for the people of many neighbouring states. Many facilities were given to the immigrants. People from various states started residing in the town of Gorkha. But the town did not enjoy such opportune for a long time. Since Prithvinarayan Shah started his military operation, he left Gorkha and resided at Nuwakot, which compelled the courtiers to shift their residences to Nuwakot. Thus Gorkha became a deserted place. Inspite of Prithvinarayan Shah's pious will to maintain Gorkha and active town, it could not retain the past activities, as all the higher officers had to shift to the new capital of the Gorkha kingdom. Later on the royal family resided in Kantipur and Gorkha became a deserted town. Hamilton describes about the town :

> "The capital Gorkha is situated on a very high hill, and was the only place of note in the territory. It is said to contain about 2000 houses, and the temple of Gorakha-

nath who is one of the tutelar deitirs of the reigning family".

During the Rana period it became just the district headquarter. Gorkha, as a town, could not develop in future.

Besides the above mentioned towns we had many habitational site scattered at different parts of the present Nepal, some of which were quite developed, active and were the trade centres at one time. But now they are just like villages some of which have some debris of the historical monuments and others do not have any thing left to tell their past glories. Msantime many new places emerged as developing trade centres. Economic actiuities specially the trade with Tibet dwindled After the Treaty of Thapathali (1856 A.D.) the trade with Tibet, once very lucrative, came to an end. The trade routes connected with Tibet are now almost forgotten which affected many habitational sites, just like the areas like Chitlang, Markhoo, Kulekhani, Bhimaphedi, Amalekhagung etc., after the construction of the Tribhuvan High way. Another reason was that the rise and fall of the towns were very much linked with the rise and fall of many states and ruling families, for example, the states of Sakyas, Koliyas, Senas, Shahs, Khasiya Mallas, Kalyal and so many others. The changing political scene of the country was very much responsible for the rise and fall of many towns. In other countries of the world the great natural calamities like earthquakes, volcanic eruptions, epidemic diseases etc., affected the habitational sites and towns. But in Nepal we do not observe such things to affect the habitational sites.

The Tarai belt which was once much inhabitated and many town developed was later on deserted, mainly because the area was much exposed to the south *i.e.* Indo-Gangetic plain, which was ravaged and plundered by the adventurous, merciless and blood-thirsty Turks and Muslim invaders. Many of the people residing in the fertile plains of Tarai, out of fear, fled to the hill area. The state which resisted the Muslim invader like Ghiyasuddin Tuglaq was conquered and the most flourished town like Simroangarh under Harisimhadev was ravaged, pillaged and totally destroyed. Such events horrified the people and deserted the area, which, later on, turned into a very dense jungle infested by the reptiles, wild animals and worst than all by the malaria. So Toni Hagen had rightly remarked that the Tarai was a malarial hell. At present when we keenly inspect such forest areas we see many debris lying under the dense forest waiting for the expert archaeologists to open them.

Another interesting feature of the habitational site during the medieval period in the hilly regions was that many habitational sites developed on the tops of the mountains, leaving the low land. The main reasons were that the elevated area was free from the malaria, because mosquitoes could not breed in such elevated and cold area. Moreover such area was strategically more safe than the low lands, as the invaders could be inspected from a far-off place when observed from the high area. The contemporary India also gives us the idea about the habitational sites, specially the rulers used to construct their fort like palaces on the top of the mountains wherever possible. The then India was infested by the invaders.

Nepal, since it is a mountainous region, had her habitational sites on the top of the mountains. Moreover the hamlets in the area were also scattered. The villages in the mountains were much dispersed due to want of spacious place for habitational sites and other facilities.

5

Position of Women in Nepal

Introduction

Position of women in general was of a subordinate type in the Nepalese social structure. Whether it was a Hindu or non-Hindu society, we have the patriarchal type of family system in general. The birth of a daughter, although not disliked, passed unnoticed in the society. For some religious performances there was and is the necessity of a daughter in the family. Since Nepalese soeiety did not suffer from the practices like that of *Tilak* (exorbitant dowry system) the birth of a girl does not prove so much agonising in the Nepalese society as in India. Once a girl was born she was given proper treatment and care by the family. The position of women is clearly mentioned by Kautilya who had written that a female would never be free. So long she is unmarried she has to remain under the protection of father or elder brother, after her marriage, she is to remain under the guardianship of her husband and when she becomes a widow she is to be under the control of her sons. When we discuss the subject on the condition of women we have deal with the various aspects like marriage system, widowhood, Sati, position of women in domestic and public life etc.

Marriage system

To talk of the marriage system of Nepal, polygamy was a common practice right from the ancient time. During the

Lichchhavi period the kings used to have many wives, one of them used to be the chief queen. Generally one who was the most favourite used to be the *Patarani* or *Mahishi*—the chief queen. King Manadev had three wives-Bhogini, Kshemasundari and Gunavati, among whom Bhogini was the chief queen. The queens had erected temples which are evidences of the freedom they enjoyed. Whether there was *swayambar* system (self-selection of the husband) or the settled marriage system is not clear due to paucity of materials. The Lichchhavi kings had married the princesses from India also, for example, Shivadev II was married to Srivastsadevi, the daughter of Maukhari king Bhogavarma and grand-daughter (daughter's daughter) of Aditya Sena, the king of Magadha. Similarly, Jayadev II married Rajyamati, the daughter of Harshadev, the king of Kosala. Since we do not have other types of sources, except the inscriptions and foreigners' brief accounts, we have very scanty informations of the polygamy.

During the medieval period also the polygamy system was very much in practice. Not only the rulers but also the nobles had many wives. The kings had harems with a large number of concubines and maid-servants. King Pratap Malla is said to have a very big harem with a large number of females. He had many wives as his inscriptions mention. When Yognarendra Malla died his thirty-three wives observed *Sati*. In this way during the medieval period the polygamy was a common practice throughout the country. The system of polygamy must have been a common feature among the common mass also.

There was no change in the system after the unification of Nepal also. The kings had many wives, for example, Prithvinarayan Shah had two married wives like Indra Kumari and Narendra Laxmi, and after his death nine wives of Prithvinarayan Shah observed *sati*. Pratap Simha Shah had two wives, one married called Rajendralaxmi and other a concubine named Maijurani. Similarly, Rana Bahadur Shah had many wives like Rajrajeswori, Subarnaprabha, Kantiviati, Lalita Tripurasundari and many other concubines.

Later on the Ranas, after their rise into power, started having their harems individually. We have many official documents which refer the orders sent by the Ranas to supply the young and beautiful girls belonging to the highercastes to be sent to the Rana palaces from the district. To cite example one order sent to the district of Jajarkot mentions that beautiful young girls of up to 10 years should be sent to the Durbar (Rana palace). Another document belonging to the period of Jang Bahadur mentions that the girl (quite beautiful, fair in complex, slim bodied etc.) should be sent to Jang Bahadur even if two or three hundred rupees should be paid. Jang Bahadur ordered Kazi Kulaman Simha that the girl should be owned not by using force but by persuasion. In those days it was a common practice to send order to the local officials to collect young beautiful girls of higher castes from the districts for the Rana palaces. Some self-conscious people did not like to send their girls whereas many people who were very ambitious used to offer their daughters quite willingly with the high expectation that if the girl (after attaining puberty) would become the favourite of the Ranas, the family would have a favour of the Ranas. Such family enjoyed higher position and got the *Bakshish.* Many of such families used to face the tragic end also. In many cases the girls when grown up fell the easy victim of the lust of the Ranas. When the females got pregnant, they were either driven out with some money to commit abortion or they were made to live outside and no recognition was given to the female and her issue. We have many such examples; one such classicial example was the case of Man Shamsher, who was called Man Bahadur so long his father, Juddha Shamsher did not become Prime Minister. Only after Juddha Shamsher, became Prime Minister, Man Bahadur became Man Shamsher. It is also believed that there were also many cases in which the pregnant women were poisoned to death, and the dead bodies were either handed over to the guardians, if the Rana mas merciful, otherwise such dead girls were buried under the fruit plants in Rana palace.

One of the strong reasons of the polygamy was the social obligations of the parents to get their daughter in marriage in time *i.e.* before the daughter attained the puberty. The wife of a Rana was called *Ranishaheb.* They used to give different titles to their concubines like *Ranishaheb*, *Nani* and so on, according to their favour. To perpetuate the polygamy among the royal family it was said that the king, being the incarnation of Lord Vishnu, should have two queens as Labshmi and Saraswati. The kings were made indulged in debauchery so that the Ranas could enjoy uninterrupted political power.

Not only among the ruling families but also among the common mass there was a tradition of polygamy. Generally the males used to have many wives, although such system caused domestic problems. The well-off people used to keep wives in different houses.

There were many other reasons of the polygamy. First, it was considered to be a social prestige to have many wives in those day. The people used to feel it a matter of prestige and masculinity to have many wives. There was a general feeling that the well-off persons or the highly statused people should have many wives. Such persons put forward their arguement that when Lord Krishna, a Hindu deity, could have sixteen thousand wives why should not a potential person should have many wives. As the feudal lords took pride in having many salves and serfs, so did the males took pride in having many wives. The poor females had neither any say or could make any protest against this. If a women is suspected of having any sort of link with any person other than the husband, such female would have no place in the society neither in her husband's house nor in her parents' house. The common mass used to keep a jealous eye on the sexual moral of their wives. Many person had also suffered from many diseases like paralysis, losing the eye-sight etc. due to over sexual indulgence.

Another reason of the polygamy was the agro-economy of the country. Most of the people earned their livelihood by cultivating land, as such a large number of man power was needed for the main occupation. Generally in the rural areas the people used to have some cattle for the sake of milk and manure. The hilly regions have scattered plots of arable land. So man power was needed for cultivation of land, collection of fodder and grazing of the cattle, looking after the domestic affairs etc. Thus a large number of the man-power was needed for all these functions. So the people used to have many wives for all these affairs. Instead of employing servants, the males used to keep many wives so that sincere and unpaid servants like persons would be available. In reality wives of such system was no better than servants.

Moreover in those days there was a general feeling among the people that larger the family greater was the social prestige. It resulted into two aspects : one was the encouragement to the polygamy and the other was unlimited number of child birth. Moreover concept of planned family had not developed. Thus the females were nothing but child-bearing machine. The birth of a son was a must duty of a conjugal life. Without a son the family line would break and there would not be anyone to continue the ancestoral worship, to perform *Sraddha* of the parents, to lit the funeral pyre. The very *Dh. rma Shastra* mentions "*Dhana Jana Briddhirastu* (let there be increase of the wealth and family members) at the time of any religious ritual among the Hindus.

Failure of procreation of a son also in many cases led to the polygamy. If the first wife failed to give birth to a son, the husband married the second wife. In some cases the first wife herself proposed the second marriage of her husband for the continuity of the family line The marriage of many wives for the want of a son was a common practice not only in Nepal but also in many countries.

Whether the polygamy was also due to the presence of excess number of females in the society cannot be accurately said due to the want of the census report of ancient and medi-eval periods. But the census report, 1981, shows the excess number of the male in the Nepalese society. Latest Statistical report shows that out of 15,022, 839 population, there were 7,695,336 males and 7,327,503 females.

It can be said that the polygamy existed in Nepal mainly due to the social, economic and cultural reasons. The selfish motive of the males had also played a vital role in the system at the cost of the peaceful conjugal life and career of the females.

Polyandry

On one hand the polygamy was a common practice in the Nepalese society, on the other hand there was the system of polyandry in certain communities. Generally in the northern area of Nepal the people of Tibetan origin had and have this system. A woman took all the brothers (or sons of a family) as her husbands. The wife of the eldest brother was the common wife of all the brothers. That sort of family had an interesting system of family life. One male was to remain with the wife, whereas other husbands would be far from the family. They used to have a routine of sharing the life with the wife, as the Pandav of the *Mahabharat* epic. Thus by turn the hus-bands would stay in the house, whereas the others would go afar : one would be busy in grazing the cattle, as they had to go afar for grazing due to the want of pasture, another would go to a distant place to purchase necessary goods for domestic use and so on. The whole function of the family was allotted to the male persons in turn so as only one husband got the opportunity to live with the wife.

In the polyandary system the female played the vital and dominating role in the family as the male in the patriarchal family. The duties of the husbands were performed on the will of the wife. Up to this time the system prevails in certain communties In that family the wife plays the key role in the family and the husbands have no option but to obey her. Generally she provides the equal opportunity to all her husbands in turn to be at home.

One document clearly mentions that polyandry was in vogue among the people of Tibetan origin. Another document mentions an order sent by Prime Minister Bam Bahadur Kunwar Rana that the Amali and Dwares of Pansayekhola should not give trouble to the Tibetan emigres from Kerong and Notse. During the Tibet-Nepal war (1855-56) the Tibetans from Kerong and Notse had come to Nepal to settle as the Nepaless subjects in 1911 B.S. These people had the tradition of one woman having all the brothers (two three of any number of brothers) as her husbands. The Prime Ministers' order further mentions that the polyandry system to these people should be accepted and these people were permited to enjoy their tradition.

The polyandry system was in vogue in various parts of the country *i.e.* wheroever the people of Tibetan origin resided. The Sherpas have the polyandry system. In Karnali region specially in the northern area the people had and have the system. But now because of the age long contact with the people having polygamy system, the polyandry has become more and more obsolute. Only in the remote areas it is still in vogue as a common social system.

When we open the pages of history we came across the term *Strirajya* (matriarchical system) in ancient time. Atkinson has mentioned the existence of *Strirajya* in the Kumaon hills in ancient time. In those days also the polyandry was in vogue, which continued on in certain aborigine tribes.

The main reasons behind the system were the economic, cultural and past legacy. When we observe the system, we find that the wife of the eldest brother does not generally allow her brothers-in-law to marry any other woman. She offers her-self as their wife and her argument is that the presence of many females in a family would cause the break-down of the family, thus the ancestoral property would be fragmanted. Thus to *keep the family intact and save the family property being divided the polyandry has played a vital role.* It is the female who declares the father of a particular issue. Moreover the system survived with an objective of maintaining the cultural heritage of the community These people were also eager to maintain their past cultural legacy for which they (a group of the people belonging to Humla) had also applied to the central government of Nepal that all the Bhotiyas belonged to the same community as such the Bhotiyas of Barha Thapalya should be exempted from *Chandrayan* as the Bhotiyas of Sat Thapalaya Sathi Khola. The request was granted by Bhimsen Thapa. They were made to pay *Chandrayan* (tax) as they did not observe the Hindu system. These people must have been charged of *Chandrayan* as they had the system of polyandry and others. The government also willingly complied with the request of those people.

Early marriage system

We have the early marriage system since days yore. Due to the paucity of material we do not exactly know about the early marriage in ancient Nepal. But it was in vogue during the medieval and modern periods in the Nepales history. Although it can not be ascertained with epigraphic evidence in ancient period, it can be assumed that there must be early marriage system then also, as it was believed that the daughters must be given in marriage before they attained the puberty. We have story of Goma, a Brahmin girl, being married at the early age of seven with an old man of seventy years. Marriage of a daughter before puberty was the main concern of the parents. This social obligation had also put the parents in the most embarrassing position. The social system must have been in existence in the ancient period also. We have many epigraphic evidences of the early marriage from the medieval period.

Rajalladevi, born in 1347 A.D. was married to Jayasthiti Malla, the well known Malla king, in 1355 A.D. at the age of eight. Generally there was a tendency of getting the daughters married at the age of eight or nine years. We have many other examples of the Malla kings. Almost all the Malla kings were married at an early age. Parthivendra Malla died at the early age of eighteen. At that time he had many wives among whom twenty-four observed *Sati.* The early marriage system was a common social feature not only in the Kathmandu Valley but also in various kingdoms of the then Nepal, Prithvinarayan Shah himself was married at an early age. Later on during the Rana period also the early marriage system was much in practice.

Jang Bahadur himself, born on June 18, 1817 A.D., was married in 1828 A.D. and his eldest son at the age of eight. Similarly King Prithvi Bir Bikram Shah was also married at an early age. King Tribhuvan, had become the father at the age of thirteen. The early marriage system was practised not only among the higher social status people but also among the common mass. It was a common practice in the society to have the young girls of six, seven or eight years married. If the girls were not married in time the guardians or the parents had to suffer much social criticism; not only that, people used to suspect on the character or physique of the girls.

Such social system compelled the parents in many cases to have their daughter married without much consideration about the character, economic condition and many other aspects of the bridegroom Consequently, many of the married women had to pass most miserable life. Once the daughters were married, the parents felt that their moral duty was fulfilled. The traditional society compelled the females to suffer all sorts of hardships and maltreatment from the part of husband and the family members. The parents had also no alternative but to advise their daughters to face the misbehaviours. Many young girls who had the dreams of leading very happy conjugal life had to pass the most wretched life without any warm embrace from their husbands. In many cases the maid-servants were more happy and enjoyed more facilities than those maltreated wives in the houses. There was a common local version in the society that the fate of a girl was always like that of vanquished people. Another traditional belief which enforced the early marriage system was that the girls would be socially recognised only after marriage.

The common mass also felt pride in case their daughters were married in time. We have many reports which mention that prior to 1951 A.D. the girls who were still sucking the mothers' breasts were also given in marriage. In those days the children were breast fed up to three-four years if there was no next issue. Both the young pairs under teenage used to play together without knowledge that they were husband and wife.

Thus the main reason behind the early marriage was the social tradition, which was very difficult to be challanged. Up to 1951 if the girls were not married during teenage, they were suspected on many imaginative thoughts and we have still many such females who had to pass unmarried life, as they were not married in time. Such unmarried daughters are considered as the great social burden to the parents. Early marriage, thus, if in one hand relieved the family burden, on the other hand it had also spoilt life of many innocent girls in the Nepalese society.

Widowhood

In the Nepalese society widowhood was one of the common features from the ancient time. The ancient inscriptions (belonging to the Lichchhavi period) mention many widows who had constructed temples and consecrated lands. An undated inscription of Chabahil mentions that a Chaitya with fiasco wall paintings based on the story of *Kinnar Jatak* was constructed after many years' hard labour. Big plot of land with the annual income of forty-five *Manika* (measurement of crop) was consecrated for a trustee of the Chaitya. Moreover another plot of land with annual income of twenty-eight *Manika* was granted for the feast to be arranged by the Sangha (Vikshu) and daily worship of Lord Buddha. The construction of the temple and grant of land were made by a female. Most probably the female was a rich widow, so she could construct such an artistic monastry and consecrated a big plot of land. Similarly, another Abhiri widow of a noble family, had constructed a temple of Lord Shiva, which was named as Anuparameswor after the name of her husband Anuparam. Rajyavati, the mother of Mandev, had also donated wealth to the Brahmins. In this way there was the system of widowhood during the Lichchhavi period.

Later on during the medieval period also we have enough references of the widows. Generally some of the active queen-mothers used to look after the administration as the regents.

During the early medieval period we have Padumalladevi and Devaladevi, both the widows had taken very active role in the history. Padumalladevi was the mother of Rudra Malla, who was the defacto ruler of Nepal during the first quarter of 14th century, was active in the political and cultural activities, whereas Devaladevi, the widow of king Harisimhadev and sister of Rudra Malla, although a refugee in Nepal, had fished in the troubled water of political situation of Nepal and grasped the whole political power for three decades *i.e.* 1336 to 1366 A.D. She was virtually the *defacto* ruler during the period. Later on, also we have many examples of widows like Ganga Rani of Bhaktapur, Lalmati of Lalitpur, Kumudini, the mother of Jaya Prakash Malla and so many others. Generally the wives of the royalties committed *Sati*, but as it was not compulsory we have references of many widows. Most active queen did not immolate herself and such queens used to play very active role in the politics.

During the modern period also the tradition was almost the same. There were many widows, for example, Rajendra Laxmi, Lalitatripurasundari, and so many others. Among the common mass also since the *Sati* was not compulsory there was the system of widowhood only among those who wanted to lead the dedicated pious life in the name of the deceased husband. This sort of leading the austere and pious life was called the maintenance of *Sati Dharma.* Although the Hindu religious texts have laid much emphasis on the *Sati* system for the widows, they have also given an option which was called the *Sati Dharma.* Many of the widows had observed *Sati Dharma* and had led a very hard life as any Hindu widow of India.

But in reality the widowhood in Nepal was not as acute a problem as in India. We have many Hindu and non-Hindu communities which had permitted the widow-remarriage although the system was not much appreciated. It is one of the specialities of the Nepalese social life. In the non-Hindu communities, specially the Bhotiyas, Sherpas and others, since the polyandry was in vogue, the problem of the widowhood hardly arose, as all the brothers used to be the husbands even after the death of the elder husbands. In the Hindu communities also the remarriage system was in vogue. To cite examples, Nayak Devi, a widow, was married by Jagat Simha during the early medieval period. Similarly, Rana Bahadur Shah married Kantivati, a widow. But this sort of remarriage was much abhorred and criticised. Inspite of this, the widow remarriage was much in vogue.

There was a common practice of marrying the widow sister-in-law (*Bhauju*) by the brother-in-law (*Devar*) in Nepal for quite a long time. According to the system in case the elder brother died the younger brother used to keep his sister-in-law (*Bhauju*) as his wife. This system was in vogue among all the communities *i.e. Char Varna Chhatis Jat* in Nepal. During the last days Bhimsena Thapa issused an order which read that the system of marrying the duly married *Bhauju* was a great sin. Since it was a forest area (backward country) whatever had happened let it be (although it was a heinous sin). Since some regulations (according to the Hinduism) had to be framed it was ordered that if anybody, who, except the Kiratas, Limbus, Lapchas, and Jumlis, would deliberately take the *Bhauju* as the wife, would henceafter be punished according the prescribed rules. The rules, declared on the basis of the social status, were very severe. Thus it is evident by the decree that the widow-remarriage was a common practice among the Upadhyaya Brahmins, Kshetriyas, Rajputs, Sannyasis, Khasas, Vaisyas, Magars, Gurungs, Ghales, Newars, Damais, Sunars, Kamis, Sarkis, Gathiens, Hurkyas, Valamis, Majhis, Danuwars, Sunuwars, Murmis, Bhotyas, Chepangs, Varais, Paharis, Kuhmals Daranus and others. These peoples were to undergo very severe punishments like shaving of head, outcastes and banishment, cutting of organ, confiscation of the whole property, enslavement and death sentence. Thus the people were checked from widow remarriage by such severe punishment. The widow the remarriage (*Bhauju*) by the *Devar* was checked. But the Kiratas, Limbus, Lepchas and Jumlis were permitted to continue the practice.

The edict further reveals the fact that the widow *Bhauju* could remarry only the *Devar* but not anyone other else. The practice was also being prohibited by the edict which laid down very severe punishment to the *Devar*. Thus, as already mentioned, the time when in India the intellectuals like Raja Mohan Roy, pioneer to modernise India, was pleading the cause of widow-remarriage to uplift the down-trodden and miserable condition of Indian women, Nepal, under Bhimsena Thapa, pushed the gear in the near side by probihiting the existing system of widow remarriage in the name of civilising the barbourous society. Anymay the then Nepalese society prior to the implementation of the edict was more practical, realistic and advance from the present day point of view. But after the forceful implementation of the edict, the widow *Bhauju* was compelled to pass the miserable and curshd life.

To worsen the situation the other members of the family always had suspicious and hatred eyes of the widow. The poverty and avarice of wealth always made the other members of the family more and more crude towards the poor widows. The system of *Bhauju Behorne* (taking the *Bhauju* as wife) had guarranteed the ancestoral property intact. The *Bhauju* could not demand the partition of the ancestoral proparty in the case of *Bhauju Vehorne*. Fragmentation of property, movable and unmovable, was checked by the system. This edict might have rescued those widow *Bhaujus* who were quite unwilling to be life-partners of the *Devars*. About it also a big question can be raised as to what extent the widows could enjoy the freedom in a male dominated society.

Remarriage of the females

But the remarriage of the females was in practice in many cases from the ancient time. The Lichchhavi inscriptions have clearly defined under what circumstance a female could get remarried. Visnu Gupta's inscription mentions that a woman used to remarry in case of death, abscond, becoming an ascetic or moral degradation and some other unbecoming things of her husband. Thus there was a long tradition of remarriage in ancient period. The remarriage of a woman on the above conditions was not liable to punishment only in case the woman could give birth to a child. The inscription further reveals that there were women, who were indulged in the debauchery many times due to sexual dissatisfication with their husbands, were of bad moral character, were fallen from the *Charitra Dharma* (Moral Character) and were frustrated from the first husband and were too much licentuous in sex moral. Under such circumstances also if a women could give birth to an issue after remarriage she was not to be punished. Thus the edict has clearly mentioned the existence of remarriage, although with contemptuous feeling. The ancient treatise *i.e.* Kautilya's "*Arthashastra*" had also permitted the divorce from the part of a woman if the husband had migrated to a foreign country for ever, fallen from the character, become an impotent or a traitor or a murderer. But Kautilya did not permit remarriage to a woman, whereas the *Narad Smriti* permits the remarriage on certain conditions. Whether Vishnu Gupta's edict was a reform to raise the condition of the then women or a retrogation to the womenkind is a matter to be further explored It is most likely that it was an attempt to control the females by laying the condition that she would not punished only in condition she could give birth to a child. But the remarriage of the females was contemptuous act from the part of the females as the basic Hindu texts appreciate and expect a docile and dedicated wife. The concept of *Patiparameswor* or *Patibratanari* or *Patidevaprana* was much cherished in the traditional Hindu society. But the heterogenous character of Nepalese society demanded some relaxations in the strictness of the Hindu laws. Thus from the ancient time the remarriage, polyanry, and widow remarriage were in existence in Nepal. It continued a social legacy during the medieval period and also the present time. The remarriage, widow remarriage and polyandry exist in many communities. The Sherpas, people of Tibetan origin, and many other communities continued to have polyandry. But now it is being gradually looked down upon and the different brothers of the families belonging to those communities, in which polyandry exists, started marrying separately.

Newars have certain specialities in their social system. The systems of *Belbibah* (the system of marrying the young girls before the mense starts with Subarna Kumar in the form of *Bel* (fruit) is a unique feature prevalent only among the Newars in Nepal. It seems that the *Belbibah* was practised only by the common mass during the Malla period, as the Mallas themselves did not adopt the system. Because of this system the Newars females were not deemed to be widow even after the death of their husbands as their first husband was the God. So the *Sati* was not a necessity among the Newar women. The system of marrying with the God was practised by the Nayyars of India also. Among Newars it is a must ritual among all from the highest class, except the Brahmins, to the Chandalas. The Brahmins used to give their daughters before the latter had menstruation. Among Newars the remarriage and widow marriage were common practice although not much appriciated, we can cite many cases of the remarriage among Newars. Among certain castes in Newars if the young girl's husband was at the deathbed she could get the divorce from the husband by returning the ten bettle-nuts to the dying husband. Such females were easily remarried. If the married women could not lead the happy married life with the husband such woman could also demand the divorce from the husband and remarry. The remarriage of the females in Newar society was an accepted system. Thus the position of females among the Newars was much better. Wright says :

> "The marriage tie is by no means so binding among the Newars as among the Gorkhas. Every Newar girl, while a child, is married to a bel-fruit, which after the ceremony is thrown in a sacred river. When she arrives at purberty, a husband is selected to her, but should the marriage prove impleasant, she can divorce herself by the simple process of placing a betelnut under her husband's pillow and walking off. Of late years, however, this license has been somewhat restricted and a divorce cannot now be effected in so simple a manner. Widows are allowed to remarry."

Such system we find in many other autochthonous communities in Nepal also but there were other communities also which had strictly controlled the activities of women. Any person who had eloped other's wife was cut down by the first husband which was a common practice up to the time of Jang Bahadur. Wright has written :

> "The Gorkhas punish breaches of conjugal fidelity most severely. An erring wife is imprisoned for life, and the dishonoured husband was expected to cut down the seducer with his Kukhri the first time he encountered

him. Sir Jung Bahadur has however placed restrictions on this custom, as he found it open to much abuse...."

In the far western region during the time of Khasiya Malla period there was a mention of *Jarikar*, which means the charge levied on the eloper or the marriage-expenses to the berieved husband or both. Might be a certain amount of the charge went to the state treasary also. In that way the elper could take the wife away from the first husband. This system seemed to have been in existence among the autochthonous communities. Later on Jang Bahadur's Code (1854 A.D.) had explicitly categorised and fixed the marriage expenses according to the social status of the people concerned.

Role of woman in political life

Let us now examine the role of women in the political aspects from the ancient time. Although the patriarchical family system prevailed in the Nepalese society, the females of the ruling families had played very important role in various walks of life. While dealing with role of female in the politics we have to deal with the females of the ruling families, as in those days politics was the concern of only the ruling family and higher officials.

The females had played very active role in the political life in Nepal. The chief queen was called *Mahishi*, *Patrani* and *Maharani*. The suffixes *Sri* and *Devi* were added in the name of chief queen, for example, Manadev I had three wives but the suffix of *Sri* and *Devi* were used only to Bhogini which signified that she was the chief queen. Moreover the chief queen was also coronated along with the king at the time of coronation ceremony. The chief queen as the *Mahishi* has also some say in the administration of the country. The queen-mother was called the *Rajamata*. On the basis of *Hindu Shastras* the queen was considered as Laxmi or Saraswati, the consorts of Lord Narayan, as the king was considered to be the incarnation of Lord Narayan. We are not in position to explain the exact role of the queens and queen-mother during the ancient period in the then Nepalese politics due to the paucity of sufficient evidences. But the references of the queens like Rajyavati, Bhogini, Kshem Sundari, Gunadevi, Vatsadevi, Rajyamati and the wife of Amsu Varma (Name unknown) in the Lichchhavi inscriptions give use some hint that they might have played important roles in the politics of the country.

The contemporary documentary evidences like *Thyasaphus*, other documents and the *Vamsavalis* have also given us a lot of informations about the active role of the queens and others in the then politics of Nepal. Nayak Devi, the daughter of Budra Malla, the *defacto* ruler during the first quarter of 14th century, was considered as the successor. It was a unique incident in the history of Nepal in which the, female was considered as the heir-apparent. Although the princess did not play any active role in the then politics of Nepal, the bridegroom of the princess enjoyed the very important position in the political scene of Nepal. So there was a struggle among the courtiers to get the hands of the princess. A prince was brought for the princess from Varanasi. Unfortunately the bridegroom was murdered by the local jealous courtiers. At such a time Devaladevi, although a refugee, could capture the power and became the *defacto* ruler for about there decades *i.e.* 1336 to 1366 A D. in the history of Nepal. Devaladevi was tactful and could win over the competent and strong feudal chiefs special Aneka Ram. She was also very competent, dashing and strong lady who could handle the then anachronic political situation. She had brough Jayasthiti Malla from outside to make him a bridegroom for her grand-daughter Rajalladevi, who was the daughter of Nayak Devi. Rajalladevi had also enjoyed higher position in the political arena being the daughter of Nayak Devi and grand-daughter of Devaladevi.

Devaladevi could control over many kings who had ascended the throne during her *defacto* rulership. It is because of her Jayasthiti Malla could rise to power and, later on, became the king. Devaladevi was called "Mahadevi"; and contemporary colophons mentioned her with all regal title. She had led the army in the battles. Thus she was one of the very successful rulers of Nepal.

We have many other queens and queen-mothers who had played the active role in the politics. Riddhi Laxmi had ruled the country as the regent of her minor son Bhupalendra Malla, the king of Kantipur. She, with the help of the chief Kazi Laxminarayan Joshi, had ruled the country during the minority of the king. Similarly, Ganga Rani had also worked as the regent in Bhaktapur. Queen mother Kumudini had helped her son Jaya Prakash Malla to restore his lost throne. Dayavati, the wife of King Jaya Prakash Malla, had conspired against her husband and staged a *coup* and enthroned her minor son Jyoti Prakash in 1746 A.D. For four years she ruled Kantipur with the help of the *Kazi* Taudhik.

But one thing we must keep in mind that excepting a few cases whenever a kingdom were ruled by females there used to be weak government. These females in many cases became the tools of the courtiers. They made some of their favourities as the Chief *Kazis* and they themselves became just like the puppets of such courtiers, under which circumstance the rival courtiers were victimised and killed in a could blood way. The administration suffered a lot. Such events we find in the history of not only medieval period but also modern period; and not only in Nepal but also in different parts of the world. In Nepal we have seen the adverse effects on the political history whenever the females or hen-pecked rulers ruled. Moreover the presence of many wives and concubines in the court, all equally ambitious and struggling for power, made the situation worse in many cases. Intrigues and counter-intrigues were the rampant characteristics of the Nepalese politics, as we have seen. The clashes among the queens had resulted into many unhappy incidents. Rise and fall of many persons led to the most tragic political scenes.

In Gorkha we have seen the very active role played by the queens One of the queens of Rama Shah was considered as the guiding lady and also an incarnation of Goddess Bhagvati. The main spirit behind the account was that that particular queen had very actively helped the king in the administration of the country. We can cite another example of Queen Chandraprabhavati, wife of King Narabhupal Shah. It is described that King Narabhupal Shah lost his mental balance after 1737 A D., after which there was a big political problem. At such a time competent queen Chandraprabhavati ruled the country and at the same crown prince Prithvinarayan Shah was also trained in the administration.

After the rise of the house of Gorkha and conquest of the Sena Kingdoms of eastern Nepal and the Mallas of Kathmandu we have more detailed informations about the role of the queens in the politics of Nepal. The queens played the vital and decisive role whenever the kings were weak. Such roles of the queens had not only weakened the politics of Nepal but also harmed a lot tothe ruling dynasty as the history of Nepal revealed. During the reign of Pratap Simha Shah, Rajendra Laxmi and Maiju Rani, the queen and the concubine of the king, could not pull on well Maiju Rani, although a kept-wife being a favourite of the king, had much influence in the politics. She, along with her some followers, had full control over the reins of administration and had also caused the clash between the two brothers the king and his younger brother Bahadur Shah; which ultimately lad to expulsion of the prince. There was no love lost between the two brothers but the presence of Maiju Rani and her supporters did not allow them to have close relations Married and chief queen Rajendra Laxmi was overshadowed After the death of Pratap Simha Shah, Maiju Rani and her supporters persuaded queen Ranjendra Laxmi to observer *Sati*. But due to her own sagacious brain and alertness, Rani Rajendra Laxmi saved herself, ordered Maiju Rani to immolate herself after the birth of her child, as she was pregnant than and banished Vraja

Nath Pandit, after branding him on the face. To do all these things she had taken the help of Bahadur Shah who was called back to Kathmandu immediately after the death of the king.

Had Maiju Rani and her supporters succeeded, the history of Nepal would have taken a different turn. What might have happened to the minor king Rana Bahadur Shah in the absence of his own mother cannot be said in the context of the then political situation Maiju Rani could have done anything to the orphan minor king.

Rajendra Laxmi and Bahadur Shah played every active role in the history of Nepal, as the regents of the minor king Rana Bahadur Shah Later on again there was clash between the two ambitions regents, which led to the death of many brave courtiers. At last Bahadur Shah was once more compelled to pass exiled life at Betiab. Rajendra Laxmi ruled over Nepal for nine years during which period she had united Kaski, Lamjung and Tanahun. She can be called one of the dashing and brave queens of Nepal. Unfortunately her life was curtailed by the than fatal disease tuberculosis.

We have many other active queens who had played very active role in the history of Nepal Rajrajeswori, Subarnaprabha, Kantivati and Lalitatripurasundari, the wives of King Rana Bahadur Shah, were quite active during the reign of Rana Bahadur Shah. Rajrajeshwori, being the Senior-most queen, had her say in the administration, but the clash between the two co-wives Rajrajeswori and Subarnaprabha had its effects in the then politics. The king and the queens, all of whom were in early twenties were not matured enough to fish in the troubled water in the then complicated politics. *Baisis* and *Chaubisis* were just merged. At such a time very matured decisions were needed. The situation was exploited by the seasoned courtiers for their personal benefits. The courtiers were divided into groups loyal to their own patrons Moreover Rana Bahadur Shah, being infatuated to a widow Brahmin named Kantivati, wished to marry her. Rajrajeswori had only a daughter whereas Subarnaprabha, although a concubine, had a son, as such both of them although the queens had the womanly nature and were jealous of each other Hence Rajrajeswori prompted the king to marry the third wife so that she could have one more supporter against Subarnaprabha. The opportunist courtiers also not only expressed their whole-hearted consent but also prompted the king to marry Kantivati. It was only those few traditional courtiers who expressed their discontent in the intercaste marriage. At last the king married the widow Brahmin Kantivati, who, in due course of time, became the most favourite queen. The courtiers had to endeavour to win her vouchsafe so that they could enjoy the power. Kantivati's say prevailed in the than court and administration.

Kantivati gave birth to a son named Girvanyuddha Bikram Shah, who was declared as the crown prince within a short time. Thus Rajrajeswori could avenge Subarnaprabha and at the same time Kantivati was also satisfied. Thus the clashes among the co-wives of Rana Bahadur Shah had affected in the political realm of the country. Within a short time Kantivati suffered from tuberculosis, after which both Rajrajeswori and Kantivati started persuading the young king to abdicate the throne in favour of his minor Son Girbanyuddha aged one and a half years. The ardent desire of the diseased queen was to see her son enthroned before her last breath, while Rajrajeswori, out of jealousy of Subarnaprabha, wanted the abdication of the king before Rana Bahadur Shah's fickle mind would change. Thus the king, mentally upset due to the fatal disease of the most favourite queen and much pressurised by the senior queen, favourite queen Kantivati, and the courtiers, who always acted according to the will of Kantivati, was persuaded to abdicate. Thus to please and keep the last will of the dying favourite queen Kantivati, the king abdicated the throne and declared the enthronement of Girvanyuddha. He declared himself the "Swami."

As the king was much engaged in having the medical treatement of Kantivati, senior queen Rajreswori worked as the regent and had the royal seal with her. She started, with the help of the courtiers, ruling over the country Meantime Kantivati succumbed to the fatal disease, as its result ex-king Rana Bahadur Shah almost became insane and started ordering in the most abnormal way to avenge the death of his most favourite queen. At such a time Rajrajeswori had to take the most cautious steps In due course of time there ensued clash between the courtiers and the ex-king. The regent queen was put in the most odd position. When he could not stand against the courtiers, who might have been instigated and prompted by Subarnaprabha, Rana Bahadur Shah fled to Varanasi. After a few days, Rajrajeswori also followed Rana Bahadur Shah. Thus now Subarnaprabha became the regent of the minor king and had the full control over the administration of the country. She was successful to have the full cooperation of the courtiers named Kirtiman Simha Basnet and Damodar Pande, who became all powerful only after the mysterious murder of the former (Kritiman Simha Basnet). Thus the jealousy and mutual clashes of the co-wives of Rana Bahadur Shah had brought about so much change in the Nepalese politics. The situation of civil war between the ex-king and courtiers emerged, not only that Rana Bahadur Shah had to pass his days as refugee in a foreign land.

Rajrajeswori, who had gone to Varanasi following Rana Bahadur, could not remain in peace and harmony with the arrogant and licentnous ex-king; so she returned to Nepal. To know of her return, Subarnaprabha wished to check her on the way. But Rajrajeswori, a very courageous lady, was endowed with all the qualities of regality, as the result of which she braved and won over all the persons assigned to check her advance to Kathmandu. She, with the golden sword in her hand, marched ahead with the evergrowing followers. When the army was sent to arrest her at Thankot, the soldiers, instead of arresting her, showed their sincere loyalty to her. Thus followed by such followers she entered the royal palace and took the reins of administration under her control. Moreover she tried to keep the ex-king in Varanasi for ever, so that she would be able to rule the country uninterferred by anyone else. She was a very courageous, brave and strong ruler and played a very active role in the then politics of Nepal. But her regency did not last long, as Rana Bahadur Shah returned to Nepal from Varanasi with the determination to average all those who had made efforts to keep him in Varanasi for ever. The people and army of Nepal showed the same sort of loyalty, which they had expressed to Rajrajeswori All the attempts of Rajrajeswori to stop the advance of Rana Bahadur Shah failed.

The main persons who tried to check the approach of the ex-king were given severe punishments. Regent Rajrajeswori along with some of her favourite maid-servants were expelled to Helambu, where she stayed so long she was not summoned by Bhimsena Thapa to immolate herself as *Sati* after the assassination of Rana Bahadur Shah. Thus Rajrajeswori, who had played an active role in the history of Nepal for a decade, was put to death in the name of the holy ritual *Sati*, generally performed in a voluntary way for the salvation of the deceased husband.

Thus being freed from the dynamic, dashing and bold queen Rajrajeswori, Bhimsena Thapa ruled the country for three decades unchallanged by anyone else. For that also General Bhimsena Thapa had to take the help of the very young queen named Lalitatripurasundari, the youngest wife of Rana Bahadur Shah. He declared the queen as the *Rajamata* (Queen-mother); thus the regent of the minor king. Rani Lalitatripuriasundari in return always continued on bestowing all the blessings to Bhimsena Thapa. The mutual understanding and cooperation made both of them most powerful Because of Bhimsena Thapa, Tripurasundari could become *Rajamata* and because of the *Rajamata* Bhimsena Thapa became more and more powerful. One after another titles like General and Commander-in-Chief were conferred on Bhimsena Thapa, who remained all powerful so long the *Rajamata* was alive. The death of Lalitatripurasundari eclipsed the faith of the most powerful man in the country. Thus what we see is that, howsoever competent, brave andvigorous a man might be, the faith of the person depended upon the favour and disfavour of the queens in the then polities of Nepal.

Bhimsena Thapa, who was the most powerful person for so many years, gradually faced humiliations and started losing his grip in the palace as well as in the daily administration since after the death of Lalitatripurasundari. Moreover in the then politics after the death of Lalitatripurasundari, the two queens of King Rajendra Bikram Shah *i.e.* Samrajyalaxmi, the senior queen and Rajyalaxmi, the junior queen, became the decision-makers of Nepal. Unfortunately both of them were just like the two poles of opposite directions. Senior queen was opposed to the Thaps, whereas the junior queen was in favour of the Thapas. The personality clashes between the two queens once again brewed up the most dangerous conspiratorial politics affecting the fate of the king and the courtiers. Senior queen in order to bring about the downfall of Bhimsena Thapa sent an order to Ranjung Pande, the son of Damodar Pande, to come back from Varanasi. Ranjung Pande, who was passing his exiled life there, returned to Kathmandu, started-serving the senior queen voluntarily and got back his ances toral property seized by government after the execution of Damodar Pande and his own expulsion. Rani Samrajya Laxmi sought the advices of Ranjung Pande to bring about the downfall of the towering personality of Bhimsena Thapa. Having got the blessings of the Senior Queen, Ranajung Pande instigated many local officials and people to send their complaints against Mukhtiyar Bhimsena Thapa At that time Rajyalaxmi could not exercise much influence of the king as the latter was much under the domination of the senior queen. King Rajendra was just a puppet in the hands of the queens.

The period from 1837 to 1845 is a classical example of chaotic politics in the modern history of Nepal. Both the queens were so much inclined and determined in fulfilling their own objectives that they had the least thought of the consequences. Samrajya Laxmi and Ranajung Pande were successful in bringing about the fall and death of the great statesman Bhimsena Thapa. The king, a helpless figure, could not think of what might befall on him when he let the unhappy incidents occour. However autocrat was Bhimsena Thapa, he had a very high respect and dedication to the crown. The king was the most respected figure in the country. The queens with all the womanish jealousy started creating all sorts of problem. At such a time as ever there was no shortage of courtiers who were cunning enough to fulfil their self interests; and such courtiers were divided into three groups *i.e.* group of the senior queen, group of junior queen and the group of the king. For some time the group of senior queen was most powerful and that of junior queen the weakest. Two queens became so ambitions that they aspired the abdication of the king and enthronement of their own sons. The womanish admancy of the senior queen became so strong that she started threatening the king by leaving the palace and sheltering at the Pashupati area. She had demanded that she should be delegated all administrative powers from the king, who was too weak to encounter any of the two queens. In the continuation of the dramatic departure from the palace, she had gone to Hetuada on the way to Varanasi. There she died of malaria in October, 1841 A.D.

The death of Samrajya Laxmi did not solve the problem. Those courtiers, who had been actively supporting the senior queen, now adopted the crown prince Surendra as their leader. The situation, instead of improvement, worsened. The junior queen now became quite aggressive and was in search of a strong person who could help her achieve her political objective. Prince Surendra, uncontrolled by his father the king, created all sorts of horrors; and none within or without the court felt themselves secured and safe due to the immaturity of the prince. All the government employees right from the Mukhtiyar to the sepoys drafted a petition which was presented to the king by all of them on December 7, 1842 A.D. It was the first event of this kind in the modern history of Nepal. The king was compelled to delegate the whole power to the queen Rajyalaxmi in January 1843, after which Rajyalaxmi got full power to rule the country constitutionally.

Had the queen been able to rule the country comperently she would have become one of the great rulers of Nepal. But instead of controlling the situation she started planning to enthrone her son Ranendra after compelling the king to abdicate. In this context a brave person like Mathbar Simha Thapa was butchered in the most cold-blooded manner. The folly of Rajyalaxmi, later on, led to most Sanguine incident called Kot (court) Massacre in the history of Nepal on 14th-15th September 1846 A.D. Jang Bahadur a very cunning opportunist and expert in fishing the troubled water emerged as the *Mukhtiyar* and Commander-in-Chief Queen Rajyalaxmi did not know what was lurking behind the scene which proved mo t dangerous to her as well as to the crown of Nepal. She was still expecting that Jang would fulfil her ardent desire. Leter on when Jang Bahhdur not only bluntly refused to set aside Surrendra and enthrone Ranendra but also sternly warned the queen that if she would ever do anything against the rightful claimant to the throne she would have to suffer the punishment prescribed by the law.

Queen Rajyalaxmi became quite furious at the unexpected answer. Now she, with the help of some of the courtiers conspired to assassinate Jang Bahadur. Unknown to her, Jang had already won a maid-servant of the court in his side, who was sending all the reports. Thus at that time two women played very active role, one to assassinate Jang and another reporting him plans made against him.

Rani Rajyalaxmi's role in the politics of Nepal proved most harmful. She, having arranged the whole plan, to assassinate Jang, sent for him, but clever Jang Bahadur was already informed of the plan by a maid-servant of the court through Pt. Vijaya Raj and went straight to the king with all his followers. He got the permission from the king to wipe out the conspirators and also got the title of Prime Minister. Then Jang made the *Bharadari* decide the expulsion of the Rani on the various political charges Rani Rajyalaxmi now labelled with the charges of treason was compelled to go the Varanasi to lead her remaining part of her life. Along with the queen, King Rajendra and prince Ranendra also went to Varanasi. Thus most powerful queen was expelled from the, country. The follies of the queen led to her own expulsionl curtail of the royal power and rise of a new regime in Nepa *i.e.*, Rana regime

One interesting characteristic of the modern history of the Nepal was that whenever the females played active role in the politics there were adverse effects and much bloodshed. These females had not properly utilised their powers and were quite active only to fulfil their selfish interests. Many a times they became just the tools of some highly ambitious persons. When the highly ambitious persons succeeded in fulfilling their objectives, they set those females aside on one or the other pretext. Many a times the family clashes also effected in the active participation of the females in the political arena of Nepal. Such example we can cite in the case of 1885 *coup* staged under the leadership of Bir Shamsher, one of the Ranas.

During the Prime Ministership of Ranaudip Simha (1877-85 A D.) there were clashes between the sons and nephews of Ranauddip Singh. Moreover there was a lack of unity among the females of the royal family members *i.e.* the daughters of Jang Bahadur through different wives like *Sri 5 Jetha Badu Maharani, Sri 5 Mahila Badu Maharani,* (married to crown prince Trailokya) and Kanchhi Maiya wife of

Trailokya's cousin brother) and Chirbirie Maiya, and wife of Trailokya's cousin brother. Similarly two wives of Ranauddip Singh, like Haripriya Deve and other *Rani* were not in good terms. The clashes between the Jang brothers *i.e.* sons of Jang Bahadur and Shamsher brothers, sons of Dhir Shamsher, further activised the role of the above mentioned females in the politics of Nepal. *Sri 5 Jetha Bada Maharani* supported the cause of Jagat Jang *i.e.* Jang group with expectation of having her daughter enthroned as the Queen of Nepal as in the then England, because at that time Queen Victoria was reigning Great Britain. Haripriya who was also in favour of Jagat Jang called him to come back to Kathmandu. After his return to Kathmandu both *Jetha Bada Maharani* and Haripriya Devi were trying their best to make Ranauddip Simha appoint Jagat Jang as the Commander-in-Chief to meet their own purposes. Under such circumstance *Sri 5 Mahila Bada Maharani*, another wife of Ranauddip Simha, Kanchi Maiya and Chirbiril Maiya supported the Shamsher group to safeguard their own objectives. These females specially the two wives made Ranauddip Simha most confused. Under such circumstance Bir Shamshere successfully staged a *coup* against Ranauddip Simha and became Prime Minister after butchering all his rivals including the Prime Minister in 1855 A.D. The *Jetha Rada Maharani* and Haripriya Devi took asylum in the British Residency and later on were permitted to pass their remaining days as refugees in India.

Bir Shamsher rewarded Kanchhi Maiya, Chirbiril Maiya for their most active support and cooperation. Both of them highly ambitious as they were, developed the ego of being the real minister-makers and started interfering the administration, which Bir did not like. So Bir gradually tried to avoid them which alarmed them. These ladies had good relation with Khadga Shamsher, the Commander in-Chief and younger brother of Bir. Another lady *Kahili Maiya*, a step sister of Bir, equally ambitions, joined hands with the two other ladies. It seemed that when these ladies felt the cold treatment from

Bir, they started conspiring against him with the objective of installing Khadga as the Prime Minister. *Kanchhi Maiya* was the most active lady. But before anything was achieved Bir expelled Khadga to Palpa and also took action against *Kanchhi Maiya* who was also expelled having made her ride on a buffalo Thus the active role of those ladies was nipped at the bud by the iron hand of Bir. One thing is obvious that none of these females had played the active role for the betterment of nation. Their role mas most self centred as such it did not have any impact on the mass except the feeling of horror. For the common mass whether Bir or Khadga was on the chair of *Sri 3 Maharaj* it hardly mattered, so the people became quite indifferent with the political development of the country.

After this event we do not have much example of females participating in the political arena of Nepal, except the indirect role of the females of the high families. It is said that every courtier including the Ranas had to please and win the favour of the most favourite wife of the Rana Prime Minister so as to get closure to the Prime Minister. It is also believed that one of the reasons of the clash between Bir and Khadga was that the latter did not pay due regards to the illegitimate but most favourite wife of Bir. As the Ranas in general were mostly power-worshippers, they used to show much respect to such women, howsoever mean these ladies might be in origin, even suppressing their conscience. Case of Khadga can be taken as an exception.

The *Bada Maharanis* played some roles, during the 20th century also. It is said that Juddha Shamsher renunciated the Sri 3 Maharajaship and Prime Ministership because of the pressure of a sage Reshunga Mahaprabhu and the Bada Maharani, both of whom became the tools of the ambitious sons of Chandra. Similarly, Padma Shamsher, who wished to rule on the basis of constitution of 1948, drafted by his order, was also cornered by the reactionary Ranas. At such a time the *Badamaharani*, instead of inspiring her husband, coaxed

Padma to abdicate for which she isas bribed three lakhs of rupees by Mohan.

In other countries also we have found the females playing very active role in the politics but in the case of Nepal the role of females in the politics proved very dangerous to themselves as well as the nation. Many dedicated persons fell victim of those short-sighted and too much self centred ladies. Active participation of women in politics resulted in the most dangerous and sanguine episodes in the Nepalese history.

Role of the females in the promotion of culture

The females had played a very important role in the retention, growth and development of the culture of Nepal. What we observe is that the females are the real safeguards of the cultural heritage of any country. We see how the queens and females of the elite groups and big-shots have contributed in the progress of the cultural heritage of Nepal. We can cite many examples in this context right from the Lichchhavi period to the Rana period. In a Lichchhavi inscription, supposed to be the oldest inscription of the Kathmandu Valley, it is described that an unidentified woman, must be a very rich and well educated female, had constructed a monastery (*chaitya*) with the fiasco depicting the wall pictures based on Kinnara Jataka after a long years' toil. For the maintenance of the *chaitya* a big plot of land yielding forty five *manikas* of crop was consecrated. Further for the daily worship of Lord Buddha and giving feast to the members (monks) of the Sangha, a plot of land yielding twenty eight *manikas* of crop was also granted. The female must be a Buddhist, as such she had spent a lot of money in the construction of a *chaitya* and consecrated two big plots of land. Unfortunately the building, is no longer in existence. Had the *chaitya* been in existence it would have represented the art and architecture and sculpture of the period in the history. Although the very building is physically missing the existence of the inscription gives an information of a woman (most probably a widow) constructing a monument in those days.

We have other examples of the wives of Manadev I constructing different temples on their own choice. Manadev I had repaird the Changu temple, constructed the Man Vihar and Vishnu Vikranta image in the name of his mother Rajyavati, giving us much information of Man adev's inclination towards the Vaisnavism But his wife Kshemsundari had constructed a Saiva temple and placed a phallus in it. In S.S. 419 (97 A D) Gunavati, another wife of Manudev I, had constructed a temple and placed a phallus in the name of her deceased father Kinnara Varna Thus two, out of the three wives of Manadev I, were the followers of Saivism, although their husband Manadev was more a Vaishnavite. Manadev's daughter Vijayavati had also constructed a Shiva temple and placed Vijayeswor Linga in 505 A.D. Besides the queens and princess, a femcale named Vijayaswami, wife of Samrat Grihapati, had placed a diety of Goddess Vijayeswori Devi at Palanchok in 503 A.D, The Goddess placed by Vijayaswami might be the present Palanchok Bhagavati, one of the masterpieces of stone sculpture of the Lichchhavi period. It is the oldest example of Shakti worship of Nepal so far available epigraphically.

Later on Abhiri, wife of Anuparam, a powerful person, had constructed a Saiva temple and named it as Anuparameswor, after the name of her husband. She had donated wealth and other things to the Brahmins and ornaments, land, etc. to the temple. She had also conscerated land for the daily worship of the God and maintenance and repairment of the temple. Abhiri seemed to be much religious minded and was much dedicated to her husband, as it is mentioned that she had called herself "*Patidevaprana.*"

Similarly during the medieval period also many women of royalities, noble and rich families had shown much interests and contributed to the rentention, promotion and development of the cultural heritage of the country. They had constructed the temples, granted land for the daily worship and repairment and maintenance of those temples. We can cite many examples of the females in this respect.

During the modern period we have also certain examples of the females who had constributed in the promotion of the cultural heritage of Nepal. We could have expected a lot of such activities during the period, as the formation of bigger Nepal resulted into more economic resources, but unfortunately we do not have much examples of females' contribution in this respect as expected; during the early modern period most of the time was spent on warfare and politi.al conspiracies, not much activities were performed in this aspect. We do not have any substantial contribution to the credit of Rajendra Laxmi who had ruled as the sole regent. as she was quite busy in warfare and conspiratorial politics. In compare to the ancient and medieval periods, the females of the modern period did not seem to be so much enthusiastic in such activities. To think of the constructions of the temples and other cultural activities, the modern period has very little contribution in the history of Nepal.

Subarnaprabha, second wife of Rana Bahadur Shah, had constructed a big temple in the Naxal area. Similarly Lalita—tripurasundari, the youngest wife of Rana Bahadur Shah, had constructed a temple of Tripureswor Mahadev, after which the locality of Tripureswor in Kathmandu gradually emerged. Moreover a construction of a bridge to connect Lalitpur through this locality enhanced its importance. Regent Lalita-tripurasundari can be credited a lot for the construction of other temple. and others also like Rana Mukteswor Sunadhara and many other temples outside the valley also. In this activity, General Bhimasen Thapa had rendered much cooperation to the regent.

The Rana Prime Ministers also did not seem to have given much freedom to their wives in contributing to the promotion of art, architecture and cultural activities. Among the Ranis of the Ranas, the name of Karma Kumari (wife of Dev) is still memorised because of the drinking water taps in the route from Anlekhagunj to Simra. Those taps were also constructed by Dev Shamsher in memory of his deceased wife.

As a whole we see a changing trend in the role of women in regards to their activities relating to the promotion of cultural heritage of Nepal. The females did not play that active role which they had played during the ancient and medieval periods. During the early modern period they could not play such role as there were much military activities. After the military activities were over some attempts were made by the queens in the construction of the temples and other things in the Kathmandu Valley and outside. We find a large number of temples and other religious shrines made by the queens. After 1837 A.D. once more the court became the hot-bed of intriguous politics, after which the Ranas emerged as the autocrat rulers.

Those Ranas took more interest in collecting money for their descendents and had to construct palatial buildings for their own use and their issues. Jang Bahadur had constructed an examplarily marvellous palace at Thapathali. Moreover he had to spend money for other palatial buildings for his sons like Jagat Jang, Padma Jang, Ranbir Jang and others. Jagat Janga's palace at Manohara was a palatial building. After him Bir Shamsher took much interest in constructing very luxurious palaces like Phohara Durbar, Lal Durbar etc. which surpassed the Thapathali Durbar in many respects. The equipments of the palaces were imported from Europe. Moreover from his time onward the Ranas collected as much money as possible to deposit it in Calcutta Imperial Bank or elsewhere. How can we expect the Rana females spending money on the construction of the temples and *pati pauwas* in Nepal? Moreover the Ranas had dominated the females so much that we can not expect any philantrophic activities from them. Pramode has vividly picturised the position of women in the Rana palace in these words :

> "Most of the ladies of the Rana family were very unfortunate women. Though they were married to the rich and powerful Generals and Colonels they were just like dummies and they had no say in domestic affairs. The husband was the master, dictator and also an incarnation of God to his wife. The wife was nothing but a child producing machine. Even if the husband committed the most horrible sex crime, in the presence of the wife, the wife had to be a silent spectator. Jung Bahadur was the man to introduce harem in his house."

Under such circumstance how can we expect the Ranas and their females donating, consecrating land to the dieties and constructing temples. The male Ranas were busy in safeguarding their chairs and life, hoarding the national property and indulging in debauchery, whereas the females tried their best to satisfy the never satiated sex hunger of their husbands suppressing all their personalities and self ego.

Females of the common mass were ever anxious and willing to voluntur for the religious and cultural activities. They used to undertake fast (*Vrata*), worship Gods and Goddess and participated actively in the fairs and festivals.

The females among the common mass seem to have played very active role in the economic field also. The males were to earn for the livelihood of the family and the females' role was rather more hard. These women had to look after the whole family, prepare food and manage the whole domestic problems. Besides, they assissted their husbands to cultivate the land, sowed the seeds, cleared the weeds and stored the crops. Generally the males felt themselves free after bringing whatever meagre income they could bring. It was the female who exploited her whole mental energy in managing the domestic affairs; and she got half-bed. Moreover she had always the fear in mind that she would have to cope with other co-wives of her husband.

Sati System

Sati system was in vogue since the historic period in Nepal. It is quite probable that the system came into existence because of many reasons *i.e.* social, economic political and others. Right from the ancient time in different parts of the world the death of the widow along with the deceased husband was in practice. Where the corpse was burnt to ashes, the widows had to immolate themselves and where the dead body was buried, the wives of the dead person were buried alive.

It is quite probable that the Lichchhavis had maintained the tradition of self immolation which they had observed in India. But the *Sati* system was not compulsory then. We have seen many temples constructed by the widows in the name of their deceased husbands. Manadev I's mother Rajyavati was prohibited by his son to immolate herself. Similarly Abhiri, a wife of a noble, also did not become *Sati.* Thus what it seems is that *Sati* system, though in vogue, was not compulsory then.

Similarly during the medieval period the *Sati* system was in vogue, although not compulsory. But one interesting thing during the period was that observation of *Sati* became more strong among the royalties and the nobles. In many cases many queens and concubines were immolated along with the dead king. The death of Yognarendra Malla led to the immolation of thirty-two wives. Similarly when Parthivendra Malla died his many wives and concubines had to observe *Sati.* Even among the royalties, many queens did not become *Sati,* such queens used to compel others whom they did not like or whom they felt as rivals to immolate. There was also a regulation that once the widow decided to become *Sati* and ascended the funeral pyre she must become a *Sati.* If she fled away from the pyre out of fear she was outcast and she had to pass her rest life as the *Chandala*. So when a widow was to be burnt, first she was tied very tightly with her husband and many big logs were pressed on her, so that she could not flee away. Moreover the musical instruments were played in a very loud sound so that the widow's horrible cry could not be heard. Sometimes many pyres were also made to accommodate many wives. The *Johar* system of the Rajputs of India seemed to have made strong impact on the Nepalese society also.

The *Sati* system (self immolation of a woman along with her dead husband) was in practice in Nepal-specially among the Kshetri castes since the ancient period. But it was not compulsory in all cases. If a woman had a son of minor age, she was not to immolate herself along with her dead husband. The case of Rajendra laxmi can be cited as an example. She worked as regent of her minor son after the death of her husband, King Pratap Singh Shah. Similarly, if a man had several wives, it was not compulsory for all the wives to commit *sati*. In 1816 when King Girwan Yuddha Bikram died, only his senior queen became *Sati*. Sometimes, the rulers used this system to strengthen their power and prestige in the country. Bhimsen Thapa compelled Rajrajeshwari, the eldest wife of Rana Bahadur Shah, whom Bhimsen took as a very strong rival to commit *Sati* after a few days of Rana Bhadur's death, while his (Rana Bahadur) other wives - Subarna prava and Lalitatripura sundari did not become *Sati*. In 1839 King Rajendra issued an order prohibiting women of twelve years or less to commit *Sati*, and in 1846 when Gagan Singh was assassinated, his wives were saved from self-immolation by the intervention of Queen Laxmi Devi. Jang Bahadur was against this "inhuman" system from the very beginning, but he was sure that the system could be terminated only after discouraging it. Oldfield had recorded a few instances when Jang used his influence to prevent *Sati* among his relatives. Through the Code of 1854 also the Nepali Prime Minister did not end the system, but discouraged it to a large extent.

The Code forbade the commitment of *Sati* in following cases :

(a) If the widow was below 16 years.

(b) Irrespective of age of the widow, if she had a son of less than 16 years.

(c) If she had a daughter of less than 5 years.

(d) If she had two or more husbands.

(e) If she was pregnant at the time of he husband's death.

In this case, the concerned woman was not allowed to become *Sati* even after the birth of her child.

Subject to above conditions, other women were allowed to become *Sati* along with their dead husbands. But the relatives of the concerned woman were duty bound to persuade her not to commit *Sati*. Contrary to it, if the relatives or others compelled any woman to commit *Sati* against her will by intoxicating her or otherwise, the person to light the pyre was to be imprisoned for 6 years along with confiscation of property if he was the son of the concerned woman. In the case of others, the punishment was more severe *i.e.* life imprisonment along with confiscation of property for the Brahmins, and death sentence to others. Similarly, it was the duty of the relatives to prevent a woman, who was not entitled to become *Sati*, from doing so. If they failed to do so, the person to light the pyre and other persons allowing him to do so were to be punished by having their property confiscated, even if the concerned woman had immolated herself by her own will. The Code did not mention punishment for those who compelled a woman to become *Sati* against her will and despite the fact that she was not entitled to do so. But we can safely presume that the punishment would be most severe, taking into consideration the punishment awarded to persons for compelling an entitled woman to become *Sati* against her will.

According to the Hindu custom, one a widow sat with her dead husband on the prye to immolate herself, she was considered a dead person. If she jumped from the pyre to save herself, her relatives were to kill her by throwing stones or beating her by sticks. The 1854 Code challenged this evil practice of the Hindus. For killing such a widow, the Code had fixed the punishment of life imprisonment with confiscation of property. The Code, however, could not place such a widow at her original caste status. It was mentioned that if such a widow jumped from the pyre to save herself, after the pyre had been lighted, she was to be given *Patiya* of holy water and would be excluded from rice among her relatives. But, if the incident took place before the pyre was lighted, the widow was entitled to have *Patiya* of water and rice as well.

In Nepal, the *Sati* system was not limited only to wives of the dead husbands. Mothers used to become *Sati* in favour of their dead sons, and servants, including slaves, used to immolate themselves along with their master's wife. The Code, however, ended these practices. If any person encouraged this system or allowed it to be continued, he was to be given capital punishment or life imprisonment along with confiscation of property, in accordance with the caste group he belonged to. The accomplices were to be punished, by having their property confiscated.

From the above discussion, it is clear that the Code did not completely end the *Sati* system, but discouraged it by imposing some conditions and fixing severe punishment in major cases. But it seems that the law could not discourage the system to a large extent due to two reasons. Firstly, it was difficult for the government to ascertain the exact year of the concerned widow or her son or daughter, partly because the decision was to be given within a few hours. Secondly, as the victim had already died, there was hardly anybody to complain about it. The government could hardly control the affairs settled by the family members through mutual consent.

As already mentioned, the 1854 Code only discouraged and not ended the *Sati* system. Bir Shamsher advanced the case by making it obligatory to receive Prime Minister's permission or that of a higher official (in the case of far-off districts), to commit *Sati*. The people were warned not to become *Sati* without necessary approval, even if it might delay the funeral procession for some days. The violation of the rule could be panished even by death sentence. Thus Bir tried to discourage the *Sati* system to a maximum extent. But we do not know what type of instructions were given to the high officials of the districts in this connection. Did they only try to persuade the concerned woman or prevent her from becoming *Sati* by any means ? Whatever may be the case, this discouragement made it easy for Chandra Shamsher to abolish the system in 1920. In terminating the centuries old religious system the Rana Prime Minister gave two explanations-religious and moral. It was declared that the Hindu texts made no difference between committing *Sati* and remaining faithful to her dead husband for the whole of her life. Hence the woman was to follow the latter path instead of self-immolation along with her dead husband. It was also mentioned that several persons misused this "sacred" system by artificially convincing or compelling the concerned woman to become *Sati*, and thus misappropriating her share of property.

The whole chapter on *Sati* system was repealed, and a new provision was made prohibiting the systsm throughout the kingdom of Nepal. The amended law made the relatives, *Jimdars Talukdars* etc., duty-bound to prevent such eventualities in their areas. If it was reported to the government offices, the concerned officials were to prevent it by persuading the concerned woman and by informing the relative of the provisions of the new law. The persons, who permitted such an event to take place, and even their accomplices were to be punished as murderers. If anybody instigated the case mainly to appropriate the property of the concerned widow he would be deprived of the same, and would be punished accordingly.

As a whole we can say that the position of female in the Nepalese society right from the Lichchhavi period up to 1951 was quite miserable. So it was natural that a woman of Lichchhavi period prayed that let her not have rebirth as a female in the next life. The females were treated as the subordinate beings. They were supposed to be dominated and controllrd by the males whether a father, husband or a son. They were supposed to immolate themselves as *Sati* at the death of their husbands whereas the husbands used to remarry other wives a few days after the death of their wives. They could enjoy as many wives as they could and had always a jealous eye on their wives' activities. The females were treated as the means of entertainment as well as the child bearing machine. Generally the well-off people and big-shots treated the females more a means of entertainment than the child bearing machines, whereas the common mass took them as a child bearing machine. The females, generally us they were very jealous by nature, were the hurdles of their own sex also. They always laid many hurdles and obstacles for their own freedom. It might be due to the age long oppression with which they were used; any attempt to emancipate the females was considered as an unwanted thing. In this the selfish interest of the males was lurking behind.

The admiration of maintaining *status quo* in the society regarding the position of women had its positive effect also. The women can be considered as the main safeguard of the social tradition. The always aimed at maintaining the tradition of the society intact. On the other hand because of ignorance and illiteracy the females took all the oppressions as the part and parcel of their life. Only those who were well educated and understood their miseries cursed the female life; hence they wished let them not to have rebirth as a female right from the beginning of historic period in Nepal. The females were given some facilities like the social security of their dowry *i.e. stridhana*, exemption of death sentence, and the right of permitting substitute of the females to suffer the punishment.

The females were also condemned as the main cause of family breakdown. So long the brothers were unmarried, they were generally united, but after the marriage the joint family system gradually broke down.

Whatsoever may be said about the facilities and concessions given to the females, it can be said that the position of the woman was quite wretched and they were treated just as the tools, child bearing machine, source of entertainment and also source of all miseries of the family. The *Shastras* were not less responsible for the miserable life of females.

6

Food Habits

Introduction

Food habit and culture of a nation generally depend on many factors such as the climate, availability of the items, culture, religion etc. In a cold area the people eat and drink such things which may keep them warm; so they take more meat, liquor and spices. Similarly, the food habit is also much determined by the availability of the food items. In some places the rice constitutes the staple food, whereas in other place the millet is the main item of food; so is the wheat. The types of vegetables, fruits and cereals also depend upon the growth of these items in various parts of the world. The variety of food items depended very much on the cultural development and knowledge of a people. Less advance people used to take the same item in the most simple way. They did not know how many varieties can be prepared out of the same items. Similarly, religion has also played a determining role on the food habit and culture of a people, for example, the Hindus do not eat the beef because beef-eating is strictly prohibited by the *Hindu Dharmashastras*, whereas, *Islam* does not permit to take pork. The Islamic rule is so strict that it does not permit the Muslims even to touch pigs or pork. But the Christainity allows the people to eat both the pork and beef. On this basis we will deal with the food habits and drink of the people of Nepal since ancient time.

Factors determining the food habit and culture in Nepal

When we consider about the food and drink of Nepal, we have to consider some of the above mentioned factors so that we can do justice on the subject. We have to consider that although Nepal has remained predominantly a Hindu state we have had many non-Hindu autochthonous communities also right from the ancient period. We have Hindu and non-Hindu peoples. The Hindus used to eat only those items of food and drink which were permitted by the Hindu Holy texts. They did not eat things like pork, beef, chicken and others. The staunch Hindus like Brahmins and others did not take onion, garlic, buffalo's meat, pork and beef etc. Up to the very recent past, the high caste Hindus had to purify themselves even when they happened to touch the pigs. Similarly, the high caste Hindus were not permitted to drink liquor. We have two types of Kshetriyas *i e. Matawali Kshetrivas* and *Tagadhari Kshetriyas. Matawali Kshetriyas*, residing in the far western Nepal, used to drink alcohol and did not wear sacred thread; hence they were considered as low grade Kshetriyas. Similarly the code of Jang Bahadur classified people into two groups-*Tagadhari* (sacred thread wearing people) and *Matawalis* (alchohol drinkers). But now people of all grades and castes, except very few staunch and orthodox people, feel themselves proud in eating and declaring that they had eaten and drunk all those prohibited things. Nowadays Brahmins have also become consumers of alcohol and other prohibited items.

The people of the northern area, due to severe cold, were greater consumers of meat and alcohol to keep themselves warm. Upto the present time inspite of much persuasion and information of the hygienic values, the people of hilly areas hardly take any green vegetable. In the name of vegetable if they ate any thing they ate potatoes, otherwise not at all. The varieties of green vegetables were not grown and the people never felt it necessary to consume these things. Some of the vegetables which they grew were fermented and taken as the *Gundru*. This sort of process made the people easier to store the vegetables, whereas in the Kathmandu Valley the green vegetables were dried up in sun and then boiled to eat. The varieties of food items were eaten according to the environment as well as on the availability of the things. In those days it was impossible for the people of the northern area to eat the mangoes, jackfruit and other food items of the tropical area, because of the non availability and difficulty in transportation of those things.

Moreover the richness and knowledge of the food items depend upon the cultural development of the people also. The people of the Kathmandu Valley had the advantage of exposure to both the north and south. Moreover the coming of the various groups of the people also enriched the cultural heritage of the valley, which became the centre of the country in many respect. People of the valley had thus rich culture. More they were cultured better the knowledge they had in many things. In this way they had better knowledge of the food items.

How a people, living in bare necessity and having very little knowledge, could prepare different varieties of delicious food. Their main concern was to meet the bare necessity and maintain their livelihood with much hardship. Such type of people could hardly think of rich varieties and delicious food. They ate what they had and what they knew. In this respect the people residing in the Kathmandu Valley had knowledge of the rich varieties of food items. The food habit and culture are also determined by the economic condition of the people. Economically well-off people go in search of many new nutritious items which they could afford. On the basis of some these observations it will be proper to deliberate on the food and drink of Nepal through ages.

Food items in ancient time

During the Lichchhavi period *i.e.* ancient period there were mainly two groups of people *e.g.* Hindus and non-Hindus.

Their food habit was determined by their religious tradition and other factors.

People mainly consumed cereals. Rice constituted the chief staple food. Paddy was cultivated widely wherever it could be produced. Many of the inscriptions clearly mention the rice output from the land. Whenever the land was consecrated to any temple or monastery it was mentioned on the basis of the rice production. Generally in Nepal the summer crop was the rice production in the warm areas. We do not exactly know the crop produced in the hilly region during the summer, as maize was introduced in Nepal only after it was brought to India by the European traders. Similarly we do not know whether the millet and soyabean were also produced by then as the inscriptions do not mention anything about them. Wheat was the next important crop of Nepal. It was and is still an important winter crop. A Lichchhavi inscription mentions *chhogun* which means wheat growing forest. Barley was also used as one of the items of food. Joshi has written that barley and millet must have been the most important crops of Northern Nepal during the Lichchhavi period. During the period edible oil must have been produced by pressing *Hamhung* (sesame) and *Kumhung* (probably mustard), as is evidenced by the Sanga inscription of Amsuvarma.

The Lichchhavi inscriptions reveal the widespread and popular undertaking of animal farming like the rearing of poultry, swine, fish and *Mullas* (buffaloes or sheep). The farming of those animals were definitely for table purpose. To think of *Hindu Dharmashastras*, no orthodox Hindus could eat the chicken, port and buffaloes. So the raising of the chicken, swine and buffaloes served the meat items for those non-Hindu communities like the Kiratas and lower strata Hindus *i.e.* the untouchables. In the contemporary India also the orthodox Hindus abstained themselves from eating the pork, chicken, onion, garlic, alcohol and others. The Lichchhavi inscriptions reveal that the taxes raised on the farming of swine, chicken, *Mallas*, and cultivation of *Palandu* (onion) and *Lasoona* (garlic) were, later on, exempted. Thus what we observe by this statement is that the farming of those things were in existence; and the Hindu rulers, who did not use them, imposed tax on such things. Later, on, the rulers, realising that these things constituted main food items of the major number of the subjects, exempted the taxes which resulted into the popularity of the rulers. The mention of those animals like swine, fish, chicken and Malla reveal that these animals were reared to serve the table of the non-vegetarian non-Hindus and lower caste Hindus. Onion and garlic were also well farmed and eaten by the people. The non-vegetarian Hindus must have eaten goat's or lamb's meat also.

Among the fruits, mango is mentioned in the inscription. There must have been other types of fruits also in those days. So Huien Tsang has mentioned that Nepal cultivated various types of cereals and the country was abound with fruits and flowers. Due to pancity of the sufficient materials we are not in a position to write much in details about the food and drink of the period. The food habit of the hilly region must have been different from that of the people of the Kathmandu Valley. There must have been various types of drink including alcohol, beer and others. Fruit juices must have been taken by the people.

Food habit and culture of medieval period

We have detail information about the food and drink of the medieval period. The contemporary documents, foreigners' accounts and many traditional feasts which continued from medieval period upto the present time like the feasts given in the *Guthis*, temples and Newari traditional feasts give us a lot of information on the subject. Many new crops were introduced and many new food items were also adopted as the part and parcel of the food habit in Nepal. In this respect the Newars of the Kathmandu Valley showed their talent and rich cultural heritage in this respect. The Newars had so many varieties of food items which no other communities in Nepal ever had. They could have those things because of their contact with North as well as with the South and at the same time their prosperity also made them possible to spend much on it. Moreover the Newars had the long cultural heritage which they maintained intact. They seem to be particular in having delicious and nutritious food. The Newars in the Kathmandu Valley had also taken much pain in exploring new varieties of food. Before describing much in details of about it, let us, first of all, deal with the various items of the food available in the various regions of Nepal. The food habits and drink of the period continued upto the present time.

During the medieval period also rice continued to be the main staple food in the Kathmandu Valley and other regions where Paddy was produced. Wheat and barley were the winter crops of the country. We do not exactly know from when the maize was introduced in Nepal. But once the maize, Soyabean and millet were produced they became the staple food in the hilly region. But in the Kathmandu Valley the maize and millet were considered as the *Ku-anna* (evil grain). It is described in a *Vamsavali* that the pulses were imported to the Kathmandu Valley, some grains of corn were found in the bags of pulses. The ruler of Bhaktapur immediately worshipped Gods to pacify. Thus the import of such grains were considered evil in the Kathmandu Valley. Potato was also brought to this part of the world from the west only after it was brought to India during the sixteenth century. Kirkpatrick mentions that till the eighteenth century patato seeds were brought from India for sowing in Nepal. So during medieval period potato was not acquainted with the people.

The common mass of the hilly and remote areas had very little to eat. They had the millet, soyabean, *phaphar* (local crop) and other crops. In some of the very remote areas like Humla, Jumla, Mugu, Dolpa and others they had only *phaphar*, millet, and some other local cereals. Generally they had very little items to eat. In some places they still take *Sishnuc* as the green vegetable. Only the rich persons can provide to eat rice, pulse and vegetable like potatoes. The people still have to ration the food supply to the members of their family on the basis of the crop available to them. If they have bumper crop, they have enough to eat and no need to ration the food. Besides these staple food, they eat the wild fruits like *Kaphal*, *Ainshelu*, peaches, apricot, oranges, and whatever was and is available. Very recently in the northern area the apple farming is introduced and it has become very profitable to farm it. In such remote hilly areas in the season these people have enough of fruits to eat and they produce more than they can consume. Pokhara was famous for orange. Similarly Dhankuta, Dharan and many other areas were and are still well-known for the fruits specially the orange. But the hilly people used to have pure food to eat, although limited in quantity. Inspite of scarcity of food they were and are quite healthy, sturdy, plump and muscular in physique.

Meat

Among the hilly people, generally the non-Hindus took any thing eatable and nutritious. They ate buffalo, pig, garlic, onion, and some of them even beef. Regarding the beef, the people used to eat meat from the dead cow and bullock. It seems that the non-Hindus used to slaughter cow or bullock to eat meat. Hamilton has written that the Kiratas used to eat beef. Moreover the people of Tibetan origin also used to eat beef. But later on the Hindu rulers gradually discouraged the cow-slaughter by charging heavy fine on the people who killed cow. For example at certain areas Gorlang, Aru, Khoparlang, Syartana of Gorkha people of Tibetan origin resided, the people used to kill cow. But the Shah rulers fined one and a half rupees to the cow-slaughter. Similarly, Jayaprakash Malla had issued order to impose a heavy fine on those people who killed cow. In this way the cow-slaughter was gradually discouraged. Later on Jang Bahadur's Code had also strictly prohibited the cow-slaughter. Any person found killing a cow intentionally was given death sentence. Thus with an intention of maintaining the Hindu religious spirit, the cow-slaughter was strictly prohibited. The beef eaters were referred to as the monsters by Hamilton. But the untouchables and non-Hindus used to eat beef. when a cow had a natural death or when a cow died of accident *i.e.* falling from the hill while grazing. It is said that the beef eating people used to push a bull, ox or a cow from the steep hill and used to take its meat to save themselves from the charge of slaughtering a cow. Uptil now we have communities which eat beef.

The Hindu non-vegetarians used to eat the meat of goat, sheep, deer, wild boar, wild fowls, duck, fish etc. in the hilly regions. The Brahmins, Kshetriyas and other higher caste people did not take chicken, buffaloes, pork etc. During modern period also the system continued. But the Newars used to eat buffalo meet. A pig was not touched even. Any contamination with the pig made a man impure. Such person had to purify himself by bathing and sprinkling holy water. But a pig was sacrificed in certain deities like Gorkha Kali in Gorkha and Navadurga in Bhaktapur. The *Prashad* (offerings to Goddess) contaminated with the pig's blood was and is eaten by all the people irrespective of the caste. It was and is an exceptional case.

About the eating of the buffalo's meat by the high caste Newars we have an interesting traditional belief which mentions that Hari Simha Dev and his followers had fled from Simroangarh after being badly vanquished by Ghiyasuddin Tughlak. While fleeing from place to place in the forest for shelter they had a dire shortage of food and were almost at the point of starvation. One night in dream Hari Simha Dev was told by the Goddess Turaja Bhawani, his ancestoral diety, which he carried along with him, that he and his followers should kill and eat the meat of any animal they would find in the jungle on the next morning. On the morning while going for a hunting they found a buffalo which they first of all sacrificed to the Goddess Turaja Bhawani and ate its meat. This is how the eating of buffalo's meat is justified. As to what extent this story is to be relied upon cannot be said exactly. Hari Simha Dev and his people did not eat the buffalo's meat as the Hindus of the Tarai area and India do not still eat it howsoever poor they are. So they (Hari Simha Dev and his family members) might have eaten it only under compulsion. What it seems is that the people of the Kathmandu Valley, although they were Hindus, had eaten the buffalo's meat long ago. There was a traditional Hindu belief that the meat of long tailed animal like buffalo should not be eaten, as such they did not eat the meat of long tailed sheep imported from India also. But the Newars used to eat buffalo.

The Newars of Kathmandu Valley had many varieties of the food as compared to the hilly people. The documents explored by Chunda Bajracharya have revealed the details of the food items provided to the guests at the time of Bhupatindra Malla's marriage. At the time of marriage ceremony of the Malla King or a prince an extensive food preparation was made to provide feast to the people belonging to the various localities and social status. So for the preparation of almost each item (main) different persons were given the responsibility. Those persons were called in different names according to their works, for example, persons preparing meat was called "La Bhandila" ("La" means meat and "Bhandila" means cook), one who prepared sweets was called "Mari Kami', one who made curd was called "Dhaubhadila" one who made flattened rice was called "Baji Bhandela" and so on. Above all of the various types of cooks, there used to be chief person called "*Naya*".

The varieties of the food items depended on the types of the feast and also the economic condition of the person providing feast. The feast given on the religious occasion and same other like-wise functions was different from that of marriage, tonsuring ceremony and others. It will be appropriate to classify the various items of food for the correct information of the period.

Sweets of medieval period

The varieties of the sweets acquainted with the then people of the Kathmandu Valley were *Jhila* (round sweet), *Jahangir Wala* (round sweet), *Chulama* (found sweet), *Khaluta* (elongated sweet), *Chapamari* (?), *Chaphumari* (?), *Mithai* (sweets made of flour and milk) and *Sakhar* (a type of brown sugar), as sugar was not produced then), *Julebi* (a type of sweet), *Khaja* (a type of sweet fried with ghee), *Durumari* (bread made of milk), *Takakala* (?). *Satkala* (a type of *laddu*), *Kachari* (?), *Matha* (?), *Ati* (?), *Chhuchunmari* (bread of wheat flour), *Chatamari* (bread made of rice flour), *Tavamari* (bread made of baked paddy), *Ani* (?) *Rebuwa Mari* (?), *Pheni* (a sweet of wheat flour fried in ghee), *Chakumari* (sweetmeat or a wheat flour bread mixed with molass or brown sugar), *Sagamari* (?), *Yomari* (rice-flour sweet fiiled up with molass and sesame), *Puri Mari* (rice flour bread fried with ghee), *Khadabala* (?), *Laddu* (round sweet : there were four types of it *viz. Satkaranka*, *Muka* (mu ?), *Siyewa* and *Taya* etc. Besides these sweets, there were also other sweets like *Lakhmari* (gaint sweet), *Gulimari* (small pieces of sweets), *Kalimari* (brown sugar mixed sweets), *Ainthyamari* (a type of sugar coated sweet) and others. These varieties were used at various occasions, for example, the *Lakhamari*, *Ainthvamari*, *Mithamari*, *Kalimari*, *Gulimari*, and some other sweets were generally used on the occasion of marriage ceremony. Most of the sweets, which were purely typical Newars' production, are dry and brown sugar coated ones, so they could be taken months after their production without getting spoilt. Such Newars' sweets are *Lakhamari*, which are made in different forms and sizes, *Ainthyamari*, *Gulimari*, *Kalimari*, etc. The *Yomari* seems to have been copied from Tibetans and the people belonging to further North even Korea. Koreans prepare *Yomari* like sweets. The Newars put the molass and sesame instead of minced meat in the *Yomari.* They had so many varieties of sweets because they had the opportunity of having contact with the people of the North as well as the South. *Julebi, Jahangirwata* and some other sweets were copied from India. The prosperity of the Kathmandu Valley also permitted them to explore and find out new types of food items. The Malla King had also encouraged in such thing as they had given patronage to the cultural uplift and development.

The Malla inscriptions also mention various types of food items like the flattened race, *Chatamadhe*, *Mnatamadhe* (soyabean bread), *Chakumadhe* (sweet meat), *Dudumadhe* (bread made of milk), *Yalamadhe* (*Yomadhi*), *Laddu*, *Kshera*, *Thiramadhe*, *Chhọchatamadhe*, etc.

The Newars are still observing the various traditional occasions ia which they eat different types of food. They still eat certain particular food item on certain special occasion. On *Sithinakha i.e.* on the sixth day of *Jestha Sukla Pakshya i.e.* moon-lit fort night, the Newars eat *Chatamari* of various types, and *Wo*, a type of preparation of various pulses. Simple *Chatamari* is made of rice flour mixed with water and cooked on pan. Special preparation of it is made with egg, or minced meat or pulses. *Dosa* a south Indian preparation, is also made of rice flour and some vegetables like onion, potato and some other spices, whereas no such vegetables are put in *Chatamari*. *Wo* is made of pulses like *Mayem, Moo, Musu, Kasu*, Bhuti, (all cereals) *Musya*, (Soyabean), *Phasi* (Pumpkin), *Chhukhtlain* (carrot) and others. On *Srawan Sukla Purnima* (full moon day) the Newars take *Kwati* and *Chhuchunmari*, whereas the Parbates and other Hindus observe it as *Rakshya Vandhan* only. The Kumai Brahmins also take cereals. *Kwati*, a Newari word, is a combination of two words like *Kwa* which means various cereals and *ti* means liquid. Thus *Kwati* is a type of *dal* of various cereals mixed up. Some people prepare it only out of cereals whereas some mix meat also.

Similarly some mix *Chhuchumari* with it. Although we do not exactly know when did it origin, it is definite that it is a legacy of a long time back. The other people of Nepal have immitated the Newari tradition of taking *Kwati* in course of time due to the close contact. On the Kartick full moon day the Newars take *Saki* (the elephants-leg) and flaked cereals. Similarly, on the Marga full moon day the Newars eat the *Yomari* since days yore. A *Vamsavali* mentions that the people of Kathmandu had taken the *Yomari* from the time of Amsuvarma. *Yomari* is somewhat like *Momo*, the Tibetan dish. The Newars later on made varieties of *Yomari* like the *Yomari* with the *Khuwa* (milk condensed to solid), *Yomari* with minced meat like *Momo* but different in shape, *Yomari* with black pulse minced etc. *Yomari* is still in use among the Koreans. It is supprising to note now the two peoples inhabiting in such distance have the acquaintence of this sweet. Might be at one time in the days yore these two peoples had very close cultural ties. On the first day of Magha called *Magha Sakranti*, *Ghui* (ghee) and *Chaku* (molass) are eaten along with yam. In this way the Newars adopted tradition of eating various things on various occasions.

Food items during the Medieval Period

Generally during the medieval period the rice constituted main staple food among the people of the Kathmandu Valley. Wheat, the winter crop, was used for the preparation of various types of sweets for the rich persons and *Chhuchumari* (bread) was used by the poor people. Millet and other local products were used by the common mass of the hilly areas befor the introduction of the maize. But soyabean was produced in Nepal long before. The soyabean was also used to prepare the bread. Besides these, various green vegetables like mustard, spinnach, pumpkin, onion, garlic, and others were taken. Regarding the non-vegatarian food meat of various animals like, Tibetan goals (*Chyangra*), sheep (*Bheda*), local lambs, castrated goat (*Khashi*), goat (*Boka*), chicken, duck, deer, wild fowls, pig, wild boar, buffalo, fish, etc. was eaten. The chicken, pig and beef were taken by low class people. Buffalo meat was extensively used even by the Newar community. The Indian Hindus and the high caste Hindus outside Kathmandu Valley did not take buffalo meat; they felt that they might lose their caste by eating it. It seems that the Newar Hindu Brahmins observing Tantric ritual used to take buffalo meat also, otherwise the Newar Brahmins also abhored it. But the buffalo meat was not considered as uneatable *i.e. Abhakhya.* The pig's meat was eaten by the both Hindns and Buddhists on special religious occasions after the pig was sacrificed to Navadurga in Bhaktapur as *prasad.* Similarly, the Manandhars make their youngsters take pork after the pig was sacrificed to a deity on *Balachaturdasi* day. But it was and is still a special practice as a part of the ritual, otherwise the buffalo's meat constituted their main meat item.

The cereals taken were black pulses, soyabean, leading like *Bhuti, Simpu,* peas (big and small), *Musu, Mu, Kwala, Pamaye* etc. They were prepared in different ways like *Dal* or *Wo* or just boiled with spices.

About the rice also the Newars at it in different ways which were given names according. The varieties were *Nasakaoja Dhauja* (rice mixed with curd), *Duruja* (rice boiled with milk), *Chakuja* (rice prepared with molass), *Kastioja* (rice with honey), *Puwakeja* (*puwa* rice cooked) *Mukaoja* (rice with *mugidal*), *Khiraja* (rice boiled with milk and brown sugar, now with sugar), *Haradioja* (rice boiled with turmeric), *Gheraja* (boiled rice with ghee), *Goraduoja, Musuraja* (rice boiled with *musur*, a type of pulse), *Masa Khichari* (rice boiled with *masa*, a type of pulse). Besides there was and is *Muja* (rice boiled with *Mu*, a type of pulse). The *Muja* and *Haradioja* are still served to the patients because they are believed to be easily digested.

About the food and drink, Desideri wrote in the 18th century,

"Rice is their principal food, either cooked or crushed and roasted; the latter served as bread and as a relish. If they eat meat it is generally buffalo. They drink water and a nasty liquor made of a certain millet which grows in this country and is the staple food of the very poor. A kind of beer is also made from wheat or rice, and drink arac distilled from raw sugar."

Thus it seems that up to that time maize did not seem to have occupied the status of being staple food among the people, otherwise Desideri should have mentioned it. According to Father Constantino Loro, wheat was scarce in the Kathmandu Valley as such wheat was not allowed to be distilled. People got their drinks from sugarcane also. Buffalo meat was sold in shops at a considerable price.

The hilly common people might have taken millet as a staple food, whereas the royal family and very rich people used to take rice, because it was not grown in abundance in these hilly area. The Hindus of the area did not take buffalow, whereas the aborigine people took it.

A document of Gorkha, belonging to the later medieval period, gives us same hints about the food and drink of the royal family of the state. It mentions the expenditure on the rice, edible oil and ghee The objects was acquired for the royal family. Generally the common mass used to eat millet, maize, soyabean and other things as the staple food. Frequent references of the expenditure on these objects in the government account denote the acquisition of those things for the royal family. *Masa i.e.*, black pulse was also referred which meant the use of it as the pulses. Betelnut was also purchased. It signifies that the betelnut was also taken by the royal family members. Nepal does not produce betelnut which was imported from India Expenditure on *Khashi* (castrated goat) and *Bheda* (sheep) signifies the use of the *Khashi's* and lamb's meat, whereas the buffaloes were purchased for the sacrifice in the different temples. In those days the meat of the buffaloes was eaten by the low caste people, whereas the people of Tibetan origin and other aborigines used to eat the beef also. But the Shah kings, who were Hindus, discouraged the used of beef by imposing heavy fine called *Govadhakara* (tax on cow-slaughter) and *Brahmadanda* fine for purification. Ghee and edible oil were used; edible oil was used to fry and make curry of the vegetables and meat. Ghee was put in the rice and also in the curry. Well-to-do family used lot of edible oil and ghee in curry. The various types of the spices were *Hinga* (asfobeia) and *Jera* (cummen seed). There is also a reference of *Kukhura* (chicken) but the high caste people did not take chicken and hen's egg either.

Feasts

We have some informations of the feast given to the whole people of Bhaktapur as well as those of neighbouring states like Kantipur and Lalitpur on the occasions of the marriage ceremonies of Bhupatindra Malla and Ranajit Malla, the then crown princes of Bhaktapur. The feast continued for many dsys, for which the people had to pay the levy. The long list of the food items levied and served shows that the Milla kings were also very much particular about the feast. Many varieties of meat of various animals, various cereals (*ghasa*). fruits, alcoholic beverages, and other were served. The schedule was fixed for the feast for the people of different localities. To consult the document it is evident how much meticulous were the Malla kings to maintain the cultural heritage of the country.

One intersesting thing is the frequent use of the pork during the medieval period. The non-Hindu people took the pork which is also refereed to by Daniel Wright in 1877 A.D. Wright has written, "The former (Magars) eat pork but not buffaloes' flesh; while the latter (Gurungs) eat the buffalo but not the pig. "The pork was used in various occasions during the medieval period in the Kathmandu Valley. A document with the detail account about the construction of a *Kwatha* (fort) mentions the pork being served to the people while a feast was given. Moreover the pork is mentioned in the list of the goods supplied for the worship of *chatkghar* on the *Adhi Vashan Pooja* day of Kwatha. The pork was prepared in a sour taste. In the same document there are many references of the pork. Similarly in the detailed account of the construction of the famous *Nyatopola* temple of Bhaktapur, pork is referred very frequently. It is mentioned that when the temple was being constructed a levy called *Shevaku* was also imposed on the people of Lalitpur who were supposed to offer the pork, a buffalo, a pig and four ducks etc. Thus pork was one of the popular non-vegetarian dishes not only of Bhaktapur but also of the whole of the Kathmandu Valley also. It is no surprise when the non-Hindu aborigines like Kiratas (who used to taken beef also), Magars, Tamangs, Lepchas and others took it. Among the Hindus, as already mentioned, only the low caste people like the Sarki (cobblers), Podes, Chyamakhalak and others took it. Whether the frequent references of the pork or pig were meant for the dishes of the those low caste Hindus and non-Hindu pork cating people or of the Hindus even from the riluatistic point of view? It can be assumed that it was used for ritualistic purpose even for the Hindus on the basis of the frequent references of it. Up to the present time the Manandhars (Buddhists) provide the pork along with others to their youngsters on the Balachaturdasi days after a big *pooja*.

Spices

The spices used during the medieval period were *ij* (cummon seed), *Mulaye* (black pepper), *Hi* (aesfobiea) *Palu* (ginger), *Halu* (turmeric), *Chi* (salt), *Chika* (edible mustard oil), *Sun* (dried ginger), *Sukumela* (green cardamon), *Yala* (black cardamon), *Golochan*, *Beharada*, *Pipi* (a type of black pepper), *Sashe Awwat* (?) *Naikya* (coconut), *Misri* (sugar), *Makhan*, *Dakha* (dried grape), *Khwashin* (walnut), *Khayeguli*. *Imu Supachuna* (?), *Goye* (bettlenut) etc. Besides these there were *Ika* (a type of sesame), *Paka* (a type of mustard), *Tu* (mustard seed), *Malebhata* (green and red pepper), *Dhaniya* (coriandar) *Jw no* (a Tibetan spice), *Tejapata* (leaf of cinnamon) *Dalachini* (cinnamon), *Methi* (fenugreek), etc. Some of them were produced in Nepal and many were imported from India and Tibet also. Ghee and edible mustard oil were generally used for the preparation of the meat and vegetables curries.

Introduction of new crops

The food habit seemed to have been changed in the modern period due to contact with the western would as well as introduction of new crops in Nepal. During the early modern period there was a gradual introducation of maize and potato. Upto the 17th century maize was considered as *Kuauna* (evil crop). Later on maize became one of the major crops of the hilly area of Nepal. The introducation of maize as a crop in India and its impact in the hilly region like that of Nepal had much effect on the agronomy of the area. Maize became more popular in Nepal in the 18th century. But Irfan Habib is of the opinion that maize occupied the position of an important crop in India only in the 19th century and it was probably unknown in the 17th century. Potato which has become the most popular vegetable item was unknown to Nepal upto the medieval period. Krikpatrick has written that in 1793 A.D. seed of potato was imported from Patna. It was introduced in the eastern Himalayan region only a few years before 1848 A.D as Hooker, who had visited there in 1848 A.D., found it recently introduced. In this way he introduction of these two new crops had their obvious impact on the food habit of the Nepalese in the hilly region. Both of theme became very popular and nutritionus food items. Potato became the most important vegetable in the whole of Nepal.

What it seems is that the Gorkhalis who had conquered the Kathmandu valley must have changed their food habit after their settlement in the valley. They had now the rich varieties of food crops in the valley in contrast to the limited varieties of the crops they had in the hilly region of Gorkha. They came gradually in close contact with the Newars who had rich varieties of food items. Although the Gorkhalis conquered the valley, they were gradually influenced by the cultural heritage of the valley. Thanks to Prithvi Narayan Shah, the sagacions statesman, who adopted and patronised the cultural heritage of the conquered area. The Parbatiyas in due course of time adopted many of the food habits of the Newars, which we find later on.

But Kirkpatrick had expressed his low opinion regarding the varieties and qualities of the vegetables of the Kathmandu valley. He has written that before his departure for Kathmandu from Bengal he was informed that the Kathmandu valley grew a lot of qualitative green vegetables. Let us quote his own words :

> "I had heard, before my visit to Nepal, that out most esteemed kitchen vegetables did not only grow there much in higher perfection than in Bengal, but that the propagation of them was annually continued from there own seed, whereas the short duration of our cold season admits but of a scanty and degenerate produce not to be depended upon.... The only kitchen vegetables we met with here were cabbages and peas, both of which were of the worst kind. They have the Tibet turnip, but cannot raise it, any more than the potatoes, without renewing the seed annually."

It is quite possible that Kirkpatrick was given an exaggerated information about the vegetables so he had a very high expection of them in the Kathmandu Valley. But the vegetable production was not so poor either in quality and quantity as he observed during his short duration in Kathmandu. The valley used to produce many kinds of green vegetables like spinnach, carrot, mustared plant, sesame plant and others. Kirkpatrick has described about the yam and asparagus which he considered to be the main substenance of the poorer people.

Hamilton has described two types of summer craps like *Gheya* and *Puya* (both paddey), wheat, barley, millet (there were two types : one cultivated in the higher part of plain and other in the hilly region) maize (by the time Hamilton came to Nepal, it had become popular in the hilly region), different types of pulses, mustard, sesame, sugarcane, raddishes, ginger, cucumber, fenugreek (*methi*), garlic, sweet potato etc.

Hamilton has rightly observed on Kirkpatrick's comment on vegetable production of Nepal that Kirkpatrick had commented from European outlook. He has remarked "Most of the European kitchen vegetables have been introduced : but they are only to be found in the gardens of men of distinction, and in very small quantities." But he has not mentioned the names of the new vegetables introduced. One thing we must keep in mind that the judgement of the food habit cannot be accurate on the basis of what a foreigner observes. If we are to judge the food habit of Europeans we do it from our point of view. We can comment that the method of food preparation of Europe is too poor in because they just boil and eat the food without substantial quantity of spices, ghee and edible oil and others, about which they take pride that their preparations are very hygienic and scienfic. We can say that the western food in tasteless and very poor quality, and as primitive as that of early stage of civilization. Generally the westerners visited foreign country with the superiority complex and comment on any thing which differed with their system, say about religion, way of life, and others. Only a few Europeans visit Asia and Africa with free mind and did try to judge the Asian or African system in an unprejudiced way. We have our own way of life befitting to our ecology, culture and tradition, which is not necessarilly satisfactory to the westerners. Hamilton writes about our food in this way ;

> "Rice is the great article of support in Nepal. Along with their rice the poorest people eat raw garlic and radishes; they also fry radishes, fenugreek, or lentiles,

> in water mixed with salt, capsicum and turmeric. To these, people in more easy circumstances add oil or ghiu; and those who are rich add a great deal of animal food. Even the poorest are able occasionally to sacrifice a pigeon, a fowl, or a duck and of course they eat these birds. No Hindu eats any meat but the flesh of sacrifices; for he considers it as a sin to kill any animal for the purpose of indulging his appetite; but when a sacrifice has been offered, the votary may without blame eat what the Deity does not use. We observed, that even the Rajputs in Nepal were so found of animal food, that, to the utter astonishment of our low country Hindus, they drank blood of the sacrifices as it flowed from the victim."

Hamilton's observation is also not fee from defects. He has written on the Nepals food habit with very little knowledge. It does not seem entirely correct to write that the Hindus did not take meat unless it was that of a sacrifice. The rich people used to have varieties of meat served on the table every day. The food habit, as already mentioned, depended on many factors. Moreover about the drinking blood of the sacrifice, it was only limited to the Tantric type of rituals which the Hindus of India did not follow.

Food habit of the Ranas

Later on with the growth of closer contact with the Englishmen, we have the gradual change in the food habit among the big-shots and rich people. The British Residency was established in Nepal after Anglo-Nepal war (1814-16 A.D.) Nepal came closer with the British. Moreover after the completion of the unification of Nepal there was much mobility of the people from one part of the country to another part. That mobilisation also had its effect on the food habit. People started knowing of new items of food. The Kathmanduites came to know of *Gundru* (fermented green vegetables), *Dhindo*. (corn or millet powder boiled), and other things. Similarly, the outsiders came to know of food items of Kathmandu. Moreover as Hamilton had written foreign vegetable seeds were more and more imported. New vegetables were introduced. Various food production from different parts of the country were brought to Kathmandu to swell the number of dishes and to make the food items more tasty and nutritious. When different communities with different food habits resided in the same place it was natural to bring about gradual change in the food habit wittingly or unwittingly. Moreover the rich persons started copying the food habit of the West as well as that of the Muslims. The Newars' food habit was influenced both by the Chinese and Indian system since long. In due course of time the Ranas copied the Western and Muslim dishes to a large extent.

The Ranas had the opportunity of visiting England and other European countries. So they had the knowledge of western food items and also took interest in the Muslim dishes. They employed the Muslim cooks to prepare special dishes. But as tradition bound they were they did not allow the Muslim cooks to touch the food. The preparations were made on the guidance of these Muslim cooks. Specially the Rana Prime Ministers used to have all sorts of various food items served at the time of meal. As the hundreds of females were kept ever ready to satisfy his sex desire so were the food items made available according to his wish. The big-shot Ranas used to have many goats, chicken, ducks, wild fowls, wild boars and all sorts of seasonal vegetables within their big palace compound These animals and fowls were used to serve the dishes of the Ranas. Similarly delicious fruits like grapes, *mausami*, *anar*, apples and many other dried fruits like cashewnuts, walnuts, figs, and others were imported. It is said that there used to be detailed list of the food items served to the Prime Minister who had also fixed the list of the food items served to the king.

Moreover the menu depended upon the personal taste of the person also. Prime Minister Bir Shamsher was very much interested in various types of dishes prepared in different ways. Muslim cooks were employed. Generally a castrated goat, an uncastrated goat, two or three fowls of all the varieties available, a wild boar once a week, three *pathi* (12 litres) of mustard oil and three dharnis (one dharni =2½ k.g.) of ghee per day and similarly all sorts of delicious fruits, local and imported, and other varieties of cereals were allotted to the king by the Prime Minister. Various types of meat preparations, pulses, vegetables, milk, fruits were served on innumerable golden plates. In those days gold plates and trays were used for the king, queen, crown prince and princess and Sri 3 Maharaj and his queen, whereas the other Ranas were served on the silver plates and trays. Moreover before the items were served. They were tasted by the chief cook called *Khanchhama*. It was done with two objectives *i.e.* one was to taste the cooked food and other was to check whether some thing alse otherwise was mixed up. There was also a tradition of cooking one *pathi* (approx 4 k.g.) of rice for the king. Although there used to be many varieties of the dishes served to the king, Rana Prime Minister had much more varieties of the food items prepared by the Brahmin cooks. Hunters were employed who had to bring certain number of wild fowls, deer etc., fishes by the fishers so on every day. Pramode Rana has written about Jang Bahadur's food habit in this way :

> "His food were always cooked by caste Brahmins. He took his meals in the kitchen, sitting on padmasana, in which the floor had been purified with cowdung and red soil. There were Muslim Khansamas (chefs) in his house. They guided the Brahmin cooks to prepare Mughalai dishes. While serving food the Brahmin cooks tied their mouth with a white cloth just to check the germs and other things coming out of the mouth. In private parties bread, meat, yoghurt, fruit etc. were generally served. Rice was never served."

It is said that Bhim Shamsher liked the meat of the *Bandel* (tamed wild boar) of 18 months old. So on every fourth days a *Bandel* was killed. Similarly Juddha Shamsher is described to have much interest of delicious, tasty and different varieties of food. While eating sometimes he used to order for something like liver, tonguc, heart and so on; immediately the servant used to rush to the place where the animals were reared in the palace, killed the animal and took the specific part and rushed with that to the kitchen. He is also described to take rice from Jumla. Fishes of Kulekhani were prepared. Almost all the Ranas used to have many animals like goat, *Khashi*, *Bandel*, ducks, chicken, wild fowls, ginny fowls, partriges and many others reared within their palace. Cows and buffaloes were also kept for milk. There was a feeling that meat of the animals with long tails should not be eaten by the Hindus, as such the buffaloes and the long-tailed lambs were not killed for the well-off people.

Besides these things, later on, biscuits, cakes and others were also imported to Nepal for the Rana palaces. Generally the well-off people ate the vegetables and meat prepared with much spices and fat (ghee and mustard oil). The vegetables and meat used to float in the fat. Similarly the juice of the imported fruits like orange from Nagpur, grapes, *Anar* (pomegranete), and others were taken by the Ranas whereas the common people had to fall sick to eat a fruit, imported from outside, that also on special advice by a medical doctor. Generally the common mass used to eat the local fruits like apricots, peaches, plums, cucumbers, guavas, plantains, oranges, various types of citrous fruits like *Jyamir*, *Bhogate*, *Jhamsi*, lemon, etc., wild fruits like *Chiuri*, wild berry like *Ainselu*, and fruits imported from warm areas of Nepal like mangoes, *lichis*, jack fruit, pine apple etc. Some big shot people specially the Ranas had brought improved varieties of plants of the fruits like apricot, peaches, guavas, oranges, vine, mangoes and others and planted them in their gardens.

Drinks

Regarding the drinks, we do not exactly know as to what type of drinks were prepared during the days of the

Lichchhavis due to the paucity of epigraphic evidences. There must be some drinks like fruit juice (for the high caste people) and breweries to the lower caste Hindus and non-Hindu tribes. Might by the Hindus might have taken *Somaras* as prescribed by the ancient Hindu texts. We have lot of informations about the drinks served during the medieval period. Although there was a prohibition for the high caste people to drink alcohol, the Newar high caste people also took it lavishly as the *Tantrism* they adopted and followed required them to take it. Generally, the Tantrism, which became quite popular from the medieval period, emphasised on *Matsya* (fish), *Mamsha* (meat), *Madira* (alcohol) among the food items, even during the rituals. In an auspicions occasion the Newars take *Sagan* (in Newari and *Sagun* in Nepali) in which meat, fish, *Wo*, boiled and fried agg and alcohol are still given as auspicious ritual in the occasions like when a man is promoted or when he is to go out, or any other occasion. Thus alcohol is a common and accepted drink. But the high caste *Parbate* people were strictly prohibited from taking alcohol. The alcohol was lavishly used by the autochthonous communities like Bhotiyas, Magars, Gurungs, Kiratas, Tharus and others. They made alcohol of the millet, fruits and other things. The Newars prepared various types of drink out of rice, fruits and millet. Various types of alcoholic drinks were *Kalathwan*. *Ajithwan*, *Katathwan*, *Karithwan* *Kejulithwan*, *Hyaunthwan* (varieties of beer) etc , and *Ayela* (wine). According to Miss Chunda, *Kejulithwan* was used only on a certain religious ritual whereas others were used in both religious and social functions Desideri had also given a brief account of alcoholic drink in his account which runs.

> "They (Newars) drink water and a nastry liquor made of a certain millet which grows in this country. ...A kind of beer is also made from wheat or rice, and drink arac distilled from raw sugar."

The available documents of the medieval period refer different varieties of drinks like *Sakhati* (water mixed with brown sugar), which was offered to the people on different occasions, specially on *Akshyatritiya*, *Tetulashiti* (waterboiled with Tulashipatra a harb), *Saseti* (?) *Misriti* (water with *mishri*, a type of sugar boiled). *Ambayati* (juice of Amala), *Anarayati* (juice of pomegranate), *Chakuti* (water and molass), milk, *Lasti* etc. There was *Khaluti* which was provided as medicinal drink when a man suffered from fever. There must be other types of drinks. In the hilly areas also various types of fruit juice, *Mahi* (churned curd), milk, *Sakharapani* (water mixed with brown sugar), *Misri Kandha* (water, *misri* and ghee boiled) etc. were taken.

During the Rana period new type of alcoholic drinks were brought into use by the rich Ranas due to their contact with the European countries specially England. By religion the high caste Hindus were probihited to take alcohol, whereas in their private life the law was not followed. Promode has written that the ethic was strictly followed by Jang Bahadur who never offered alcoholic beverages in public and private functions. Whether Jang himself took it secretly is doubtful, as an incident gives a hint about it. But the Ranas' private life was much panicy due to the alcoholic drinks Pramode Rana writes ;

> "They (Jang's sons) enjoyed drinking wines and spirits and imported alcoholic drinks in large quantities... Almost every evening the young sons of the Prime Minister (Jang) hosted drinks and dinner parties in their homes.... The invities very willingly joined the parties and drank freely.... Every alcoholic drink was then classificed as wine in the Rana houses. But the most popular drinks were John Exshaw No. 1 Cognac and French and Portugese red wine. They often drank straight and consumed severals bottles in one sitting. Some of the young ladies were also addicted to alcoholic drinks."

The Ranas used to import the drinks from abroad. Excessive drink among the nobilities was a common feature. But the people were scared to comment on that because the people might fall victim of the wrath of the Ranas. Jang Bahadur had once made a person pass his urine in the mouth of Kazi Karaber Khatri, a courtier, in the presence of the Bhardars in the court of Jang Bahadur, as Khatri expressed his doubt of Jang's alcohol drink. About the drinks Wright has written in 1877 in this way :

> "The Newars, and most of the lower castes, consume a considerable quantity of a coarse spirit called Rakshi, which is distilled from rice and wheat. It is prepared by families in their own house and there is no tax on it when made merely for home consumption, but a license is required if it is to be sold. Amongst the Newars the consumption of this is habitual, but drunkenness is after all not very common among them, except on the mela days and during the season of transplanting the rice."

Here Denial Wright has made a partial observation about the habit of drink. He has mentioned that only the Newars and lower caste people of Nepal were habituated to alcohol drinks, where as Pramode Rana has clearly written that the Ranas were also addicts of the alcohol drinks. Pramode Rana has also written that many of the Ranas were so much addict to drink that some of them had succumbed to death. The high officials and caste people also used to drink alcohol but secretly. Any person, exposing the licenteious private life, would suffer examplery punishment, as such their private life was kept much secret. Pramode Rana has cited an example of Jang Bahadur's brutal treatment to Karbir Khatri, on whose mouth a soldier was commanded to pass urine in the presence of all the courtiers at Thapathali Durbar when Karbir Khatri expressed his doubt about Jang's drinking alcohol during his visit to Europe. The Ranas, puffed up with power, sometimes used to go mad and give very cruel punishments to the innocent people, for example once a tailor took the dress folded to a Rana palace, but by mistake the dress was folded not in a proper way. At that the tailor was beaton to death. We have other examples also. Although Wright did not write directly about the high caste people taking the alcohol, there is a hint to think about it. He has written :

> "The higher classes are supposed not to touch spirits, as they would lose caste by doing so. Strange to say, however, no trade is so profitable in Nepal as that of importing brandy or champagne."

According to the *Dharmashatras* the high caste people were not supposed to take alcohol. On the basis of the *Shastras* the Code of Jang Bahadur had classified the people into two groups *i.e., Tagadhari* (Sacred thread wearing people) who were supposed not to take alcohol, onion, garlic, tomato, chicken etc. and *Matawali* (one who drank wine) who could take alcohol, onion, garlic, tomato, chicken, and others. Although such regulations were framed they could not be implemented on the Ranas. So the rules were meant for the common mass not for higher class. The Code of Jang Bahadur had also provided different are more severe punishment to the *Matawalis* than that for the *Tagadharis* on the same punishment, who were considered superior to the *Matawalies.*

Besides the alcohol the tea was also taken as a drink among the people. Wright has mentioned :

> "The higher classes, and the lower too when they could afford it, consume a large quantity of tea. This is imported from Tibet. It is prepared in two ways; either boiled with spices, when it tastes like weak negus; or made with ghee and milk when it resembles weak chocolate."

He has further mentioned that the tea preferred by the Nepalese was the brick tea. The English type of tea was taken by only a few people of higher class who had visited Calcutta. In this way the modern type of tea taken with milk and sugar was used only by those people who had the opportunity of going to Calcutta or other parts and their employees. But the common mass who had been to Tibet were used with the Tibetan tea. The people residing in the northern side and in the south were used to take Tibetan tea and western type of Tibet. But the people in the middle belt did not take the tea as a common drink. It became a popular drink among the common mass only after 1951 A.D. One drink among the Nepalese also used for medicinal purpose was the water boiled with ginger, turmeric, salt and other spices. It was used when a person suffered from common cold. Water boiled with the leaves of *Tulashi* (a herb) was also taken for medicinal purpose.

In those days the people eating buffalo's meat and pork were very much hated. The Newars, who used to drink alcohol and eat buffalo, were looked down upon as inferior people. The feeling became so strong that even those Newars, who became close to Ranas and were given high posts like *Bada Kazi* or *Kazi* and others, also gave up eating the buffalo's meat and drinking albohol publicly, although both of those things were used in their *Aganudevata* (family deity) worship. Those very Newars also started behaving their neighbours and kiths and kins using them (meat of buffalo and wine) as low grade people. They felt themselves elevated in the social status by abhoring those things in public. Similarly other communities like Magars, Gurungs, Kiratas were also very much looked down upon as the *Matawalis* and drunkards.

Food habit and culture of modern period

It is a big task to discuss in details about the food habit and culture of the modern period. So here we are dealing it in short. The various communities had various courses of food items on different occasions. Moreover, the food items served on occasions made it clear that what sort of occasion was being observed, for example, the Brahmins did not serve meat at the feast given on the occasion of the daughters's marriage, but in case of son's marriage, the meat was served. Similarly, the course of food differed from caste to caste among Newars also and also on various occasions. Preparations of the same thing differed from caste to caste etc.

Regarding the staple food, the hilly people used to eat *Dhendo* of millet or maize and *Gundru* (fermented green vegetables). Besides these, they used to eat yam, elephants-leg, potato and other things. The rich people took rice, pulses, vegetables, curd, milk etc. Meat was the occasional dish served. In the Kathmandu Valley, the people took rice, *dal* and vegetables in general as the staple food, whereas the rich people of Tarai also ate rice, *dal* and vegetables, while the poor people took *Chapati* (bread of wheat flour), a green chilly and a lump of salt. But all these agrarian people used to forget their economic constraint when there was any occasion of feasting like religious feast, fairs or rituals like marriage or tonsuring ceremony etc. The cultural richness can be judged on the food culture and habit of a people. The Ranas and nobilities started copying the western and Mughal system. But the hilly people retained their own traditional system, who did not show much interest in immitating the food items and habit of other people, for example, the Khas, Magars, Tamangs and others who were also the subjects of the Mallas did not develop to enrich their food habit inspite of their contact with Newars since long.

Generally the Parbates provided the cooked rice, some vegetables, pickles, meat curry, *Chatane* of sesamum and curd at the feast on the occasion of marriage cremony. There were many such places in Nepal where rice was considered as the most delicious food. So serving of cooked rice was the delicious item they could provide. It is also said that in same part of eastern region the rice was so scarce that a handful of rice was taken there just to give *Tika* on the Dasahara occasion. The hill people had *Kashar* (a round sweet made of wheat flour, sugar)and *Puri* (wheat flour *Chapati* fried in ghee) as the sweets. The *Kashar* has become so deep rooted in the culture that inspite of having knowledge of various sweets at present it is a must on the marriage ceremony among the Parbates. Instead of cooked rice, the flattened rice is also served. As already mentioned the Brahmins served meat only on the occasion of son's marriage but not on the ceremony of daughter's marriage. The Tarai people used to serve the curd, flattened rice, sugar, vegetables and some sweets like *Jilebi*, *Laddu* etc. in the feast.

The Newars had and have the maximum varieties of the food items among the Nepalese. Among them also in the modern period the food items differed from caste to caste and occasion to occasion. In general the Buddhist Newars have still maintained the food culture of the rich tradition of Newars which the high caste Hindu Newars have almost given up and have also forgotten traditional food culture. These high caste Newars have very simple type of food items, whereas the Buddhist Newars still are very particular of their rich food culture. The Newars served the various items of food one after another and a person acquainted with food culture of Newares would know that the feast would be over after serving such and such things, for example, curd was served in the last among the Buddhist Newares and the fruits among high caste Hindu Newars. The course of the food also differed according to the type of festival or ritual. The most pompous feast given was on the occasion of marriage ceremony.

The items of the food served were and are still numerous among the Newars. The flattened rice was and is the main item. The varieties of meat served were *Sapu* (a part of stomach), *Kimala* (minced meat), *Khago* (a part of stomach), *Gorama* (meat prepared with rice flour), *Challa* (dehyderated liver, kidney, spleen, heart cooked as curry), *Chhakula* or *Takula* (a big piece of meat weighing about two hundred grams prepared as curry or *Kawab*), *Chhyalla* (*Sinki*, intestine, fat and local beer cooked as curry), *Takha* (meat prepared and freezed), *Pukala* (fried meat), *Bulla* (beer and meat cooked), *Lago* (present meat ball), *Lapi* (present meat cutlet), *Sanyakhuna* (fermented fish cooked with the juice of meat and freezed), *Sapumhicha* (marrow sewn in the intestine and fried), *Hainyula* (a meat curry with a large quantity of ginger), *Nhyapu* (brain boiled and fried), *Me* (tongue-boiled and fried), *Swan* (lung boiled and fried), *Senlapukagu* (liver boiled and fried), *Nugase* (heart boiled and fried), *Kachila* (minced raw meat mixed with spices), *Sekuwa* (roasted meat), *Sukula* (dried meat), *Hikwa* (blood), *Ghohi* (blood from internal part of body), *Tisya* (marrow), *Paunla* (meat tasting sour), *Haku Chwayala* (roasted meat with spices), *Mana Chwavala* (boiled meat with spices), *Janla* (flesh from the back part), *Basupa* (a kind of cutlet). Thus the Newars had and have different varieties of meat preparations for the feast. All these sorts of meat preparations were made on certain special occasions. They were and are still served to the new bridegroom and other respected persons. The Newars seemed to have been influenced by the Chinese way of giving feast. The guests were served with such a large quantity of food items that one could not do justice to them. The guests used to leave much food as waste. It was thought that the food should be supplied in such a way that the guests must leave a large quantity as waste and on that basis also the standard of feast was judged. It was also said that one third of the food was eaten, one third was taken home (like sweets) and one third was left as waste. It was a traditional feast. The waste food was not thrown away; it was given to the *Chyamekhalas*, the sweepers, who used to dry it on sun and consumed it later on.

Moreover there was an interesting habit of the Nepalese regarding the eating of meat. The Nepalese ate and eat the skin, intestine and head of the animals and birds killed or sacrificed. Among the Newars the head of the sacrificed animal was taken as *shi*. The head of the goat was divided into eight parts like two eyes, two ears, nose, two jaws (right and left) and tongue. They were and are given as *shi* to the male members of the family according to seniority. Inspite of abundance of food items it is obvious that the food of the people was very poor in calories.

While thinking of the food culture of Nepal, we find the Newars very meticulous in retaining its age long culture. They have various types of courses of food items according to the type of the rituals. Richest varieties were provided in the marriage cermony. There are not only various types of meat preparation but also various types of cereals which are called *ghasa*, a general term for all the cereals. About the *ghasa* among the Newars, there are symbolic significance also. There are five, eight, twelve, twenty four and eighty four varieties. The number of the varieties of food items depended on the different rituals, castes and others. Regarding the eighty four varieties it was a common usage among all the people as the term *Chaurasi Vyanjan* denotes. The *Chaurasi Vyanjan* was prepared on certain occasions like, *Annaprasanna* (food feeding ceremony), marriage ceremony and others.

About the food, Daniel Wright writes :

> "The Brahmans of course live in the same way as their brethren in the plains of India, but the bulk of the population consumes a great deal of flesh than is customary in Hindustan. The Gorkhas eat chiefly the flesh of Khasis, or gelding goats, which are imported in great numbers both from the Teria and northern hills. The higher classes also consume large quantities of game, such as deer, wild boar, pheasants etc. The wild pigs are caught when young, and kept and fed like domestic gigs in England. ...The Newars are great consumers of buffaloes, and also of goats. sheep, ducks and fowls. The sheep they eat are all imported from the hills to the north and west, as they will not use the sheep from the plains of India, because they have long tails. The former (Magars) eat pork but not buffaloes' flesh; while the latter (Gurungs) eat the buffalo but not the pig. ...It is not very often, however, that the poorer classes can indulge

> in flesh, and the greater part of their food consists of rice and vegetables, which are generally plentiful throughout the year. They are specially fond of garlic, both raw and cooked, and of radishes. The latter they use in a semi-fermented or rotten state called Sinki, the smell of which is something unutterably abomiable."

The account is mostly of the people of the Kathmandu Valley. Wright has not mentioned about the hilly people in details, as he was not much acquainted with the food habits and culture of the remote parts of Nepal because in those days no Europeans were allowed to travel freely in the remote parts of the country. The Rana's policy was to keep the country unexposed and the people isolated.

With the closure contact with Europeans many new vegetables were introduced, but due to the want of detail information we do not exactly know which one vegetable was introduced in which year, for example, cauliflower, tomato, varieties of turnips and radishes and others. In those days the local varieties of paddy were grown, the yield of which was poor. With the dawn of democracy Nepal is exposed to the world. As such due to closure friendly relations with the states of the world hybrid chicken meant for eggs, broiler chicken for meat, *Bangur* for pork, Chinese varieties of paddy (highly productive), varieties of vegetables, Israeli carps and so on are introduced in the country.

The chicken and hen's eggs were not taken by the high caste people and Buddhists up to 1951 A.D. Only after the dawn of democracy there was also democratisation in the food habit. All sorts of social taboos were gradually ignored by the people after 1951 A.D. To do away with the social taboos in the food the foreign embassies had also contributed unwittingly. When the dinners were served to the leaders and high rank government officials of all the castes, the chicken, buffalo's meat, liquor, onion, tomato and many other prohibited things were served in various foreign embassies. Thus people of higher caste like Brahmins, Kshetriyas, Rajputs, Thakuris and others got drunk and ate all those things.

To conclude about the food and drinks, we can say that the people did not have much awareness about the hygienic food. The food used to be too much spicy and fatty. The attitude of the people was that more the fat like ghee and mustard oil richer and more delicious and luxurious was the food. It is said by many old persons that they used to eat eggs, fruits and even meat very rarely. They did not have much sense of nutritional value of the food items. The main objective of eating food seemed to be primarily maintenance of life only. In regular diet the people had low calories but once there was any festival, they took too heavy food. The Newars were so much indulged in feast and the Parbates in luxury that a proverb "The Newars were spoilt by feast (*bhoj*) and the *Khaye* (Newars' terminology for the Parbates) by luxury" came into common use. During the Rana period, the common mass were so much psychological oppressed that even the rich persons (subjects) who could afford did not eat delicious food. The delicious food items were considered as the privileges of the Ranas not of the subjects. The ignorance of scientific knowledge and poor economy also made the people much traditional in their food habit. Although Newars had some knowledge about it, want of scientific knowledge of the food led to many diseases like the goitre, Beriberi and others which they took for granted as the curse of God. In those days while the privileged people suffered from indigestion and over-feeding common mass from malnutrition and underfeeding. The common mass ate only two meals a day, as their economy permitted that much. Many people waited a feast of festival to eat nutritional and rich food. It is said that even the Newars who had a rich food habit and culture used to wait for his birthday or *Tihar* to eat the eggs and fruits.

7

Dress and Ornaments

Introduction

Dress and ornaments of a people are very much determined by the geographical factors, economy, culture, the contact with the neighbours and also the regulations of the rulers. At a glance on our national dress we can surmise that our dress is the outcome of the evolution of a long period influenced by many factors. The Nepali cap, the copy of the Kashmari cap, is prepared by the skilled Nepalese in our own way. The coat is borrowed from the British. Nepalese pronounciation of the English waist-coat is *Est Coat*. We have made certain modifications in our upper garment (*Leveda*) which seems to be the legacy of the age old upper garment copied from Rajasthan. The lower garment *Suruwal* is also a modification of *Salwar* of the Muslims or Rajasthan. Socks also seemed to have been copied from Englishmen. Thus because of climatic reason, that is, to keep warm and the contact with the outsiders we have been able to produce our own national dress. Although at present our national dress comprised of cap, coat, waist-coat, *Labeda*, *Suruwala*, socks and shoes, we have different types of dress at different time and places.

Dress and ornaments in ancient time

Let us now trace the history of dress and ornaments of our ancestors through ages. Regarding the dress and ornaments of ancient times we have very scanty informations referred here and there. *Mulasarvastivad vinaya*, a Buddhist text, mentions that the Kathmandu Valley had a very rough and cold climate, as such the Buddhist monks used the leather shoes in the Kathmandu Valley although the Buddhist rules and regulations did not permit the wearing of the leather shoes. Considering the climatic hardship Lord Gautam Buddha had also permitted it. Kautilya's *Arthashastra* mentions that *Bhingishi* woollen clothes of Nepal were very famous in the India market. The word *Bhingishi* seems to be the ancient form of the present Newari word-*Bhingu* which meant better one. It seems that fine and rough woollen cloths were woven in those days in Nepal. The fine one was used by the royalties, nobles and rich people while the rough one by the common mass. The woollen dress might have been used in the winter days whereas in the summer days thin muslims were used. The reference of various groups of traders coming to Nepal during the days of Lord Buddha also gives us hint that various types of goods including textile goods were imported to Nepal. Thus the then people must have been well acquainted with the Indian goods which the traders had brought to the valley for sale. Besides the woollen cloths the people must have used cotten textile and silken goods. The cotton cloths might have been used by the common mass in general whereas the silk fabrics by the richer section of the society.

The Chinese envoy Wang Hiuen Tse had referred the dress and ornaments of Nepal. *Tang Annals* contain the account given by Wang Hiuen Tse regarding the dress of Nepal during the seventh century. It is described that the people of Nepal kept short hair, pierced their ear lobes for ornaments of bamboo and horns. The people wore one single dress which covered the whole body. Since it is an account of an eye-witness there can not be any doubt about it. But the question before us is whether all the people rich or poor used bamboo or horns only as the ornaments. The very Chinese account mentions that King Narendradev was dressed with fine clothes embroidered with pearls. He had also ornaments of pearls. If we are to believe the *Tang Annals in toto* the people under the Lichchhavis should be said quite poor. The account, however contemporary it was, cannot be generalised. The rich people must have adorned themselves with ornaments made of gold, silver, pearls and various other stones. The Indian traders who had frequented Nepal since days yore must have brought various types of ornaments or materials for ornaments. In those days even males used to adorn with various ornaments like necklaces, rings, armlets and others. The account of the *Tang Annals* must be that of the ascetics or the very poor people regarding ornaments.

Similarly regarding the dress it is described that the people wore a single dress covering the whole body. About this Joshi has guessed "It was something of the sort of a one piece dress like the *Jama*-garment which is yet used in specific ceremonial occasions." About this also there is enough scope to raise questions. If it was an account of the people residing in the remote part of Nepal who were not much exposed to the outside world it can be easily taken for granted. But when it is generalised a dobt arises. The dress mentioned must be either a particular dress for certain occasion of the very poor common mass or the overgarment to cover the whole body in order to save from the severe cold. The royalties used very costly dress embroidered with silver thread and pearls and others. The Lichchhavis who had come from Vaisali and had constant link with the foreign (India) traders were difinitely well advanced and must have the skill of knitting the various types of clothes. In the contemporary India, Mauryas, Sungas, the Imperial Guptas and Vardhans were the rulers. Specially the Imperial Gupta period is described as the golden age in the history of India. Much development had taken place in all aspects of the human life. Under such circumstance how can we satisfy ourselves that the then Nepalese wore only a piece of cloth to cover the whole body.

The Lichchhavis themselves were one of the most advanced people of 6th century B.C. They had deep aesthetic sense of life which is clearly revealed by this account, "...the Lichchhavis were very handsome to look at and passionately loved the use of different kinds of colours in dresses and other belongings," It is also described that the Buddha gazed at their (Lichchhavis) beautiful dresses of varieties of colours in Vaisali. Whether such people remained satisfied with only a single dress covereing the whole body. Moreover the *Tang Annals* has vividly described that king Narendradev decorated himself with the pearls, rock crystals, mother of pearl, coral and amber. The king had ear-rings of gold and pendants of jade, and breloc belt ornamented with the figure of Buddha. Thus the account of the *Tang Annals* mentioning a single dress and ornaments of bamboos and horns must be that of the people who were so heavily burdened with the taxes that they had to remain satisfied with such dress and ornaments, otherwise the richer section of the society and the royalties enriched by the heavy taxes paid by the people wore costly dresses and ornaments imported from India. The Lichchhavis had also highly advanced textile industry on which the government levied *Chailakara* (tax on textile industry) in Nepal. As in Vaisali in Nepal also the Lichchhavis might have introduced gaudy dresses. This system seems to have been continued in Nepal for many centuries. Up to the present time the Jyapus in group (the descendants of the Lichchhavis) wear uniform dress on special functions like *Matataya* in Lalitpur. Dr. Jha had also rightly expressed his view which runs :

> "Men belonging to well-to-do families must have worn well prepared gaudy dresses. The Lichchhavis could not have forgotten their passion for dresses and decorations with which their ancestors of Vaisali were so much connected. On the contrary they could have brought with them those fashionable ideas to Nepal. It is no

> wonder that the modern love of the Newars of the valley for gaudy and colourful garments is the perservation of the old Lichchhavi tradition."

Whether there were rules and regulations relating to the dress to be used by the different caste people or not cannot be exactly said due to paucity of the detailed informations. It seems that there must be certain rules and regulations relating to the dress and ornaments. The lower caste people like the *Chandalas*, who existed during the Lichchhavi period, must not have been allowed the costly dresses. Such lower grade people had to be satisfied with very simple dress.

Regarding ornaments there were rules and regulations during the Lichchhavi period. It seems that the common mass were not allowed to put on different types of ornaments. An inscription mentions that Vishnu Gupta, a defacto ruler, being pleased with the people of Dakshinkoli Gram, had permitted them to wear on other ornaments except the *Kalli* (anklet), *Vaju* (armlet) and *Paujeb* (an ornament used on the leg like anklet). It is also mentioned that the people were already being granted some facilities regarding ornaments. On the basis of this account it can be expressed that the people could wear on ornaments only on the special permission of the rulers, otherwise they could not use the ornaments. It is now quite evident that the common mass during the Lichchhavi period were being governed by the rules and regulations to wear or ornaments. The ornaments in this context might be gold ornaments. Wearing of *Kalli*, *Vaju* and *Paujeb* was the special privelege of the higher class people only. Thus as referr-edin the *Tang Annals* the common mass had to be satisfied with the ornaments of bamboos and horns. The above mentioned inscription clearly mentioned that the permission to wear on ornaments was given to the people of Dakshinkoligrama only; in that cases also the above mentioned ornaments were not permitted to others. Thus the common mass were not permi-tted to wear on ornaments.

Moreover the Tang Annals had further described that the people used to have short hair up to the eye brows and having a long ear-lobes upto the shoulder was considered very appreciable. The appreciation of having long ear-lobes is still prevailing. The people feel that a person having long ear-lobe is considered to live long.

Codification relating to dress

It seems that the political anomalies which prevailed for some centuries had its effect in the social history also. The Hiudu rules and regulations which had been strongly implemented were ignored. So social evils from the orthodox Hindu point of view had crept up. Jayasthiti Malla who could restore law and order in the state formed a committee of learned Brahmin scholars to frame rules and regulations relating the social, economic and cultural life. These regulations, as were based on traditional orthodox Hindu tradition, seem to be too much oppressive to the lower caste people. The Code of Jayasthiti Malla besides many other regulations had explicitly mentioned certain rules and regulations about the dress and ornaments which were in practice up to the dawn of democracy. According to the Code, the *Kasais* (butchers) should put on half sleeved dress only, the *Podes* (one who cleaned the latrines) should not use the caps, shoes and gold ornaments. Similarly Rama Shah had also codified in Gorkha. According to his Code, gold anklets should be used only by the members of the royal family. Permission to use the gold anklets by others had to be sought from the king. The people violating the rulers were punished. It was considered that gold was divinely as such gold anklets could be used only by the queen who was considered as an incarnation of Goddess Laxmi as the king was considered Lord Tishnu. The Code of Jayasthiti Malla has also prohibited the *Podes*, *Kasais* and *Charmakars* to roof their houses with tiles. They were commanded to pay high regards to the high caste people. That is why up to some years back these people used to refer the high caste people as *Baje Bajai* (grand father and grand-mother) : these words were used to express high respect. They were not allowed to touch the high caste people nor were they allowed to reside within the city. They were allowed to reside in the slump area near the rivers and not allowed to enter the fortified area after the sunset.

Dress and ornaments during Medievel period

Dress : Thus after the Code of Jayasthiti was framed the lower caste people had to be satisfied with sleeveless dress and so on. With the restoration of law and order there was a smooth sail in all aspects of life. In course of time Nepal prospered as the trade interpol between India and Tibet. It had the apparent effect on the dress and ornaments of the people of the Kathmandu Valley. Regarding the dress we have certain accounts of the Christain missionaries who had frequented the Kathmandu Valley :

> "Father Ginseppe Da Ascoli, who came to Nepal (Kathmandu Valley) on the way to Tibet wrote about the dress of the people in 1707 A.D. thus, "Inhabitants are dressed like the people of Denmark." Father Desidari had written about the dress in 1721-22 which is as follows : "They wear wollen or cotton jacket reaching to the kness and long trousers down to their ankles, a redcap on their head, and slippers on their feet; when it rains men and women go barefooted. Nobles and even the king himself, make no use of saddles, but sit on the horse's bare back with their legs hanging down, or at most have a horse-rug."

The woollenor cotton jackets mentioned in the account were the *jamas* which we find the people using in the traditional rituals up to the present time. The jacket might be the legacy of the Lichchhavi period. The Newars use the *jama* just like that of the Mughals in the traditional festivals and rituals. The people who perform the traditional rituals still maintain long hair which is tied behind the head but not like that of the Sikhs. In summer the ordinary people might not have worn the trousers, whereas the royalties wore the trousers also. Generally the attire of the males included *Pagadi*, a cap or turban (by the royalties) made of wool, silk or cotton, *Jani* (cloth used as belt), trousers, *Jama* or *Angarkh* (Skirt, long on reaching up to ankles), *Bhoto* (clothes used by both male and female) etc. A document of the medieval period gives us detail information about the dress and ornaments of the period used by the Mallas. According to that cloths imported from various towns of India like Varnasi, Patna, Agra, Tirhut, Dacca, Gorkhapur, Kanuaj, Bodhanpur, Nagpur, Bhagalpur etc. were well known to the people of Kathmandu, specially the royalties and nobilities. Tibetan and Chinese goods were also available in Nepal. Some clothes were of very costly varieties, for example, one *Sari* cost Rs. 100/-. Cloths embrioderid with silver thread (*Tasha*) with valuable stones and pearls were also in use. The names of various types of clothes were *Patuka* (long cloth used as belt), *Jama* (fackot) *Suruwal* (tunic) and regarding the cap, the royalties used *Pagadi* and the nobilities and others other varieties of caps.

Females used *Sari*, *Bhoto* or *Lon* (*Cholo*, Nepali version for full sleeved blouse) and *Ga* (*Khasto* in Nepali, an over garment to cover the body). The *Saris* used to be very long ones about thirty yards in length. Such *Saris* were used by the royalties nobilities and rich persons. It was a tradition to offer *Sari* to the girls reaching the age of twelve years. Only the adolscent females used *Saris* whereas the young girls wore *Bhoto* and very huge female *Jangawal Suruwala*. Among the Newars when a girl observes her twelveth birthday, she was offered a *Sari* taking into consideration that she had become adolscent. Royalties, nobilities and rich females used the imported fine *Saris* whereas the common mass used hand woven or handloom woven rough *Saris*, because it was considered that if the females who had to do manual work like cultivation, assistants of masons and other works would wear on fine cloth that would not last long. Moreover they could not afford to use such costly *saris* also. They had to work in dust and mud so they used the black coloured rough hand woven *saris* with red border. It is a tradition that the females with husbands (*Sadhuwa*) should wear on red dress, put *Sindur* on the head and brow and wear glass bangles, whereas generally the widows were and are not allowed to use red dress, *Sindur* on the brow and head and glass bangles with the exception of those who have got the *Dikshya* among the Newars. Those Newar widows coald use red dress but not the glass bangles, yet generally they do not use red dress as *Sadhuwa*. At the time of marriage ceremony, the females wore special type of dress like *Bhoto* also called *Lan* and petticoat type *Jama*, both made of *Tasha* (silver thread woven cloth). All sorts of ornaments were also used by then. Red colour called *Ala* was besmeared on the leg.

In those days generally the common mass used the hand woven dress, for which King Mahendra Malla had encouraged and instructed that the persons should go out to learn skill from outside. The Malla Kings were much interested in the different types of dress which are represented in various statues and paintings. Generally the status and paintings give us the idea that the light fitting trousers up to ankles and equally tight fitting long jackets flowing up to the knee or feet were used. They used both gorgeous cloured and light coloured plain cloths. They wore *Pagadi* with pearls, diamonds and various types of stones; aroung the waist they had *Jani* (belt like cloth). The shoes were just like the Rajasthani shoes *i.e.* pointed shoe without lace. Dr. Regmi does not seem correct when he wrote "No leather shoes seem to have been in use." But foot-wear of straws and fibre of *Ketaki* were made by a section of Jyapu caste. The Mallas and nobilities wore the shoes even made of leather, but the leather shoes were made of caw's leather. The various inscriptions installed at different temples have mentioned that no shoes are permitted in the temples. Royalties, nobilities and rich persons used the slippers made of cloth and sole made of thread and the very poor persons used the slippers made of straw and *Ketaki* fibres also.

Regmi's assumption of no use of leather shoes was because he did not see the shoes in the statues of the royalties and others placed in front of the temples. It was the tradition that no one should use shoes in the temples. The statues placed in front of the temples denote the devotees, as such they were not supposed to use the shoes. Palanchok, an area in the kingdom of Bhaktapur, now in the district of Kabhre-Palanchok, was very famous for the shoe production up to three-four decades back in the Kathmandu Valley.

Ornaments : There were various types or ornaments used by the then persons. Gold and silver were imported from Tibet and various types of stones from India and Tibet. Necklaces of gold, pearls emralds, coral ete. were used by the royalties, nobles and other rich persons of both sexes. The females used various types of ornaments which had different names, most of which have become obsolute now. The different names of the ornaments were *Taya Nyapusikha* (five chains wrought together to be used on the head), *Tikha* (necklace hanging up to the breast), *Chandrahara i.e. hara* shaped like *Chandra* (moon like chain). It is conglomoration of many chains hanging from neck up to the chest, *tuti baki* (an anklet shaped in such a way so as to cover the feet, used for a bride), *Pyakha Angu* (finger rings generally used by females on special occasions like marriage), *Angu* (finger rings), *Shikha* (chains of various types used by the royalties and silver for common mass), *Lun Churi* (gold armlets), *O Churi* (silver armlets for poorer and lower caste groups), etc. Newar females used to pierce many holes around the ear for ornaments but never pierce the nose, whereas the Parbates used to pierce the central as well as the left or right side of the nose for the use of ornaments. Regarding the dress and ornaments of the medieval period we can still have the idea about them to see *Kartick Nacha* of Patan and living Goddess Kumari of Kathmandu who use the traditional dress and ornaments up to the present time.

With the lapse of time there was change in the political scene of India as well as that of Nepal. The mighty Mughal empire had its fall and there was the scramble for power in India. The natike states which did not like to remain under the yoke of the British, sought the military aid of the Franch, as France was the only potential power which could cope with the British in the European continent as well as in other parts of the world. The petty states of the Mallas, Senas, *Baisis* and *Chaubisis* were all merged and a bigger Nepal was formed. Meanwhile there was fast growth of British power in India which ultimately reduced the whole of India into a British colony. Bigger and stronger Nepal was a big threat to the rising British power in India. Had the personnels of English East India Company tactfully dealt with Prithvi Narayan Shah in the initial stage most probably the court of Nepal would not have suspicious eyes on the British. The mishandling of the affairs made the court of Nepal very suspicious of the Britishers and the court drifted farther away from the Britishers which ultimate led to the Anglo-Nepal war (1814-16 A.D.). After the war friendly relationship developed between Nepal and company's government. British Residency was established in Kathmandu. Under such circumstance let us now deal with the dress and ornaments of Nepal which were also influenced by the French and British.

Change in dress and ornaments

Prithvi Narayan Shah had laid emphasis on the indigenous textile products for his subjects. His feeling was that he had achieved so much in unification of Nepal by wearing rough cloths called *Chyanga* and *Panga* so posterity should also be satisfied with the indigenous clothes. By using the local products in one hand we could save our national property while on the other hand local cottage industries could also be encouraged. The great king wished to develop the local cottage industries by showing them the samples from outside. Because of their poor economy the Gorkhalis could not afford to use so much luxurious and pompous dress as the Mallas of the

Kathmandu Valley or the Sena kings. But after the unification they had better economy and could afford much for the better dress. Moreover the royalities and the courtiers came in close contact with the urbanised people of the Kathmandu Valley, who were difinitely richer in dress and ornaments.

In the initial stage the Shah Kings had used the *Jama, Pagari, Suruwal*, slippers and various types of ornaments. Even the males used the ear-rings, armlets, necklaces, finger rings. The females used *Cholo, Saris, Patuka, Khasto* (over garments) and various types of ornaments. They used nose-studs, which Newars never used. Later on Bhimsena Thapa, in the way of modernising the Nepali army, introduced western dress in the army. Perhaps up to that time there was not much difference between the dress of the soldiers and other civilians. Now Bhimsena Thapa introduced the then French drees in the army. He himself wore the French uniform and also made the king wear French dress in formal occasion. Thus a revolutionary change took place in the drees system of the army. They were French cap, full sleeved full shirt, half-pant in summer and full pant in winter. A long tape was tied around the ankle and above upto the knee to make the soldiers more efficient in marching. Similarly foreign military boots were imported. By that time Britishers were well established in India where they introduced their dresses. In India also certain communities like Parsees also immitated the European dress system. The frocks of the Englishmen, long coat, ties and bows were also used in India. In the name of modernisation the willing communities like the Parsess and Anglo-Indians (females) started exposing their bodies also.

About the dress and ornaments, Daniel Wright, the contemporary eye-witness as the surgeon of the British Resident, has written :

"The Gurkhas are decidedly the best dressed part of the population. In summer they wear paejmas and a jacket, or long tunic, of white or blue cotton, with a kamarband, in which is invariably fastened a Khukri, or large heavy crooked knife. In winter they wear similar clothes padded with cotton, or, if they are able to afford it, lined with fer. The headdress is generally a small closely rolled turban of dark cloth, but they often wear a loosely folded pagri, or a gaudy little skull-cap, ornamented with tinsel and braid."

"The poorer classes of the Newars were in general little but a waistcloth and a jacket of course cotton or woolen cloth, according to the season. Some of the wealtheir, particularly merchants who have visited Tibet, wear a handsome dress, consisting of very full short trousers, a long tunic and a fur-edged cap. Some of the men, especially the inhabitants of Harisiddhi, wear a long robe like a woman's gown, reaching to the ankles, and gathered into numerous plaits at the waist. The headdress of the Newars is a small skull-cap of black or white cloth, thinly wadded with cotton, and generally turned up for an inch or so at the border. The dress of the other races varies from those already described."

"The women of all the races dress much alike, wearning a cloth by way of petticoat, gathered into a mass of plaits in front and almost touching the ground, but short behind, barely reaching the knee. Besides this, they wear a jacket, and a sari (shawl or sheet) which is either worn as in the plains of India, or wrapped round the body like a broad kamarband. Headdress they have none. The Newar women may be distinguished from those of the other races by having their hair gathered into short thick club on the crown of the head, whereas the others have it plaited into a long tail, ornamented at the end with a tassel of red cotton or silk."

"All the women wear a profusion of ornaments, such as golden or brass plates with jewels on the top of their heads, necklaces or beads (coral or gold), rings, earring of peculiar slapes, nose-rings etc. The handsomest, or at any rate the most peculiar, ornaments are worn by the Bhotiya women, and consist of neck-laces of agate, coral, and others stones, massive chains, silver amulets of great size, bracelets of shells, and the like."

"All classes are very fond of flowers and use then greatly for ornamenting their hair, especially on festival days. Both men and women generally have flowers stick in their hair or behind their ears."

Dress of the Ranas

In Nepal after the establishment of Ranarchy there was a gradual tendency towards the immitation of western dress and some modifications in the dress of females. But the iron grip of Ranas made the change very slow. We find the change in dress firstly among the Ranas and in copy with that the people higher status also gradually changed their dress. Jang Bahadur's visit to Europe had also brought some effects on the dress and ornaments. It is described that Jang Bahadur's dress had very much impressed the Englishmen in London. Later on the Ranas had developed the new style of the dress. The coat and waist coat of the English style were used in the Nepali dress. Similarly the *Labeda* (upper garment) and *Suruwal* (lower garment) were used along with the shirt (an English dress). Those Ranas, who had frequented India, started copying the western dress not in public but inside their palaces. They started wearing the sleeping-suit, dressing gown etc. Even in their formal dress they used the shirt and a tie which were obvious in the *Labeda* and *Suruwala*.

The Ranas used various types of caps most of which were Indian copy. When in India they wore the English suit during the first half of the twentieth century. Generally the Ranas used to go to Calcutta where they used to order the dress to the Rankeen and Company, (the then famous tailor's shop). Almost all the well-off Ranas and other nobilities were the customers of the Rankeen Company which supplied the necessities to them. It is said that once Chandra Shamsher, when he was in Calcutta, wished to visit a departmental store of Calcutta. The store was informed of His Highness's visit. When Chandra Shamsher visited the store, the proprietor of the shop escorted the Rana Prime Minister to his store. Every almirah with goods which was observed by the Prime Minister was labelled "Sold to His Highness, the Maharaja of Nepal." To see that, Chandra was stunned and returned without seeing the whole store. Another interesting story was that a very well-to-do Rana had visited the store of Rankeen Company to order for some coats. But to see so many varieties of beautiful cloths he could not make any selection. So he placed an order to make coats of all the varieties of cloths available in the shop. Thus hundreds of coats were ordered. Similarly another Rana while visiting Calcutta went to another famous departmental store of Wachael Moula. He was so much attracted with the goods displayed that he purchased all the goods of the store. Thus the Ranas used to purchase goods from the well known shops of India. Pramode Rana has also written that Bir Shamsher used to put a Chesterfield jacket tailored by Rankeen and Co. of Calcutta and shoes specially made by Watt and Co. In those days Calcutta was the main shopping centre of the Ranas. Whenever Ranas visited India, they were well respected and honoured. But the honour and respect shown to them were not for their high calibre and quality but it was mainly due to two reasons; firstly, the Ranas were considered to be pro-British rulers in Nepal and lastly, they had enough wealth squeezed from the nation to squander in vain glorious way, which the cunning businessmen of Indian understood well.

Specially the well-to-do Ranas used to import the European goods for daily uses. They squandered a lot of money to fulfil their vain glory. They also used to give away their used dresses to their employees and *Chakariwalas* (those who visited the Ranas everyday to pay respect). Such *Chakariwalas* used to feel themselves proud enough that the Ranas had been quite merciful to them. They used to call the Ranas as the *Dayasagar* or *Dharma Avatar* (fountain of mercy). It is pity to think of the situation in which the poor people of Nepal had to survive in those days. It was all due to socio-political and economic condition of the mass which made the people feel themselves bestowed with all sorts of mercies by the Ranas. They could not or did not express how much exploited they were. In one hand the Ranas were dressed with the best possible cloths available outside and inside the country on the other hand the people had to remain satisfied with the half naked dress. The poor people in the hill areas had to wear on one *Labeda* (upper garment) and a *Kachhara* (a small piece of cloth to cover the organ only) keeping the thigh naked. B P. Koirala has written that his father Krishna Pd. Koirala, who was championing the cause of reforms in Nepal, had sent a packet of the shattered clothes of a hilly person to Maharaja Chandra Shamsher to make him acquaint with the miserable condition of the hilly people. At that Chandra became so furious that Krishna Prasad had to leave Nepal for good.

The royal family also used to order the Rankeen and Company for the dress. We have not got any photoes of King Prithvi Bir Vikrama Shah with the European dress whereas king Tribhuvan's photo wearing the English suit with bow and tie are available. It seems that King Tribhuvan had used the western dress while he had gone to Calcutta or for photography, otherwise King Tribhuvan used to dress on *Labeda*, *Suruwala* Nepali Cap, Coat etc. He is also credited to have used the *Bhadgoanle Cap* (a black cap made of thinly padded and heavily knitted cap which is now used as the cap to be used by the civil servants) which made the cap very popular among the peopel. It is said that King Tribhuvan with the cap on had once come to see a football match in the public. Upto that time the Ranas used to look down upon the cap as it was used by the people of Bhaktapur. But King Tribhuvan made it quite popular. Kashmiri caps, Muslim circular cap, Varanasi cap etc. were in use among the well-to-do people whereas common mass used the ordinary Nepali cap. In his childhood king Tribhuvan used to wear on jacket like coat made of velvet with silver thread and pearls embriodered. Such dress was used by the Ranas also.

In the northern belt the people used thick clothes called *Bakhu* and *Docha* (high-naked boots made of the skins of *Bheda* and *Chyangra*) to keep themselves warm. In the middle belt the people used *Labeda*, *Suruwala*, coat, waist coat among the affluent society, whereas in the remoto hills the waist coat, jacket of raw wool, long *Labeda* and small *Dhoti* or *Kachhar* with bare foot, a Nepal cap etc. were used. In the warm Tarai region the people in general wore the *Kurta*, *Dhoti* or *Piejama* and jacket. Dress system in general differed from community to community.

The official uniform was as prescribed by the government order. Fine British woollen jacket and tunic with silver thread woven lace were used as the uniform up to certain status of the civil administrators. The breadth of the silver thread lace depended upon the status. Similarly the cap called *Chandtoda* with the plume also differed from status to status. *Chandtoda* made of gold was used from the status of *Dittha*, a civil servant. Emeralds were fixed in the *Chandtoda* belonging higher status civil servant like *Sardar* and others.

Dress of Females

Regarding the dress of females, the common mass used the *Bhoto*, *Cholo* and *Sari*, whereas the Rana females used many dresses. Pramode Rana has written about the dress of the *Maharanis* during the days of Jung Bahadur in this way. They put on gorgeous saris of about thirty metres length and enormous padded trousers inside the sari made the ladies a circus elephant in size. It was impossible to walk even a few steps inside the hall without the aid of several maids. This was the fashion in the Rana houses in the second half of the 19th century. During the summer days the ladies used to wear on thin clothes like the silk, *Dhaka* and other fine clothes, but in winter they used velvet (simple or embriodered), padded and well knitted cotton cloth or woollen closh. The *Khasto* (over garment) also were of various types from a very cheap ordinary cotton piece to highly embriodered Kshmiri woollen shawl. *Dhakha* and *Damar Kumari* were commonly used by the females. Local *Pashmina* (woollen shawl) was also used.

In the early half of twentieth century we see the gradual change in the fashion of women belonging to the Ranas and affluent society. Indian type of blouse with buttons or clips in the front instead of laces to tie the dress was used by the females. Generally the females were not supposed to expose any part of their body except hands, legs and face. Exposure beyond that was considered as shamelessness from the part of a women. Such woman used to become the centre of social criticism. So no female of a gentle character or a noble family ever exposed her body. But there was a gradually change in the fashion in dress. The blouse was generally adopted. The enormous trouser (padded in winter and unpadded in summer) gradually gave way to the petticoat. The twentyfive metres saris were replaced by five yard long saris. Similarly gradually the females of the affluent society started using the brasseries and under wears which were imported from Europe and India. Among the common mass the younger generation females used these things whereas the old generation females continued on the traditional old dress. They continued on the enormous trousers and saris. The change in the dress among the females was a very slow one, because, the society was so much orthodox that any sort of ultra modernity in dress (specially) was much commented. There was a general social version that one could enjoy full freedom in eating and drinking (since they were done in the private life) but not in outing, which also meant in dressing, going out and moving freely. By 1948 A.D. some affluent familes in the Kathmandu Valley started introducing the Punjabi dress *i.e.* the *Kurta* and *Salwar* to their young grils. At that these girls became the centre of attraction and comments were made by all the orthodox people in the society. Generally in those days the young girls used to wear on short *bhoto* or *long bhoto*, traditional big *suruwal* and *khasto* (over garment) in the Kathmandu Valley. Rich people used three layered dress *i.e.* inner layer, middle layer, which was the main cloth with various designs printed called *Damar Kumari* and thin cover. But the *Kurta* and *Salwar* became popular in a short time. Moreover the dawn of democracy in 1951 also brought a very fast change in the dress of the society.

Ornaments

Regarding the ornaments also there seem to have been changes. The ornaments from the European countries were also imported. Belgium-cut-diamonds were imported to decorate the royalties, Ranas and rich families. Before their introduction, the Varanas-cut-diamond was in use even among the big shots' families. Similarly the sari-pins, hair-clip, hair-pin, hair-roller, nose-studs and other types of ornaments were used. Tiara was used to decorate the females of the royalties and Ranas also. The males also used to decorate themselves within necklaces and other ornaments on special occasions. But in the modern age there was general tendency of not using the ornaments among the males in the affluent society, whereas among the people in the hilly areas the males also used earings and other ornaments for everyday used. The girls among the common mass used solid silver anklets. Only the people of the Tarai region used the rings around the toes and leg fingers. The silver ornaments were used among the people in the poor section of the people. The richer common mass used the armlets, gold chains or flowers to decorate the heads, and other ornaments made of gold, jades, emerald, pearls, jewels, coral and various other types of costly stones. Only the royal family members, higher class Ranas and some other persons with the permission could use the gold anklets, otherwise not. Before the rise of the Ranas, the permission to use gold anklets wrs sought from the king. After the Ranas came to power, the permission was given by the Rana Prime Minister. Formerly those very Kunwars, who, later on, became Ranas, were not permitted to use the gold anklets. After their rise into power, the royal family members, the Thakuris related to higher Ranas by marriage, *Chautariyas*, the Ranas, *Guru* (royal preceptor) and *Purohit* (Royal priest) could use the the gold anklets. But the rules of Jayasthiti Malla and Rana Shah that the low caste people should not use gold ornaments were still in vogue among the Nepalese society.

Nepal used to have gold and silver from Tibet from the medieval period. The gold ingots and lumps of gold were exported from Nepal in exchange of the coins. The Nepali traders sold the surplus gold and silver in Indian market. As such the Indians believed that Nepal was rich with gold and silver mines. The people of Nepali hence, used to have enough gold and silver ornaments. Regarding the pearls, gems and diamonds they were imported from India during the medieval period. Hazrat Mahal, the wife of Nawab Vizier of Oudh, and Chand Kunwar, wife of Ranjit Singh, the king of the Punjab, had also got asylum. Ranas became rich with jewelries after the Great Revolt of 1857 in India. In order to help the Company's government Jang Bahadur had gone to Lucknow to supress the rebellions. At that time also he had collected lots of jewels from the royal palaces of the Nawab Vizier of Oudh. After that also the refugees who had fled to Nepal to escape the punishment to be meted out by the British Government influxed in the Tarai region of Nepal. Among the refugees to get asylum the noted persons were the family members of Nana Saheb, Hazrat Mahal, the wife of Nawab Vizier of Oudh and many others. All those noted persons had brought enough jewels with them. Most of the rich females were given shelter within the Thapathali Durbar square, some of whom were treated as the kept-wives of Jang Bahadur. Jang Bahadur was successful in collecting the jewelries, gems, pearls etc. from those refugees, as such Jang and his own sons became rich with the valuable jewels, which aroused the jealousy in the minds of his nephews. Later on after staging a successful coup in 1885

A.D., Bir Shamsher spared no time in collecting all the jewelries Jang's sons had. Thus among the Ranas the descendants of Bir were very rich with the costly jewelries.

The females used to have necklaces of coins. Might be from the medieval period the necklaces of coins (both the local and Muslims) were used. Later on, when the Nepalese were recruited in the British army (British Gorkha regiments) those Nepalese, called as the *Lahures* in Nepal, brought the necklaces of the British Coins called Company in Nepal. The very rich families used the coin necklace of *Asarfi* (gold coin of Nepal) or *Ginnis* (British gold coins), whereas the common mass remained satisfied with the silver coin necklaces. *Potte* (tiny glass beads) was used by all the females rich or poor as the symbol of *Sadhuwa*. On the basis of the ornaments also it could be deciphered whether a particular woman belonged to the affluent urban family or the rich Newars or the Parbates or of the Tarai region. The profession of gold-smith both local and Indian was quite profitable in those days. Among the local goldsmiths the *Badas* also called *Lukamis* were well known, whereas the *Sunars* were from outside.

Cosmetics and Fashion

Cosmetics and fashion, equally important aspects of the human beings, reveal the attitude and skill of a nation through ages. They are governed by many factors *i.e.* the cultural background, economic condition, aesthetic sense, attitude and skill, taste etc. When we think of our own ancestors we feel the paucity of source material in dealing with the subject of the ancient and early medieval period. When we consult the ancient Hindu texts, it is described that the females used to besmear their bodies with sandal wood powder mixed with water so that there would be scent. Various types of scented flowers were put on their head to decorate themselves. *Tika* was used both by the males and females; as regards to females the *Sadhuwas* used red *Tika* and flowers and *Bidhawas* white or yellow flowers and *Tika*. Whether the females used the red painting on their leg and toes cannot be exactly. Possibly it was a practice then also. Perfume was used.

The fashion underwent a change during the medieval period. Instead of one piece cloth covering the whole body, the Malla rulers used the *jama* of the Mughal style embroidered with pearls, gems and others. Scents of various types were also used. The hair dress was also changed. The females had their hair combed forehead to back and the long hair was much appreciated. Big eyes with black eye pupil was much adored. The *Kazal* was used to the appreciation of the people. *Ko* (a powder of rice, *musur dai*, a type of pulses, and others mixed with mustard oil and water) was applied on the face and hands, so as to keep them clean and soft. Nepal as described by the foreigners, had a rough climate, so to keep their skin soft, they used to massage their body with mustard oil.

After India was reduced to British Colony many British cosmetics were introduced in India. Similarly there was a change in the fashion of the people. Now many types of cosmetic powders were also imported to Nepal. The females of the royalties, Ranas and big shots applied the cosmetic powder and face creams. The very rich persons used those things imported from England, whereas the middle class used those objects produced in India. But the common mass ramained satisfied with the traditional cosmetic. Similarly the royalties and Ranas used the French perfumes whereas the others the Indian scents. European best quality soaps were imported for them while the elite groups with meagre income used the Indian soaps. The traditional method of washing the cloth was not by using the soap but what they used to do was they put the ashes of hay on a basket and pour down the water on it. Water thus filtered was used to wash the cloth. Later on, local soap was also used. Similarly the common mass washed their heads first either with the *Pancha* (yellow clay) or the water filtered from the ashes of hay. Besides these things the mustard cake and *Rithha*, a wild fruit, which gives fume like that of a soap, were also used to wash the head. Up to the present time the Newars use the mustard cake in their ritualistic baths. *Amala* was also used for washing the head. *Rittha* was used as soap. It is still used in the hilly area. With the introduction of soap right from medieval period the soap was also used but it was limited only among the royalties, courtiers and other big shots. During the Rana period the European, Indian and local soaps were used. With the facial powder and cream, the lipsticks were also used. Similarly the nail polish became popular. Glycerine was used to keep the skin soft.

Hair style was also changed. Formerly the hair was simply combed, as already mentioned, from forehead to the back or from the centre of head to the left and right sides making a line on the centre of the head. But now in the 20th century the females of the affluent society from the royalties to the higher middle class had their hair in the forehead cut. That short hair, thus cut, was let fall on the fore-head. The hair in the rear was also plaited long or rolled. Curling hair was much appreciated among the males. During the primiership of Juddha Shamsher, his grandson General Nara brought the hair dresser from Lucknow and the barber was given permission to open a saloon. But these sort of facilities and modernity were meant for the Ranas their *Chakariwalas* and rich person not for the common mass, as the common mass had their traditional barber. We had many areas where the males also used to have long hair as they did not have barbar. In Kathmandu there were the local Newar barbars and Indian barbars. In those days the Bengali hair cuts tyle was much appreciated. These barbers used to visit their customers' houses to cut the hair. Mostly the barbers (Indians) used to wait on some places besides the road for their customers. Sharing of the head bald was and is the custom when a near relative would die. Once a common person, who had passed a long time in Calcutta, with the curling hair and *Kurta* and *Pyjama* was going around the main road of Kathmandu. He was immediatly dragged to a barber and his curling was shaved and his

Kurta and *Pyjama* were torn. This short of dress and hair-style were considered as the impact of the Indian National Congressmen by the Ranas. So the people with *Kurta* and *Pyjama* were suspected.

The fashion of the royalties and Rana females was to wear on very big frock covering the whole body which was an immitation of British ladies on special occasion such as at the time of snapping photos. But such dress was not used in functions or in daily use. The Rana families later on became the centre of the modern fashion, whereas the common mass, however rich, they could not venture to copy the modern fashion, as they were scared of the jealous eyes of the Ranas. Moreover highly fashionable females were much commented by their own status people.

To conclude about the dress, ornaments, fashion etc. it can be said that they were much determined by the social status political status, economic condition and other factors. The very regulations, relating to the dress and ornaments, as were based on the Hindu Holy texts as already mentioned, did not permit freedom to the people in wearing the various types of dresses and ornaments. Moreover politically also any change in these things was watched with jealous eyes. The changing fashion in India had its enormous impact in Nepal. The thirty yards long *saris* gave way to the five yards long *saris*. Similarly the big trousers worn inside the *saris* were replaced by the petticoat. The males started using pants, suits and sleeping dress and night-gown. Changes were mostly brought by the big and ruling families. There was a very slow and steady change in dress, ornaments and fashion among the common mass.

8

Social Entertainment

Introduction

People of any country need enjoyment to relax themselves after tiring business. They entertain themselves in many ways just like dancing, singing songs, playing games and athletics, and others. Ancient Rome was famous for gladiatoral games as the part of the social entertainment; whereas ancient greece had Olympic game. Similarly the bull-fight of Spain is still famous in the world. The types of entertainments differed from time to time, for example, in ancient times some of the types of entertainment were very crude. brutish and fierceful, for instance, the gladiatoral games resulted into death of participants. Later on such types of fierce entertainment were given up and humanitarian approach was made, so that people could enjoy the maximum without causing any harm to any body even the animals. Nowadays people enjoy by dancing, singing, games (indoor and outdoor), film shows, etc. Every nation has its own way of enjoyment and relaxation either in group or individually. The types of the entertainment gradually underwent changes due to the contact with other communities and states. Some of those remained traditional and others copied. In this context let us study the methods and types of entertainment of Nepal through ages.

Fights

The Nepalese had various ways of enjoying and entertaining themselves in their own ways : some of which were purely secular and some others religious. In ancient time *i.e.* the Lichchhavi period also we had both secular and religious types of entertainment, which are referred scantily in the inscriptions One type of the entertainment was the *Mallayuddha*' which simply meant the wrestling as a sport. There was an organisation called *Mallayuddha gosthi*, which managed the *Mallayuddha*. But about the term *Malla* some scholars have enterpreted it in different ways. Vajracharya opines that *Malla* was a kind of the buffalo in context with the *Mallokara*, where as Nepal wants to denote it as one of the varieties of the sheep in that context. But whatsoever opinions were formed by these scholars regarding the term *Mallakara* the *Mallayuddha* simply means the wrestling, which was organised by a *Gosthi* to have a social rejoice and the sport. In the contemporary India also there used to be wrestling contest among the wrestlers. In the ancient world wrestling was one of the popular sports which they enjoyed very much. The localities or the villages used to have their own wrestlers whom they adorned as their heroes. There used to be competition which was well organised by the *Gosthi* and the people enjoyed it very much.

Besides it there was also *Goyuddha* mentioned in the Anantalingeswor inscription. The reference of a grant of twenty five *puranas* allocated to the *Goyuddhapataka Vastu* (which means hoisting of flag at the time of *Goyuddha*). Moreover the Lichchhavi government had also issued an edict which mentions the reduction of the *Goyuddhakara*. In this way the *Goyuddha, i.e.*, the bull's fight was well recognised sport as such the government not only reduced the tax on the bull's fight but also allocated certain grant. The *Goyuddha* used to take place at the *Dakshina Koligrama* in those days. This administrative gesture in favour of bull fight was shown because of its much popularity among the mass. In those days there were frequent changes in the reigning families so the rulers to attain more and more popularity among the mass had shown favourable gestures in such activities which concerned large number of the population. In those days both the *Mallayuddha* and *Goyuddha* must have been quite popular games, as such the government had shown favour.

Besides these, there must have been other sources of recreation, although the inscriptions are silent. The Lichchhavis in Vaisali used to play games, and also enjoy the dancing. The famous dancers were well regarded in the society and they were considered to be the glory of the area where they resided. Such dancing girls were called *Nagarabadhus* (the brides of the town) or *Nagarsobhinis* (the beauty of the town). Amrapali was probably the most famous singer and dancer to whom Ajatasatru, the king of Magadh, had also visited to enjoy her. It is very interesting to note that we do not come across to any evidence regarding the prostitute during the Lichchhavi period. Is it possible that they did not have the *Nagarbadhu* in Nepal ? The Lichchhavis used to have very beautiful gardens where they enjoyed their life. Moreover they were the active participants in the festivals and athletics. When they came out to participate the festivals they, in groups, used all their things like dress, ornaments, even the saddles and reins of the horses or the chariots of the same colour. Such type of uniformity in dress we still find among the *Jyapus* when they participate in the festivals. The *Jyapus* still participate in the Neware traditional festivals actively, as such there is every possibility that the present *Jyapus* were the descendants of the then Lichchhavis. Unfortunately we are in want of detailed information of the various types of recreations of those days. There must have been the games of playing the dices, cowries and others. Dances and dramas must have been performed. So was the athletic games.

Festivals

Besides those secular type of recreation, the then people as any community of the word must have enjoyed at the time of religious functions. We have references of the *Dwarodghatan* and *Kailash yatras*, as mentioned in the Khopasi inscription', *Barahayatra*, and other *yatras*. Generally any *yatra* was an occasion of observing the religious festival as well as the recreation, enjoyment and feasting. The people generally used to worship Gods and Goddesses, dance and sing the songs and eat the feast in the *yatras*. Vajracharya has opined that both *Dweradghatanvatra* and *Kailash yatra* were related with Lord Pashupatinath. He mentions that the first one was in commemoration of the inauguration of the main gate of Lord Pasupatinath, temple and the second one was the *yatra* observed on the mound near the Pashupati temple which is still called Kailash. Due to the want of detail accounts of the *yatras* we are not in position to explain them in exact way. The inscription is broken and a few letters between the words Kailash and *yatra* are missing. Under such circumstance it will not be appropriate to point what exactly it was. The other words have clearly mentioned that every person (of the *Kurpashigrama* =Khopashi) should pay fifty balls or lumps of white clay for the *Dwarodghatana yatra* and *Kailash yatra*. White clay was meant for annual white washing of the main gate on the occasion of the anniversary of the inauguration of the main gate (of Lord Pashupati ?). Anyway King Shivadeva I and *Mahasamanta* Amsuvarma had wished to make the *yatras* run in perpetuity.

Barahayatra was another festival during the period. *Baraha* means the swine and the Hindu mythology mentions that Lord Vishnu in the form of *Baraha* had lifted the earth from the ocean. Thus the Hindus worshipped. The *Baraha* incarnation of Lord Vishnu. Connected with Lord Vishnu we have also a reference of worshipping and paying homage to Lord Vishnu on *Kartick Sukla Dwadashi* on which day up to the present time people visit the four Narayans situated at four places of Kathmandu. These four Narayan temples were credited to have been constructed by Haridatta Varma, a Lichchhavi king'. The people visit these temples in a way of going for picnic also. This practice is the legacy of the Nepalese tradition right from the Lichchhavi period.

The Chinese Annals give us the information that the people in those days were "very fond of scenic plays" and took keen interest "in blowing trumpets and beating drums." Thus the Chinese envoys who visited Nepal during the Lichchhavi period had seen the dramas being played as such the Chinese accounts mention the plays. Many types of musical instruments like drums, blowing of trumpets and conchshells and others were used for the religious and social purposes. Playing of the musical instruments were also used for the dances, songs and other playings.

Dr. Jha is of opinions that the *devabhṛityas* and *dasis* were meant for dancing and pleasing the gods. He is also of the opinion that the horses and elephants of which the amy was consisted would have given the pleasure from their race.

The various gardens mentioned in the Lichchhavi inscriptions must have been the centre of frequent visits for recreation. The love of natural beauty and being closure to it was also a source of enjoyment. The Lichchhavis in Vaisali had also many gardens, and parks with various types of flowers and fruits, which they enjoyed. The tradition seems to have been maintained in Nepal also.

Whether there was arehery tournament in the then Nepal as in Vaisali cannot be said due to the paucity of sources.

Medieval period

Compare to the ancient period we have more documents to inform us about the entertainments enjoyed by the people of medieval period. The contemporary documents like *Thyasaphus*, the dramas written by the various Malla Kings and other literatuers, colophons, contemparary *Vamsavali*, and the various dances which still exist as the Malla legacy reveal some of the important sources of the social recreations of the period. The

Malla kings of the Kathmandu valley were much inclined to promote and encourage the cultural activities. They themselves had taken keen interest in writing the dramas and played the active role in the dramas. Many dances like the folk dances, mask dances and others were given full patronage by the then kings. It does not mean that the other kings of the hill regions were indifferent to such activities. But in compare to the Malla rulers of the Kathmandu Valley they had very little to contribute to the promotion to such aspects. The Kathmandu Valley was comparatively well enough economically as such the valley had many sources of the entertainment.

Festivals

One of the sources of the recreation was the religious festivals which were very much encouraged, promoted, protected and financed by the rulers also. As the people were also very much religious minded, they spared no chance to observe the festival and at the same time enjoyed themselves. The festivals were the occasions for the religious performances, feasting and merry-making. All the members of the family and the guests worship the various Gods and Goddesses, offer sacrifices of the goats, buffaloes, fowls, sheep etc. and enjoy the festival by feasting, dancing and merry-making. In those days there were many festivals as referred to in the *Gopal Vamsavali* and other *Vamsavalis.*

Indrajatra was one of the festivals observed by the then people. The worship of Indra was observed since the Lichchhavi period. On the occasion Lord Indra is worshipped publicly as well as within the houses. The images of Indra are still displayed at various centres where the people worship and offer many things. The people enjoy it by taking feast. The Indra-jatra, which is still observed, falls on *Bhadra Sukla Chaturdasi i.e.* 14th day of the full moon fortnight. On the occasion besides the display of the images of Lord Indra, many dances like the dance of *Majipat Lakhe* (demon dance of

Majipat *i.e.* Manjushree Patan), Kumari dance, *Makacha Nacha* (monkey dance) of Bhaktapur, Bhairav dance, etc. were played at the Hanumandhoka courtyard, and many other places. The ten incarnations of Lord Vishnu were also displayed in the north side of Kumari temple. On the occasion the images of Bhairava were also well decorated and displayed specially at Indrachowk and Hanumandhoka palace square. The Malla kings had taken keen interest in the festival, so they had consecrated land for the occasion. *Same* (flattened rice, fried flattened rice, soyabean, fish, *Wo*, roasted meat, all mixed) and various types of beer were freely distributed to the public. The festival seemed to have been observed more and more pompously in the lapse of time. The Malla kings had shown much interest and actively participated in it. The people also enjoyed it very much as it was the occasion when they could see many dances, take the *Same* and drinks and feasts.

The introduction of *Kumari Ratha Yatra* by Jayaprakash Malla further enhanced its importance. *Kumari* (the Living Goddess), *Ganesh*, and *Bhajrav* were taken around the then Kantipur capital on their respective chariots. For three days the chariots were drawn in different parts of the town. They were followed by the various masked dances as mentioned above. It is described that Jaya Prakash Malla had introduced the system of distributing *Same* (fish, roasted meat, *Wo*, flattened rice and fried rice) to the drawers of chariots and the public). Meantime the beer in jars were poured down from the mouth of the image of Bhairawa at Indrachowk and Hanumandhoka. The beer flowed out from a pipe fixed up to the mouth of the image. The people drank the beer thus flowed out of this pipe.

The festival of Indrajatra was given so much importance because the people wanted to express their obligation to Lord Indra who was considered as the God of Rain also. The people were obliged to Him because he had caused sufficient rain for the crop. So at that time the people were quite happy because their field was having good crop and the weather was also quite pleasant neither too cold nor hot. This was is and one of the most jubiliant occasions when the people enjoyed most.

Gaijatra : Another festival the people enjoyed most was the *Gaijatra* which was observed in all the three kingdoms of the Kathmandu Valley. The occasion was observed in two ways *i.e.* in the morning the grawn-up persons or the young boys and girls dressed in different ways and masked as cows take around the main streets of the capital in the name of the deceased persons of the year. It was purely a religious festival, whereas in the afternoon the festival was observed in another way *i.e.* at that time the people besmeared with different colours and dressed in the most unusual way or masked took round the town making most witty and satirical comments. It was the time when the people freely criticised and commented on the many things. This sort or satirical comments were made for eight days, when the people enjoned full freedom even during the period of Rana autoctacy. It is said that the Rana Prime Ministers used to collect the people's opinion on that occasion. The people enjoyed the festival most jubiliantly as they had just completed their cropping season. It was the period of relaxation and enjoyment. The people took *Kwaty* (cereal mixed together and boiled) and enjoyed the satirical comments. For eight days the people enjoyed much.

Dasain was the most important festival enjoyed by the people throughout the country irrespective of the castes and kinship. On the occasion the people, however rich or poor, prepared new dresses to wear on, worshipped Goddess Bhagwati and took delicious feast according to their economic eapacity. All the members of the family, although separated, gathered together to worship the Goddess and eat together. The festival was observed most happily right from the king to the people-a pauper.

So was the *Tihar* also known as *Panchaka* which is and was observed fot five days. On the occasion besides the religious rituals the people cleaned, white-washed, illuminated their houses with the expectatian of the blessing of Goddess Lakshmi, the Goddess of wealth and took feast. During *Panchaka*, besides the religious activities the people, fully happy because of the rich harvest, enjoyed the festival most jubiliantly. Moreover the season of the *Panchaka*, festival falls on the most pleasant season of the year. Although we do not have much contemporary documental evidences of how the people enjoyed the *Dasain* and *Panchaka* festivals of the medieval period we can surmise on the basis of how the tradition of those festival still goes on. More details of how the people entertain themselves during the festivals are available, which will be written in the proper place.

Holi was another festival enjoyed by the people right from the ancient time. Entertaining part of the festival was that the people right from the royalties to the common mass put vermillion on the forehead and face, water-colour to other persons and made merry-makings. *Gopal Vamsavali* mentions that the festival was introduced in Nepal by the Lichchhavi King Manadev I. On the occasion during the medieval period, *Chira*, poles with pieces of cloths of different colours, were erected on the *Falgun Sukla Astami* and the *Holi* was observed up to the *Falgun Sukla Purnima* (full moon night). It was observed in commemoration of Lord Krishna's *Rashalila* and also the event of Holika, the sister of Hiranya Kashyapu, burning to death in the way of punishing Pralhad, the rebellious son of the demon king Hiranya Kashyapu. Moreover it was and is the occasion of enjoyment because of the spring season. The people enjoy by putting the colours and vermillion omong themselves.

Besidss these festivals there were other festivals also observed by the people of all the scattered petty states of medieval period. Local festivals of Kathmandu Valley here and are *Bisketjatra* of Bhaktapur, *Pahanchahare* of Kantipur and *Matchhandranatp ratra* of Lalitpur and others.

Sports & Games

The medieval people might have entertained among themselves by many other activities. There might have been wrestling competition *Malla yuddha*), bull's fighting *Goyuddha*), cock's fighting Sheep fighting and other games. Some documents mention some of the games prevalent during the medieval period. The existence of the *Satranja, Gajampha, Tripasha* (Dice) during the medieval period was a proof of the popularity of those games. They used to play those games to entertain among themselves. Although the gambling with cowries was a popular game among the Nepalese during the modern times we do not have clear-cut reference of the game during the medieval period. On this basis only we can not say that the game was not unknown to them. The game must have been prevalent in Nepal during the period also as were the cases of the *Satrainja* and *Tripasha*. Mahendra Malla's order prohibited the people from gambling. Yogi Narahari Nath and Baburam Acharya (eds.)-*Dibya Upadesh*, Kathmandu Prithvi Jayauti Samaroh Samiti. 2010 B.S , p. 30. The main difficulty in dealing with the subject is the paucity of the material on the subject, as most of the document dealt either on the political aspect or the religious aspect. Hence we have to surmise on the basis of what existed during the modern period as the age old tradition except those which were of innovation type like cinemas, norse-race (on the *Godejatra* festival), foot-ball game etc.

Drams & Dances

On the basis of the available material we have ample of the evidences of the drams, dances and the festivals as the source of entertainment during the period. *Gopal Vamsavali* mentions that a four-act drama named *Ramayan* was staged during the reign of Champadev. Thus we have dramas being staged from the early medieval period. *Sudhanapal* drama was staged during the reign of king Anandadeva (1147 A.D.-1167 A.D.). The king, having introduced reforms regarding the purchase and sale of the land, constructed the temple of Shiva, Tripura palace and capital and suppressed the thieves, became famous. The four-act play *Ramayan* is referred to have been staged many times. But it is not known whether the same drama was shown or different dramas of the same name were performed. The four-act drama *Ramayan* was staged on the occasion of the birth ceremony of prince Dharmadev Malla, the son of Jayasthiti Malla in 1367 A.D. also. In 1367 A.D. *Jestha Krishna Panchami Chaturaka Ramayan* (four-act *Ramayan*) was staged throughout the kingdom of Jayasthiti Malla. Twelve stages were prepared, which was written by Pandit Balsarswati, belonging to Lalitpur. The organiser of the drama was Sri Upadhyaya and Jayat Mulmi. Thus the drama seemed to have been staged in different parts of the kingdom. Although Jayasthiti Malla had not become the king of Nepal in 1367 A.D. *i.e.* 487 N.S. the scribe of the *Gopal Vamsavali* mentions him as the king.

In N.S. 497 *i.e.* 1377 A.D. *Balaramayan* drama was performed on the occasion of the *Vatukaran* of prince Dharma Malla. The dramas and dances were staged on different occasions to entertain the royalties as well as the people. The then intellectuals generally wrote the dramas on the basis of the Hindu Holy texts and mythologies. The stages were constructed and generally there used to be open theatre or stages. The audience used to sit on the floor. The dramas were staged for days on in different towns after they were performed for the royalties. Another dance called *Ashirhi* was also exhibited in 1378 A.D. We do not exactly know what sort of dance it was. In the dramas and dances the Malla rulers had also participated personally. During the early medieval period Rudra Malla, the defacto ruler, had himself danced in the stage. According to the *Gopal Vamsavali*, in 1320 A.D. Rudra Malla had personally participated in the drama named

Ratnagat staged in the presence of King Jayasi Malla. The drama was written by a Pandit of Sankhalankhu. It is also described that Dasa Bharo, who was to participate as a *Pisacha*, died as he broke away from the group and played the role separately. On the occasion of the aniontment of Jayadev according to the rite of *Nagapattabandha* in 1256 A.D., the *Nahri* dance was staged. Unfortunately we do not exactly know what sort of dance it was. It must have been a religious dance staged with the pious feeling.

On the occasion of the marriage ceremony of crown prince Dharma Malla a special drama, named *Bhairavananda*, was staged in the three sowns *i.e.* Lalitput, Bhaktapur and Kantipur. Dvijaraja, Joti Kasta Bha, Gajaa Mulami and Pandya Manaku Bha were the maeagers of the show. The people were thus entertained on various special occasions. It seems that there was no management of the dramas by the individuals in those days nor on the private enterprise, because staging a drama was a costly and too much pains-taking affair. The dramas were performed according to the *Shastras*. So the people seemed to have been entertained by the dramas organised by the royalties or by the *Pachayats*. Later on also many dramas were staged. The Malla kings themselves took interest in writing the dramas. Among the Malla kings the famous drama writers were Pratap Malla, Jitamitra Malla Bhupatindra Malla, Ranjit Malla and others. In those days the Malla kings wrote the dramas in different languages like Sanskrit, Maithali, Newari and sometimes in the mixed language. They promoted and inspired the dramas, dances and cultural activities so much that all the three Malla palaces have one *Nasal Chowk* each; the *Nasal Chowk* meant the courtyard where the cultural programmes were performed. In the Hindu tradition *Nasal Devata* was is the God of Dance. So in those days those persons or artists involved in the dance and dramas used to worship the God Nasal (one of forms of Lord Shiva in the dancing position). We have many shrines of Nasal Devata constructed during the medieval period. Pratap Malla is described to have constructed a temple of Nritya Nath temple. Wright's *Vamasvali* mentions, "He (Pratap Malla) made a beautiful image of Nritya-natha, exactly like one in a concial-shaped temple, and placed it in a large pati, newly built for the purpose, which was named Madu-nasala-deva". Pratap Malla had constructed the Nasal Chowk in Hanumandhoka. He is also described to have played the role of Narsimha in a drama. Many dramas and dances were performed in the Nasalachowk.

The famous dances of the Malla period were *Jatalan-pyakhan* (*Jataran* dance), *Gathu Pyakhan* (dance performed by the *Guthus i.e.* gardeners), *Daitya kumar Pyakhan*, *Kartik Pyakhan*, *Jala Pyakhan*, *Harisiddhi Pyakhan* and many others. Some of the dances were performed on certain religious occasions lik *Kumari Pyakhan*, *Majlpat Lakhe Pyakhan*, *Bhairav Pyakhan*, *Devi Pyakoan* and so on. Many of them are still performed on the occasion of the *Indrajatra*, *Dasain* and other occasions. These are the cultural heritages of the Malla period which are well maintained by the Shah Kings. Some of the dances like *Harisiddhi Pyakhan*, are performed only once in twelve years. *Kartick Pyakhan* and *Narsingh Pyakhan* were introduced in Lalitpur, the former was performed for one month in Kartick (October and November).

We have a reference of the ornaments and dresses meant for the dances and dramas. *Kshudaghantik*, made of gold and silver of various sizes-small and big, was used for dances. Similarly golden *Phunda* (?), *Turra* (?) and golden bracelets are also referred to as the objects of dances. These were some of the objects found in the Malla palace of Bhaktapur.

As already mentioned the drams and dances were performed on special occasions like marriage ceremony, tonsuring ceremony or coronation ceremony and religious occasions. We have a reference of *Darasana Pyakhan* being staged for five days at Bhaktapur attended by Srinivas Malla, king of Lalitpur, on the occasion of the marriage ceremony of the prince Ugra Malla, the younger brother of Jitamitra Malla, King of Bhaktapur in 1674 A.D. The group of the performers was granted ten mohars. Similarly later on there used to be competition among the dancers on such occasions, in which the dancing groups were invited to stage the performances, the best performers were awarded a handsome amount. On the occasion of Bhupatindra Malla's marriage ceremony the dancing groups of the three kingdoms were invited to perform the dramas in groups from many localities of the three principalities. It was not only on that occasion that such performances were conducted but also on many other such occasions. Similarly the rulers of principalities had invited the artists from other principalities. The artists were given lavish feasts and awards Such royal gesture of patronage and encouragemen had highly inspired the artists and promoted the cultural heritage of Nepal. In this respect the Malla Kings of the Kathmandu Valley played most important role to promote the cultural heritage in compare to the other kings of the hilly states. In the hilly states also they had their own local type of dances and dramas being performed. But due to the want of materials we do not have so much informations about them. The religious festivals and other occasions provided many opportunities to entertain the people.

Songs were the integral parts of any drama in those days. They provided not only entertainment but also a chance to get an insight into the play. Singing songs was the pivot part of the dramas. The expert songsters were the qualified actors. The classical songs were sung in a very melodious way. The impact of such activities had such an impact on the Newar community that the Newars have still maintained the tradition of singing songs. The Newars have special songs to sing in every month according to the lunar calendar. Not only that right from the medieval period the people used to have a *pati* or *sattal* where the people after their dinner used to sing the prayers and songs in the evening. We had sush *pati* or *sattal* besides almost every temple. The people used to sing songs and hymns composed by the kings and others. Besides these religious sites there were other *sattal* or *pati* in almost all localities, where the people, after the day long hard work, used to gossip, sang the *bhajans* and other songs and thus relaxed themselves before going to bed in the evening. Such tradition was in vogue up to some years back. But now the people have ignored it.

Moreover we had a *dabuli* (platform) in almost every centre of the important places or the localities, where the dances and dramas were staged either on some religious occasions or whenever the people liked. Upto the present time the various traditional dances are performed on such *dabalis* on the occasions like *Indrajatra*, *Gatjatra* and other *jatras*.

About the theatres we had generally an open air stage. The traditional plays were staged before the mostly crowded audience which enjoyed the plays with much rejoice and laughter. For such dramas also the *dabulis* whether those of Nasalchowk, royal palace or those of the localities were used as the stages. Regmi has written :

> "No curtains were used to give the background of the situation, rather the idea of the scene was conveyed through the songs which described the same. This was meant to be intelligible to those who watched the performanses...."

It seems that the curtains were not used in the early period. But the reference of the curtains meant for plays in a document, mentioning the objeets found in the Bhaktapur palace, give us a proof that they used curtains in the stage also. Might be it was a later development.

In almost all the dramas there used to be songs which were composed by the kings and others. The songs were also used to depict the picture and situation of the dramas. So the were used to communicate certain message besides entertaining the audience. Various types of *Ragas* and *Talas* were adopted for the songs in those days. One such was composed by King Pratap Malla in mixed language which is inscribed on the copper plate fixed on the doorways of the Taleju in the Hanumandhoka palace dated N.S. 792 (1672 A.D.) The *Ragas* and *Talas* referred to in the inscription are the *Saratha Raja*, *Khajit Tala*, *Dhanasri Raja*, *Garjati Tala*, *Pahadiya Raja*, *Shandala Tala*, *Chowo Ek Tala*, *Kedar Raja*, *Plan Tala*, *Bihagara Raga* and *Javanti Vela Vala Raga*. Thus a hymn tuned in various *Ragas* was composed in the name of Goddess Taleju by King Pratap Malla. Many such lyrics tuned with different *ragas* were composed and also inscribed. In those days it was believed that the music had great power to effect the minds of the people as well as the atmosphere also. Any thing could be done by the power of the music, for example flame could be caused by the *Deepak Raga* and rainfall by *Raga Malhar*. In the palace there used to be royal singers who used to entertain the royalties and courtiers. We have reference of music being played early in the morning to awaken king Chandra Gupta Maurya in the ancient India. The princesses were also trained in the dances and playing many musical instruments. *Beena* (lyre), *sitar* and others were the popular instruments in those days which continued later on also. We have a reference of the famous singer Tansen occupying an influential position in the court of Emperor Akbar in medieval India. Although we feel dearth of such informations about the medieval Nepal it can be assumed that there must have been well known singers both local and foreign during the medieval period, as the Mallas Kings themselves were so much interested in the music, dances and dramas. We have some *Bhajans* in Newari composed by the famous poet Vidyapati. It seems that the poet might have come to Kathmandu and composed those *Bhajans*.

The expert singers used to sing songs according to the time, situation and season. On the occasion of the *Basant Panchami*, they were to sing *Basaut Raga* to celebrate the beginning the spring season. Similarly the had to sing songs on the occasion of *Holi* which was observed in great pompous and granduer not only in the Kathmandu Valley but also in the states outside the valley. We have reference of *Holi* being observed in the states like Gorkha, Parbat and others. As already mentioned, the Newars still have particular song to be sung every month according to the lunar calendar; it is a vivid example of how much importance was given to the mnsic by the community. *Bhajans* song in the various temples everyday both in the morning and eveving or either in the morning or evening are the evidences of the love of the music of the community. Not only that the instrumental music of the *Dipak Raga* should be performed when the dead bodies were burnt, as edicted by Jayasthiti Malla.

In those days obtaining master in the music was a matter of great pride in the society. *Sangeeta Vidya* was highly esteemed. The *Ragas* are classified into six groups, *ragimis* thirty-six and *sutras* (Sub-groups) eight. The Malla Kings had also mastered themselves in *Sangeeta Vidya* and took pride in inscribing *Shastra Shastra Sangeetadi Sakala Vidya paranga.* Pratap Malla had mentioned *Shastra Shastra Sangeeta Sakla Vidya Pravina,* as an eulogy in his inscription. Similarly his son Parthivendra Malla had also borne *Shastra Shastra Sangeetadi Savad Vidya Parang* in his enlogy. Yognarendra Malla was also well versed in the *Sangeeta Vidya.* In this way they took pride in being well versed in the music and they themselves composed and sang the songs and played the musical instruments. The presence of the *Nasalechowk* in all the three royal palaces of the Kathmandu Valley is an evidence of the royal patronage to the music, dances and dramas. It seems that in the days yore the dancers were also invited from India on special occasions like *Holi,* as is evidenced by the *Dibya Upadesh,* in which Prithvi Narayan Shah is described to have given instruction that if the dancers from India were needed, let them come for a few days on *Holi.* Thus this instruction also reveals that there was a tradition of inviting the musicians during the medieval period, when Prithvi Narayan Shah could not restrict. Moreover it has also revealed the importance of the *Holi* festival during which the people enjoyed very much. Further the Gorkha King had said that the Newar's dances should be observed, which revealed that the Newars excelled the other communities in dancing and singing. If the other communities had developed expertees in the activities, Prithvi Narayan Shah should have pointed the other communities.

We have a community named Badi in Nepal, whose main function was to entertain people by dances, songs and even by being a postitute. It is said that they were known as Bode during the hay days of Lichchhavis in Vaisali. They had migrated to Nepal after the fall of Lichchhavis in Vaisali. But they continued their traditional occupation. The young girls of the community because the prostitutes willingly and many a times they were forced by their guardians. Such prostitutes might have been in existence in Nepal since long ago. Legally prostitution did not exist but socially it existed secretly.

Musical instruments

The movement of the characters of the dramas was guided by the rhyme of the musical instruments. The names of some of the musical instruments were *Basuri* (flute), *Dhyame* (a type of drum played on the side with a cane which was twisted into a coil at one end and the other side with the bare hand), *Bhusya* (a pair of cymbals), *Tainai* (a small plate, made of bell metal, struck with a stick), *Khwalimali* (a pair of small cymbals), *Khin* (like *Dhyame* but played by a straight stick), *Kahal* (a long straight copper trumpet generally used either in making an announcement or at a funeral procession), *Kartal* (a pair castanets), *Damru* (a small wooden, metal or clay instrument in the shape of an hourglass, covered at both ends with leather, having two small ball like objects attached to its middle by two strings so that when the instrument is turned quickly by the hand, the balls strike the ends and produce the sound. This instrument is very much syembolic with Lord

Shiva), *Neku* (an instrument of buffalo's horn), *Bina* (giutar like instrument, attached symbolically to Goddess Saraswati), *Sankha* (a conch-shell), *Sitar* (an instrument like the *Bina*), *Sarangi* (a sort of fiddle) etc. The famous musical concert of Nepal is *Pancha Boja* which is played by five persons. We have such musical instrument in Gorkha also. The concert was an auspicious and propitious one used on the auspicious occasions. Big drums and bells were also in use for specific purposes like on the occasion of worshipping Gods and Godesses. Some times they were used for emergency purpose: whenever there was an emergency either of those objects were sounded and the whole mass gathered in the palace.

Hunting

Another sort of entertainment during the medieval period was the sport like hunting. The hunting expedition was a source of entertainment only to the royalties not for the common mass. In those days only those kings who had good relations with the king of Makwanpur used to go for an expedition to catch wild elephants. The presence of an elephant was matter of great prestige and rejoice in the hilly kingdoms like the kingdoms of the Kathmandu Valley, Gorkha, Jumla, Palpa and other kingdoms. The elephants were used generally to carry the royalties and courtiers. Although the Changu inscription has mentioned the use of elephant on the military operation during the reign of Mandev I in Circa 464 A.D., we have paucity of the reference of the elephants being used in the military operation during the medieval period in Nepal, whereas in the contemporary India one section of the military strength of the states was comprised of the elephants. Inspite of the dearth of reference of the use of elephant in military purpose, the use of the elephant in military operation where feasible could not overruled in Nepal also. The elephant were used to carry the royalties and dignitaries. We have such reference right from early medieval period. The sight of elephant was a matter of enjoyment to the youngsters, who gathered at a distance with great rejoice. Moreover the people out of their traditioual feeling took the elephant as an incarnation of Lord Ganesh; thus auspicious to look at. The one tusked elephant was considered as the most auspicious, because Lord Ganesh is also described to have only one tusk. Hence it was a noble prize to have one tusked elephant. From the military point of view also a hilly state having elephant was considered as a powerful state as one with a tank in the initial stage of the invention of tanks.

Gorkha under Purandar Shah (1570-1605 A.D.) had got an elephant as a present from Tanahun; which had become a matter of great prestige to Gorkha and because of which she could cause fear to the neighbour chieftains. The Gorkha kings continued to have elephants in the palace. A document found in Gorkha reveals the various expenses for the maintenance of elephant like spices, sugarcane, bell, *daua*, ornaments and others. Jumla, the most powerful state among *Chaubisis*, had also elephant. Thus the presence of an elephant was a matter of great prestige, military importance and also entertainment where such a huge animal was not available. The elephants were found in the dense forest of the Tarai area, as such the rulers of the hilly region having close friendship either used to get elephants as presents or got permission or invitation from the rulers having Tarai jungle under them to catch elephants from the forest. A *Thyasaphu* mentions that Subha Sena, a prince of Makwanpur, had presented a pregnant she-elephant to *Chautara* Chikuti of Kantipur in N.S. 798 *Kartik Krishna Panchami* (1677 A.D.). The she-elephant gave birth to a youngster in the night three days after her arrival. King Nripendra Malla went to see the birth of the youngster. Later on the youngster elephant was taken to the royal palace as the king liked it very much. But after a few days the baby-elephant died. The inhabitants of the Kathmandu Valley had given so much importance to the elephant that all the scribes of the *Thyasaphus* had recorded a lot about the elephants. A she-elephant was dead in 1709 A.D. in Bhaktapur. This incident is recorded along with the mishaps in Bhaktapur like the death of King Jitamitra Malla (in 1708 A.D.) and Ugra Malla, sight of the comet etc. There are other references about the elephant. Deaths of the elephants were recorded with much importance. Generally in those days the elephants were brought to the Kathmandu Valley via Banepa as the *Thyosaphus* mention that the elephant was delivered at Sandesh *i.e.* Banepa at present.

Regarding the hunting (catching) of the elephant a *Thyasaphu* mentions that king Yognarendra Malla had gone to *Purva* (East) for the capture of the elephant Unfortunately we do not have the information of how many elephants were captured and brought to Lalitpur. Another king, famous for such activity, was Bhaska Mulla or Mahendra Singh, who had taken the title of *Gajapati*, Lord of the elephants. He had been quite active in capturing elephants. Such type of hunting expendition as a source of entertainment was, no doubt, limited only to a few Malla Kings who were adventurous and courageous.

The Malla Kings seemed to have collected rare animals at least for the Kathmandu Valley. The concept of the zoo as the source of recreation and its educational value do not seem to have occurred in the minds of the then people in those days. Inspite of that in those days the royalties used to tame many animals and birds for the entertainment. That sort of taming the animals and birds depended more on the personal interest of the rulers. Generally in the medieval society the king was the main source of multifarious activities of the state. As the Mallas were much interested in the cultural activities there was a tremendous development and promotion of such activities. Hundreds of the dramas and dances were performed and innumerable temples were constructed. Similarly different types of animals and birds were tamed in the palace. Birds like *mainas* (talking birds) and parrots were tamed. The royalties used to have silver cage covered with the velvet. Peacocks were also tamed because of their beautiful colour; and they were considered as the vehicle of Goddess Laksmi (the Goddess of wealth). We have also reference of the hawks being tamed to hunt the small birds. We have references of the hawk being tamed in the Mughal Court. The hawks were captured from the jungle while young and were trained to hunt and even attack anyone when instigated. The well trained hawks were very costly. The court of Gorkha had also the hawks, because the list of expenses found in Gorkha has mentioned the expense of eight annas for the feed of hawk whereas one rupee for the horse and elephant. What we see by this account is that the cost of hawk feeding was quite costly. Inspite of this the hawk was tamed both as a fashion and entertainment. There must have been hawks in the courts of *Baisis* and *Chaubisis*; the hilly areas of western Nepal continued to export the hawks up to the Rāna period. Various types of the pigeons were also much appreciated and tamed by the people. The pigeons were also used as the message carriers. Similarly dogs of various breeds and sizes were kept as the pet animals for decorative purpose as well as for the security. Some dogs were tamed for the hunting purpose. Such tamed hunting dogs were taken to catch the preys.

We have a reference of camel in a *Thyasaphu*, according to which in (1714 A.D.) the king of Bhaktapur Bhupatindra Malla had to sue for peace with Bhaskar Malla, the king of Kantipur and the king of Lalitpur by giving a camel and two elephants. One camel and an elephant were given to King Bhaskar Malla. Thus the king of Bhaktapur had camel, which was a rare animal for the Kathmandu Valley. But camel did not seem to have survived in the cold climate of the Kathmandu for a long time, so we do not have other reference to it. On *Ashad Sukla Dwitiya* 828 N.S. (1708 A.D.), a rhinocerous had broken the iron chain by which it was tied and killed its tamer. In those days to have a rhinocerous in the Kathmandu Valley was a very rare thing. How the people might have brought it here was a big question. The rhinocerous must have been carried in a cage to the Kathmandu Valley by the porters. But the rhinocerous did not survive long, because it died on

Magha Krishna Chaturthi Sunday 829 N.S. (1709 A.D.). Thus what it seems on the basis of the scattered informations is that the royalties used to have various types of animal collected from different places. If in one hand it was considered a matter of prestige of those rulers to have such collections on the other hand it served the purpose of entertainment to them. Up to that time it seems that the concept of having a zoo for the public exhibition had not developed in Nepal.

Horse riding might be another source of recreation as well as a necessity in those days. The messengars and the well-off people used the horse as the means of conveyancy. The rich people used to ride the horses as the motor-bikes at present. Horse-breeding occupation was a brisk business in those days. Jaya Prakash Mall's famous horse was named.

MODERN PERIOD

Changes in entertainments

With the beginning of the modern age we see the gradual change in the types of entertainment. Many reasons can be taken into consideration regarding the changing means of entertainment. Firstly, the untfication of the whole Nepal brought all the scattered petty states with different tribes having different cultural background under one umbrella. Thus there was an inter mixture of so many cultures, which difinitely paved way of having inter-communication and interchange of the types and sources of recreation. Secondly, the huge national treasury which was under the disposal of the rulers made them possible to explore and adopt various ways of entertainment which was not possible in the petty states with meagre income. Thirdly, with the contact with the west specially after the establishment of the British Residency in Kathmandu, the employees in the Residency brought many new types of the sports for their own purposes, which were, later on, adopted by the Ranas and the common mass also, which we will discuss in the relevant place. Moreover the

Ranas and the well-off people who frequented British India came to know various games and activities which they introduced firstly for themselves and later on their favourities were also included in them. Fourthly, in the context of world also there was a gradual change in the way of entertainment. Many new innovations which were prevalent only in Europe were introduced in their colonies. The people in the colonies adopted them; India, a British colony, witnessed many European methods of entertainments. Some of which were also introduced in Nepal under the patronage of the Ranas. Lastly, with the changing attitude of the society there was a new dimension in the scope of entertainment. The civilized society of west started evaluating the other societies in their own standard. As its result they started evaluating the other society from their outlook. Moreover there was a gradual tendency of showing themselves as well cultured and civilised on the basis of the western outlook. The enthusiast youths with western education slowly adopted the western type of sport and games to entertain themselves to be counted as well cultured and civilise in the recreation also. But such thing was possible only when the enthusiast Rana youths came forward. Thus the youths of the Rana family introduced many new sports in the country and such extracurricular activities developed fastly. The age old traditional means of recreation was also conserved by the senior ruling groups.

What we find in this aspect during the dawn of the modern preiod is that the Shah Kings were busy in the military campaign for the unification of Nepal. Inspite of this the sagacions, diplomat and competent statesman Prithvi Narayan Shah himself participated in the cultural activities, made the vanquished people feel well protected and gave full patronage to the Newari culture and tradition. So the age old legacy of the Kathmandu flourished well even under the new dynasty. The *Indrajatra* which was one of the most entertaining festival was also observed with much enthusiased by Prithvi Narayan Shah personally, as its result the Newars felt very much pleased and obliged with the new king. Similarly the other festivals were also observed and given full patronage. As such the vanquished people of all the petty states felt themselves free to enjoy their own cultural activities.

Prithvi Naryan Shah's attitude to wards recreation

But Prithvi Narayan Shah, who had experienced the drawbacks of the luxurious life, had alerted his successors and courtiers that they should keep themselves away from the glamourous and luxurious life. He seemd to have been puritanic in the dances and luxurious life. So he had advised that no foreign dancers should be permitted in the court, because such persons were not to be trusted. These dancers would expose the state secrecies. So Prithvi Naryan Shah had given an alternative that it was better to see the dances of the Newars of the Kathmandu Valley, in that case no state secrecies would be exposed to the foreigners and whatever amount would be spent in entertainment would remain within the state. Prithvi Narayan Shah's feeling was that the unified Nepal was the result of his hard labour of a long time; and the successors and the courtiers, if indulged in the luxuries and amorous life, would be undo it and the enemies would prevail. So his suggestion was that his successors should keep themselves away from the dance and other ways of amourous life. So he wished to establish a citedel in the Dahachowk area as the capital of his newly established kingdom. He had stopped the gambling in his kingdom by 1769 A.D. as one of his inscriptions mentions. The information gives us the hint that the gambling was one of the sources of recreation of the medieval period. It is quite probable that the restriction to gambling was imposed only during the life time of the great king.

Contrary to the spirit of the king, his son Pratap Simha Shah indulged in all sorts of the luxurious life The dancers got encouragement in his court. The various sources of princely recreation were revived.

Rana Bahadur Shah's interests

Rana Bahadur Shah, the grandson of Prithvi Narayan Shah, indulged more in entertainments. One of the reasons of his inclination in such life was that Queen mother Rajendralaxmi and Bahadur Shah, both of whom worked as regents, jointly and in turn also, had mad him indulged in such activities, so that the minor king would feel himself happy. Bahadur Shah made all sorts of means of recreation available to the king so that he could divert the king's attention to those things instead of administration. Moreover both of the regents were in their prime age as such also they were inclined towards entertainments. The literary figures like Shaktiballabha had written dramas with the objective of entertaining the then rulers. More attention was given to the entertainment by the then rulers.

Rana Bahadur Shah took much interest in entertaining himself by having many pet animals. According to Sundarananda, the king had many big bulls in his cow-stable. The names of the bulls were Malya, Vajya, Mangalya, Jujhya, Bhotya etc. The physicians, employed to look after the bulls, used to prepare special diet consisting of various spices like cardamons, camphor, cloves, leaves of cardomon, molass, brown sugar etc. He had taken much interest in having good type of bulls from India also, as such he had ordered Deena Nath Upadhyaya, the Nepalese Vakil in Calcutta, to obtain a pair of very beautiful and big bulls of Vijaya nagar states. According to that document it is mentioned that Vijaya Ram, the king of Vijayanagar, had ordered for a very big and special pair of bulls but the time the ordered bulls reached there the king had already died. Rana Bahadur Shah who had taken keen interest in keeping bulls sent order to the Vakil that the pair of bulls must be acquired by any means without taking any care of the amount to be involved in it. It was a very strict order sent by the king to the Nepalese Vakil that he must try his best to get the pair of the bulls at any cost. Incase of failure to get the bulls or those bulls were already dead, the Vakil should send persons to Machhilibanda kund Betha-sima (?) to get the tallest bulls bulls or oxen. We have many traditional hearsays about King Rana Bahadur's keen interest on the bulls. He used to collect bulls from within the country also. At that time he had issued orders that the bulls should not be castrated and used to plough the land. Better types of the bulls were collected from within and without the country. The text relating the order to purchase bulls either from Vijayanagar or Machhilibanderkund Bethasima and the informations he had about the animals and birds are the strong evidence of Rana Bahadur Shah's interest in the animals and birds.

King Rana Bahadur Shah had a zoo just outside his palace *i.e.* in the area where we have the centray office of Nepal Bank Limited, New Road, at present. In the zoo there were various types of animals and birds like tiger, bear, monkey, elephant, horse, deer, *Nyaku* (a type of animal), Gokarna (an animal with the ears like those of cow), *Sarangi Chakhewa*, heron, peacock. *Sarata* (?), *Battain* (a small fowl used for fighting), pigeon, wild dogs, robbits, rats, mongoose, etc. King Rana Bahadur, in his letter to Deenanath Upadhya, had ordered for the cocks of Hydrabad. He had also strictly ordered the Vakil that why had he delayed in sending the big dogs. Beautiful ducks and pigeons were also imported from India. Thus the personal interest of Rana Bahadur Shah led to the establishment of the zoo.

As Rana Bahadur Shah, Jang Bahadur had also a 200 of his own in the Thapathali Darbar, which was entirely a different world in Nepal. He enriched his 200 by the collection of fauna from different parts of Nepal at the time of his regular hunting expeditions and also from abroad. He himself used to supervise and inspect it. He used to enjoy the buffalo-fight, bull's fight, wild boar's fight etc. in his palace.

Fights of animals and birds

The cocks, *Battain* sheep and bulls were also made to fight among themselves to entertain the people. In those days the common mass also used to tame the sheep, cock, *Battain*, *Chyakhura* etc. They enjoyed at the fight of the animal and the birds. Those animals and birds conlinued to entertain the people up to the very recent past. Such birds and animals were supplied special feed. Ayurvedic tonic was also feed to keep these birds and animals strong enough. Besides them the people used to enjoy the pigeons flying for hours in the sky. There used to be competition among the people in a all these activities. Pigeons, *Battians*, cocks, and others were imported from India also. We have many ancedotes of the fights of cocks, *Battain Chyakhura*, sheep etc. The Ranas also took interest in such thing as such they had tamed many birds and animals. Even the royalties used to enjoy such fights. It is said that common people were also permitted to take their pets for the fights with the royal pets. In case the pet of a common person could defeat the royal pet, the common person was awarded one rupee and upward. It is very surprising to note why this sort of system was maintained by the Ranas. It is rather justifiable to give some cash in case of the pets of the common mass were defeated, because in such case the pets might be fatally wounded.

Kite flying

Kite flying was another means of entertainment right from the king to the common mass. Although we do not exactly know when did it start, the popularity of the game during the reign of Girbanyuddha Bikram Shah gives us ample evidence of its existence during the medieval period. The people enjoyed the kite flying specially during the festival of *Dasain*. It is still a practice among the people to fly the kites during the *Dasain* in Nepal. Generally after the monsoon is over specially the young boys enjoy a lot in flying kites. But during the *Dasain* (Dasahara) even the grown up persons enjoy it very much. We have got documental evidences of the kite flying from the time of the reign of Girbanyuddha Bikram Shah. Sundarananda, a contemporary poet, has mentioned that young king Girbanayuddha Bikram Shah, helped by Bhimasena Thapa, used to fly kites from the Taleju temple, Hanuman-dhoka'. In the kite flying also there used to be competition on cutting other's kite while flying. The string was besmeared with the many things like the powder of glass and others, so that one would easily cut other's kite. When the king's kite cut the kites of the youngsters of the common mass those youngsters were searched and given money as the award. The young boys felt very much happy and obliged. Similarly the other kings also used to fly kites. During the Rana period also the kite flying was a popular entertainment right from the king to the common mass. King Tribhuvan is also described to have taken interest in the game. Sometimes he used to fly kites from the Narayanhiti palace and other times from the building in Chhauni, which is now used as the National Museum. The common mass used to fly the kites made of Nepali paper, whereas for the royalties and the Ranas the kites were imported from Lucknow. The kites of Lucknow were very much appreciated and cherished; it was beyond the approach of the common mass. Only the *Chakariwalas* or the favourite employers of the Ranas could get some of the Lucknow kites from the Ranas. During the Rana period the kite flying was permitted only during the *Dasain* and *Tihar* festivals.

Dances Dramas

Dances, dramas were other modes of entertainment among the people in those days. About these also we find the continuity of the traditional Malla dances going on in one hand and the gradual introduction of innovations on the other hand. The traditional Malla dances were performed on the special occasions like *Indrajatra, Gaijatra* and others. The performances of the dramas written by the Mallas gave way to the new dramas written in the urdu, Hindi, Newari Nepali and Sanskrit languages. Formerly the Mallas used to write the dramas in Maithali, Bhojpuri, Sanskrit and Newari languages. Many literary figures started writing dramas in the Nepali and Sanskrit languages. Shaktiballabha was one of the literary figures who had written dramas like *Jayaratnakar Nataka* in 1782 A.D., *Hasyakadambak* (before 1798 A.D.) and others. Since Rana Bahadur Shah had taken much interest in dramas, dances and singing, such activities got much encouragement under the royal patronage as the collection of the pet animals and birds. Meantime it seems that the dancers from India were also brought to the Kathmandu Valley. Bhimsen Thapa who was the defacto ruler for thitty-one years left no stone unturned to provide all sorts of means to recreate the young kings. He himself spared times to recreate the kings like kite-flying and others which were the prevalent type of sources of entertainment. Many dancers were employed to stage dramas, dances and singing songs. His own palace was also fully equipped with all sorts of luxuries. Fine gardens were made. The Chinese gold fishes were imported to decorate the old tank like the Ranipokhari, tank in his palace and other tanks. From the time of Bhimsen Thapa, the Chinese gold and silver fishes were introduced in the Kathmandu Valley. Similarly many new trees were planted being imported from both China and India. Such trees like eucalyptus were planted in the palaces.

The dramas, dances and singing songs were, later on, organised in all the palaces of ths well-off and interested Ranas. These Ranas used to have an audience hall and stage within their palaces. One interesting feature in those days was that the dramas and dances staged and organised by the people did not have female characters whereas in the Rana palaces all the characters of the dramas used to be females. The dramas staged and organised by the public used to have young boys playing the role of the females, whereas the court plays used to have females (*Talimes*) playing the role of the males generally. Moreover the traditional dances and dramas ware performed on the platforms specially meant for that purpose, whether in Hanumandhoka or in the different localities, whereas the new dramas and dances were performed in the stages. The traditional dramas and dances (masked dances mostly) were performed in the Hanumandhoka, the symbol of royal palace, even after the construction of the Narayanhiti Durbar, a separate royal palace for the royalites, during the days of Bir Shamsher. No doubt, the king used to reside in Hanumandhoka palaces up to the early days of Prithvi Bir Bikram Shah, but during Ranauddip Simha (1877-85 A D.), king Prithvi Bir Bikrama Shah was taken to the Narayanhiti Durbar where both the king and Prime Minister resided. Only at the time of Bir Shamsher a separate place was construction for the king which is still called the Narayanhiti Durbar. The old royal palace was demolished as was much damaged by the white ants and the present palace was constructed by the King Mahendra.

Another interesting characteristic of the then dramas, (*Nacha*), was that the Urdu or Hindi language was used in dialogue and songs Nepali medium was considered undiscrable and unappreciables in the dramas. It was only in 1994 V.S. (1937 A.D.) Prime Minister Juddha ordered that the dramas should be staged in Nepali language, not in Urdu and Hindi languages, according to Balkrishna Shama. Siddhicharanshrestha has also expressed the same view. In those days in India the dramas were played in Urdu and Hindi languages; as its impact in Nepal also all the dramas were written in either of those languages, exapt some in Newari language, no matter whether the majority of the audience understood it or not. But the dramas meant for the common people of Kathmandu were in Newari language. Urdu and Hindi were for the affluent society. In the interior parts of the country local dialecte were used.

The royal palace had also a stags and hall which was called "*Nach ghar.*" So was the case in the Rana Prime Minister's palace. In those days the females, well-trained in such activities, were called *Talime*. Their main duty was to entertain their masters in showing their utmost skill. Most beautiful young girls were employed for the purpose, sometimes such females did attract the master's attention and became concubines and most favourite and powerful in the palace. One such example is the case of *Badamaharani* of Bir Shamsher who had gone to his palace in the way of dowry and she was a *Talime.* The female became the most powerful figure whose favour was sought even by the brothers of Bir to win over their brother. Right from Jung Bahadur we see special arrangement for the dances and singing songs, about which Pramode writes :

> "In the harem there were several groups of dancing and singing girls. There were some girls who were trained to perform drama in a stage. Several ustads (dance and music experts) of the courts of the Indian Nawabs and Maharajahs had come to Nepal after the Sepoy mutimy of 1857 and were engaged by Jung Bahadur. At that time Nepal literature was not developed upto the mask so all rags, gazals, thumaris and bhajans were composed and sang in Hindusthani language and dramas also were composed in Hindusthani. Some of the girls of the Prime Minister's harem danced classical dances like Shiva Tandab, Krishna Leela, Katthak etc., expressing perfect bhavs and mudras and song, Rag Raginis of Indian music in proper Tal and Sur. The Prime Minister sometimes invited his brothers and high ranking Bharadars on festivals and exhibited dance and drama performed by his Talimays."

In this way harems of the well-off Ranas were meant for entertainment. Many *Talimes* were employed whose main duty was to exhibit different shows on occasions. Later on, such *Talimes* were found in the palatial buildings of the *Gurujus* and others also But the Ranas used to have dramas and dances from those *Talimes* of their palaces. Jagat Jung also had arranged such exhibition to his own family members. He had employed many famous singers from India who were given the facilities of accommodation, handsome salary and other gifts. Bir Shamsher had interest in well decorated palaces. In the palace there was a *Nach ghar* (audience hall), a very attractive building, in the Lal Durbar compound. Many enormous chandeliers and dazzling gaslamps illuminated the *Nach Ghar*. About the dances, songs and dramas in the *Nach Ghar* Pramade writes :

> "Bir Shamsher had a deep interest and love for classical music and dances. He had engaged the services of some of the famous ustads (music experts) of India. Taj Khan, Dunde Khan and some others of Lucknow fame were at his service. These ustade had trained several Talimay girls at Lal Durbar. These Talimay girls played Indian musical instruments like Sitar, Tanpura, Tabla, Pakbaj etc. and song Rag Raginis in perfect Tal and Sur. There was a troupe of dancing girls who danced like Apsaras (fairies) and also performed classical dances like Kathak, Manipuri etc. There was an orchestra of girls who played western music on such imported instruments as the piano, drum etc. Also there was a theatrical group which was perfect in the art of performing drama. They staged plays at the decorated theatre hall of the Nach Ghar."

As already mentioned all the character of the dramas performed in the Rana palaces used to be only *Talime* feinales, whereas no females participated in the dramas managed by the Common mass. It was only in 1948 A.D. females participated in the dramas of the people. Buddhi Devi and Junu Devi were the first actresses in the history of plays of the common mass in Nepal. Otherwise males, whose moustache had not grown, used to play the role of the females. Most famous actor was Ratnadas, who was highly popular and genius as an actor and singer. Besides him there were other persons who had acted as females. They were Kanchha Buddha Vajracharya, Ganesh Bhandari, Asha Kazi Tuladhar, Chiniya Kazi, Narayan, Ratna Babu Udash, Krishna Man Dangol, chakra shrestha, Kishav Raj Tuladhar, Vijaya Kumar Malla, Rajendra Rayamajhi, Sanatan Kumar Wagle, Prem Singh

Khadka, Ramhari Shakya. Rabindra Shah, Daulat Bikram Bista, Buddhi Sagar Ranjitkar, Kakabhai Manandhar, Janani Mool, Ganesh Prasad Shrestha, Kalaniddhi Adhikari, Devendra Raj upadhyaya, Ganesh Bhandari. There evere many others who had aeted as females.

During Rana period there were many famous directors and producers. Dambar Shamsher Rana had one hundred *Tamile* females in his place. He was very much famous as a director of the dramas, which here staged in the Narayan his Royal palace, Bir Shamsher's palace and in his own palace. It is said that as he was excludid in the roll of Succession of the Primeirship his half brothers, who became Prime Ministers, made him indulge in wine, women and luxuries. He was provided financial aid also. He was very much impressed by the theatres of Calcutta. So he had constructed an audunce and a stage in his palace. He took interest in dance and dramas. His dramas were "Juhara" "Baharam," "Badshah Balkana," "Atarud Vazir," Shahazad Merikha'" "Jwahal," "Shahahind Badshahaki Ladaki Mustari shahayadi," Malika Muajma," "Khiradamanda". Nagalila" etc. The dramas played in the royal palace were "Paristanaka Badshah Firoz shah," "Gula Adam," Gulzer Shah," "Muluk Damiskaska Badshah Muzafar shah," "Muluka Hindustanka shahjada Dilaram," Parihasan," "Meharbano," Jajbno "Noorjan," "Dilbarkan" etc. Most of them had dialogues in urdu; only a few of them werein Hindi.

"Shakuntala" trauslated in Nepali by Moti Ram Bhatta from the original Sanskrit drama "Abhijnan Shankuntalan" by Kalidas was the only drama in Nepali staged by the order of Dev Shamsher, the then Commander-in-chief, in 1892 A.D. That drama was exhibited to Bir Shamsher, the then Prime Minister of Nepal and other Courtiers. Its was a revolutionary step in the history of the plays in Nepal, because up to that time the plays were written only in either Urdu or Hindi. After observing the drama, there, was a stuculus among big shots that the dramas could be played in Nepali language also. But the immature death of Moti Ram Bhatt and fall of Dev Shamsher proved a heavy blow in that step. Once more the dramas were written in Urdu and Hindi. Reactionary Ranas prepared. The Urdu and Hindi dramas to the Nepali dramas. Feeling of nationalism was looked down upon. Dambar Shamsher was an active person in directing the dramas which were meant for the royalties and the Ranas. Only yusuf was another active person to direct dramas which were staged for theRanas and the Common mass in 1930 A.D. He used to show his dramas in Urdu and Hindi during *Guijatra* and *Indrajatra.* Mean time another famous director and producer was Vaizer Man Pradhan, a duitist, whose plays were appreciated right from Sri 3 Maharaj Bhim Shamsher to the common mass. Wherever and whenever his plays were exhibited there used to be a big crowd. His plays were demanded by all the big shot Ranas, who used to compete to have his plays in their palace as early as possible. In those days such dramas could be played only for a limited number of days So Pradhan used to face a big problem as he could not comply with all the demands. Generally, he was given special permission of seven days extension to show his drama. Janardan Sama writes that the *Athpahariyas* (bodyguards) of the Ranas used to reach Pradhan's house early in the morning to fix the time of the show. Sometimes *Athpahariyas* used to kidnap the hero of the drama Ratnadas (later on Ratnadas Prakash) so that the drama could be taken to their master's palace. One of the reasous of the success of Vazir Man Pradhan was that he used to have Ratandas as the actor in his plays. People right from Bhim Shamsher, the then Prime Minister, to the common mass were the fans of Ratnadas in those days. He had started his career from 1932 A.D. as a producer.

In those days the Muslims of Indrachowk, Kathmandu, also used to organise dramas which were exhibited to the Ranas and in Common mass. Mohmad Miyan and Meer Saheb were most active in this field. They produced and directed "Gularu Jarina" in 1923 A.D. Their other plays were "Mohabbataka Phool," "Laila Majnu," etc.

Muncha was also very popular the produce: in well famed as those days. He was also as popular as Vazir Man Pradhan. So there used to be much competition among the Ranas to have his plays also.

Bal Krishna, Sama, the grandson of Dambar Shamsher, had written many dramas like "Mutuko Vyatha," "Mukunda Indira" annual day of Durbar School.

"Bhakta Dhruba" and many others. He is said to be the Shakes peare of "Nepal as his dramas were written in blank verse style. His dramas were not played as those of others. His dramas were played by the students. On particular occasion "Mukunda Indira" acted by the students of Darbar School, was exhibited on the 1994 B.S. (1937 A.D.) It issaid that after suing the drama Juddha Shamsher, the then Rana Prime Minister, ordered that hence after the dramas written in Nepali language only should he played. Prize for such plays was instituted. Bal Krishna Sama's "Mutuko Vyatha" was also played. "Dhruba" and "Pralhad" were staged in 1995 B.S. (1938 A.D.) Balkrishna was very much meticulous as a director.

Later on Puspa Shamsher Rana and Joglal were given permission to stage dramas throughout the year by the order of Padma Shamsher, the then Prime Minister. Their dramas were exhited in the Town Hall, "whoro common mass could see the dramas after paying the entrance fee.

There used to be *Kasdi Paltan Nach*, in which the Kasais, a Scheduled Caste, used to prepare dramas and songs. Similarly there were *Jyapu Nach* which was also meant for Common mass. Sometimes as many as fifty drams were dances prepared for *Gaijatra* and *Indrajatra*. Common people used to collect funds locality wise for the payment to the shows. Huge crowd used to gather to see the plays. The dances performed in the building of *Bada Gurujee* Tarak Raj Pandey were so famous that even the then Prime Minister and other Ranas used to visit to see the dances.

During Rana period the Curfew which was unposed during the night in Kathmandu was also relaxed during the *Gaijatra* and *Indrajaira* periods. The Ranas did not permit the dramas for a long time. During *Gaijatra* the permission for shows was given for eight days and so was the Case during *Indrajatra*, as the Ranas were strict disciplinarians for the people. Sometimes the Ranas extended the permission to exhibit drams of some producers for some days more. The above mentioned dramatists and producers were generally for the bigshots. Besides them there were many other producers meant for the common mass Bekha Bhai Mahajan was one of them. He was quite popular producer of dramas for the common mass. His dramas were shown in almost all the localities of Kathmandu and even in the Ranas palaces.

There were many artists who were quite popular among the people. One of such artists was Ratnadas, who was most popular. He was quite handsome, very smart in acting and was blessed with sweet voice to sing. In those days the producers used to run after him to have him as an actor in their palys. Whosoever could have him, his drama used to become hit in those days. Ratnadas, born in a low Caste in 1970 V.S. (1931 A.D.) started his career from his early age of Seven Years, when he danced as *Maruni* in the *Kasai Paltan Nacha*. Later on so long he did not have moustache, he acted as an actress. At his fourteenth year he played the role of Jarina, the heroine of the drama "Gularee Jarina". In another play "Mohabbata ka Phool" also he look the role of the heroine, whevere Munna Khan was the hero. "Laiia Majanu" was another play in which he acted as Loila and Dwarika Bhakta Mathema as Majnu. Names of the some of the dramas in which he participated were "Gularu Jarina", "Mohabbataka Phool", "Bhayankar Bhoot", "Salima Begam", "Silver King", "Haris Chanda", "Roop kumar", "Jhoola", "Bandhan", "Kangan", "Dila ki Pyausa", and many other.

Ratnadas was the child character, heroine, hero, director, singer and what not else. Quite handsome Ratnadas had very sweet voice as such he is considered as one of the best singers of Nepal. He was *The Artist* of Nepal, who was the target of the sex started maid servants of the Rana Durbars.

Some of the dramas exhibited during the days of Chandra Shamsher were 'Khel Abul Hasan', 'Madhavanala', 'Kamakandala', "Mitra Dukha haran" written by *Bahidar* Ram Krishna, "Madalasa", "Bir Pralhad", "Bir Savitri" written by a hort of writers like Kedar Shamsher Thapa and "Ekadasi Mahima" by Melawa Devi "Madan Mohini" was one of the popular dramas in those days.

In 1994 B.S. (1937 A.D.) "Salima Begam" drama was exhibited in Nepali language at Singh Durbar for Juddha Shamsher the then Prime Minister and after that it was shown to the public with the permission of the Prime Minister. It ran for three months with much appreciation. It had to be exhibited in many Rana palaces also. Ratnadas was the hero whereas Narayan the heroine. Narayan had also gained much popularity.

In the next year "Mukunda Indira" written by Balkrishna Sama was exhibited in the Town Hall. The person to play role of Indira was Ram Keshari Basnet. Along with that drama "Dilki Pyaasa" in Nepali was also played. In that drama the female roles were played by Asha Kazi and Daulat Bikram Bista.

In 1999 B.S. (1942 A.D.) "Chandidas" play became quite popular which was shown in the Rana palaces and Town Hall. The hero of it was Ratnadas and heroine Ganesh Bhandari. It ran for nine months. Meantime Bal Krishna Sama's "Pralhad" was also played.

Thus Town Hall, constructed by Juddha Shamsher, became the public theatre as well as meeting.

Besides these dramas, and dances, there was much interest in music also among the ruling people and common mass. The traditional *ustads* used to sing the traditional songs tuned to various *Rag* and *Raganis*. On the occasion of *Basantapanchami* the *ustads* sing *Basant Rag* upto the present time. In those days there used to be many *ustads* employed in the places. There used to be competition emong the *ustads* in the palaces.

On that aspect also Bir Samsher Seemed to have taken much interest. Besides the exhibition of many dances and dramas in his palace performed by the *Talimes* to his relatives and courtiers, he had employed many musicians from India also. The *ustads* employed by him were Rahim Khan, Haidar Khan Mohamad Khan and Rasul Khan who were given Rs. 884/-, Rs. 64 /-, Rs. 242/-, and Rs. 189/- per annum respectively from Kaushi Tosha Khana Office, Nepal, in 1889 A.D. In 1897 A.D. Taj Khan and Kashinath were Bir Shamsher's most favourite *ustads* who had come from Gwalior and Baroda respectively. Taj Khan got the salary of Rs. 2400 per annum.

In the palace of Bir Shamsher sometimes very exotic dances were also performed. Bir had granted *birta* lands and monetary rewards to the must impressive performers. In such dances the *Talimes* with their charming and exotic actings and songs used Dallure their masters; and some fortunate ones became the concubines *Badamaharani* of Bir Shamsher was a glaring example. The various *ustads*, local or Indians, used to train the *Talimes* other common artists (the characters of dramas) and others in the music. Bir Shamsher's interest on songs and music is revealedly the grand music conference held in *Bagari Ko Jalasa* held at Bagari in January 1900 A.D. Hundreds of *ustads* from different parts of India and Nepal participated in the *Jalsa* and song *Rag Raganis*. For several days the *Jalasa* continued. Some of the expert *Talimes* of Lal Durbar also participated in the conference Bir Samsher was so much moved by the touching *Rags* of Rahmat Khan of Lucknow fame that he immediately ordered his officers to pour down bags of silver coins on Rahmat Khan, who was nearly buried in the heaps of silver coins. Other participants were also handsomely rewarded. It is rightly written by Lord Robert about Bir Shamsher in this way. "Maharaja Bir Shamsher is extremely musical and has several well trained bands taught by an English band master".

Ustads Namak Misra and Nuruddin were in charge of theatre in the King's palace and *ustad* Bala Prasad was appointed as such in the palace of Prime Minister. Besides these foreigner *ustads*, there were many famous local *ustads* namely Bhairav Lal Pradhan, Ananda Lal Shrestha, Ram Bahadur Shrestha, and many others.

There was a gradual introduction of Western musical instruements in Nepal. Due to paucity of materials we can not exactly say when did exactly the Western musical instruments were used in Nepal. We have some ideas of about them during the days of the Ranas. Jang Bahadur is described to have witnessed and participated in the Western dances and music. He had also participated in the ball dance and others in Europe. As he took interest in it, he had also got Coaeling on the Western dances while in Europe. But the Western dances were not introduced in Nepal, because the Ranas did not wish it in Nepal. If they wished they could go to abroad specially India and enjoy it.

Bir Shamsher is credited to have introduced the western music and musical instruments in Nepal. Being enriched by the booty he got after the 1885 *Coup* he enjoyed the most among the Rana Prime Minister. As he was educated in Doveton College and stayed in Calcutta during the period of his studies, he seemed to have been influenced by the Western music and musical instruments. Moreover the British Residency had also contributed in the introduction of the Western music and musical instruments like piano, Clarionet harmonium and many others. The Englishmen took interest in musical instruments like piano, harmonium and their musical concert consisted of many. instruments unknown to the Nepalese Society. The Ranas also in immitation of the Britishers imported the pianoes and others. Jang Bahadur also had Erard's piano in his Thapathalic Durbar. As already mentioned an Englishman was also employed to train the military musical instrument players. The military musical, bands displayed their talents and occasions like the rituals functions, marriage ceremonies of the royalties and the Ranas. The Ranas and affluent class visited India also to witness dance, music and songs, dramas, cinemas and wasted a lot of money for their personal recreation and entertainments.

Gramophone record players were imported by the well off people in those days. Gramophones became very popular in Nepal. It was a matter of prestige among the well off people (the Ranas and rich people) to have a gramophone and some musical records as the Television and Video sets now a days. During the days of Chandra Shamsher records of Pyara Saheb, Mohamad Hussain, Gauhar Jan, Miss Gauhara, Master Mohan Master Nishar, Pyara Kavval. Aga Faiz, Master Rahat, Miss Dulari, Janaki Bai, Master Labbhu and Master Mohammad were quite popular in Nepal. Songs of Master Labbhu and Master Mohammad were in the month of the people of Kathmandu Everybody used to sing their songs.

In one hand the songs of Indian singersw ere getting quite popular on the other hand some Nepali emigrats in India were doing their best to contribute in the development of Nepali songs. Some of them in the British Gorkha Rejiment had played the dramas, composed and song the Nepali. *Jhyaure* (local) songs which were recorded. Dyau Bahadur Dura, Pancha Subba, Birkhe Pun and Hansarani were the famous artists of Nepal who could contribute in the growth of Nepali songs in India. Birkhu Pun and Hansarani performed their dances, sang songs jointly. Birkhe Pun was enverted to London also to show his actings and sing songs.

Setu Ram's *Kali Bhajan* was first recorded among the Nepali sons in 1917 A.D. It was in a mixed language *i.e*, Maithili and Newari. Birkhu Pun and Hansarani's haydays were in 1910 A.D. Meantime Bahadur Singh Baral and Mitra Sena jointly made a move in the development of Nepali songs. Many of his Comics, gramophone dramas, folk songs etc., here recorded. His dramas like "Dhruba Charitra" "Draupadi Cheera Harana", "Sudama Charitra", "Swasthavi" etc. dramas were exhibited in the barracks and recorded. His records become popular in Nepal also. Meantime Mitra Sena's records also got popularity. Melawa Devi, a *Talime* female of Chandra Shamsher's palace, also started having her songs recorded. Mitra Sena and Ranu Devi also had contributed in this respect. Later on Ratnadas became a very popular singer. As already mentioned he was a versitile singer, dancer and actor. He had his four songs recorded in 1940 A.D. for the first time. He song duct songs with Laxmi Devi and Prem Devi, the *Talimes* of Lal Durbar, who had been in Calcutta at that time. Ratnadas records were sold like hotches in Kathmandu. Some of his songs become quite popular and every body started singing his songs.

Besides these Nepali songs, records of Indian films were also very much demanded K.L. Saigal, Khurshid, Noorjahan and others were known to Nepali people due to their songs.

Radio

Meantime radio was introduced in Nepal. In the initial phase it was used only in the British Embassy, later on Indian Embassy, royal family and the Prime Minister Later on all the Ranas got permission to use the radio. Among people upto the dawn of democracy in 1951 A.D. Only high officials used the radio. In those days a radio was more valuable than the Television and Video set at present, because Nepal did not have radio broad casting office, as such the Nepalese used to hear foreign news and programmes. India was having a freedom movement as such the Ranas wanted to keep the people ignorant and blind of what was going on in India. Indian newspapers were censored. So the Rana authority did not wish the people liston the radio. Whosoever had radio, they had to time it in a very lo wvoice so that others would not hear it. Even during the days of Padma Shamsher famous for his liberal attitude there was a very strict control over the permisson on the use of radio. Radio had become a very useful source of entertainments. Those who had radio used to write their near relatives to enjoy the songs from radio. Nepalese used to enjoy the Indian film songs, *Bhajans* and others when the democratic movement started in Nepal, the Ranas started tighting over the radio-owners. Spies were used to collect informations as to how the radios were used. Thus, although the radio was a source of information and entertainment, the owners had to be very alert and cautious in its use.

Thus the dances, dramas and songs were the most popular source of entertainment for the common mass in the Kathmandu Valley. Whenever any dance or drama was exhibited in the rich people's (common mass) house all the people of the locality used to poor down to see the display. Such dramas were the only source of recreation in the absence of the cinemas.

But the common mass of the hilly areas had their own traditional type of dances. *Rodighar* dancing house was the most popular among the Gurung youths. The youths (girls and boys) still use to dance, sing and enjoy in the *Rodighar* sometimes the whole night. It is also called a social 'night club'. Similarly the *Bhote Shelo* is another typical dance among the youths (both boys and girls) *i.e.* the Sherpas. The Sherpas had and have their own type of dance. Magars also have their own traditional dances which continued since long. *Dohari* is a typical way of singing songs in a way of dialogue in a musical tone. A female just makes a comment cuns question or asks a male, who is supposed to answer it in a musical way. It is also said that in that way there used to be competition between the groups of both sexes. In that way the males used to elope the females also. *Rodighar* was another place for entertainment as well as love making also. Many youths of both sexes fell in love in such activities also. Similarly the Tharus, and other communities in the low lands of the Tarai had and have their own dances and songs. Thus the different communities, whether in the mountains or in the low lands, had their own type of dances, songs and dramas. But one interesting feature is that the young girls and grown up females freely participated in the dances, singing songs and dramas both in the hill area and the Tarai whereas in the Kathmandu Valley no females participated in such activities.

Hunting or Shikar

Hunting is the traditional game of recreation since time immemorial. In those days it was a favourable pastime of the royalties all over the world. The old scripturns have described and appraised the valour of the kings and nobles in the practic of hunting. The rulers and nobles of Nepal had also shown keens interest in the practice of hunting as an entertainment as well as a duty. Killing of man-eaters was considered as one of the important duties of the rulers and nobles. In this way the hunting of big animals like tiger, rhinocerouses, leopards, deer, wild-buffaloes, wild-boars, etc. was the privileges as well as an attraction to entertain themselves in those days and even now. Nepal, being a mountainious region with dense forest, is and was abound with the various types of animals since days long. Fahien had described the presence of the white elephants in the Kapilavastu area during his visit and had also described the deserted area (Kapilavastu) infested by the wild animals. Thus from the ancient times the present Nepal was rich with the wild animals, which were hunted by the rulers and others at different times. As already described the Malla Kings of the Kathmandu Valley were also much attracted towards the hunting and catching the wild elephants. The prizes of the hunting expeditions were displayed with pride. The elephants were well tamed and used to carry the royalties and the most dignified officers.

We have an account of Jaya Prakash Malla's conspiracy to imprison Pratap Simha Shah, the Gorkha crown prince, during the period of war between the Gorkhas and the Mallas. Pratap Simha Shah was allured with the pretext of hunting the wild boars at the Chisapani forest area. This incident is also a strong evidence of the popularity of hunting in those days also. Prithvinarayan Shah had also many elephants; most probably after the conquest of Makwanpur he became rich in elephants. When he entered the fortified Kantipur town to conquer he was riding his favourite elephant named "Sundarprashad". The elephants and even the horse were given names, which we will describe later on. The place where the elephants were kept and tamed was called *Hattisar*. During the reign of Rajendra Tikram Shah, the age old *Hattisar* was extended. Many elephants named Laxmi Prasad, Devi Prasad, Havada Prasad, Moti Prasad, Ambar Prasad, Sri Prasad and so on were the famous elephants during the reign of Rajendra Vikram Shah. Various types of spices, ghee, wheat floor, rice etc. were fed to these elephants. The elephant named Laxmi Prasad was one tusked elephant, as such it was considered an auspicious one. According to the Hindu tradition Lord Ganesh, the elephant headed God, also had only one tusk, so one tusked elephant was considered as if the incarnation of Lord Ganesh. Pandit Sundarananda has appraised a lot about the various elephants in the poetic way. He has also described about one white elephant found in a jungle of Nepal. Many *shikars* were employed to catch and tame the wild elephants. The Tarai area was famous for the elephants, rhinocerous and other animals, Jang Bahadur had also taken the occupation of hunting *i.e.* catching the wild elephants during his worse days. Mathbar Simha Thapa had also escaped from Nepal during the period of political chaos on the pretext of hunting in the Tarai of Nepal. About the catching of the wild elephants it can be said that in one way it was a matter of entertainment for the royalties and on the other hand the wild elephants were caught, tamed and exported to India.

Hunting as an entertainment both to the rulers and foreigners specially to the British royalties, Viceroys and dignitaries became popular during the Rana Period. The Rana Prime Ministers and their entourage had gone for hunting to the Tarai area of Nepal many times during the winter season. Jang Bahadur, one of the best marksman, was very much interested in the hunting' The trophies of Jang Bahadur's hunting expeditions were exhibited in a big hall of his palace of Thapathali. Wright, a contemporary British Residency physician, wrote :

> "After inspecting the public rooms, the stranger is shown the trophies of Sir Jung Bahadur's hunting expeditions. These consist of skull of elephants, tigers, rhinocerouses, wild buffaloes, and gayal; stacks of deer-horns of all sorts, skins of the above-mentioned animals, crocodiles and snakes, with many other curiosities. In the Elephant court are generally to be found some fine males, used for hunting wild elephants and also frequently one or two comical little young ones, born after their mothers have been caught in the annual hunting expedition."

Jang Bahadur took much interest in hunting the wild animals and catching wild elephants and watching elephant-fight wild boar's, quailts' fight etc. Almost every year during winter he used to go for hunting. In his hunting expedition he used to take hundreds of military and civil officials. In one of his hunting expedition he had taken with him 32000 soldiers, 52 guns, 300 horsemen, 250 horse artillery, 2000 followers and 700 ration officers to the Tarai forest. Actually for the hunting such a large number of persons was not necessary. In the hunting Jang Bahadur had Keeuest interest and gained fame not only within the country but also abroad. For such hunting hundreds of elephants and people were needed. So Jang Bahadur had maintained several *Hattisars* in the Tarai region, where hundreds of elephants were kept there. Jang nsed to supervise those *Hattisars* personally very often. It is described that the elephants were very sensitive and obedient to their masters. Jang's favourite tuskers were Jang Prasad, Barchha, Sri Prasad, chandra Prasad and Bijuli Prasad, which also were too much loyal to their master. The elephant Jang Prasad was so sensitive that he seldom moved without the Prime Minister's order being read to him by the officer of the *Hattisars*. The elephants were also given different status as the dogs in the police administration to detect the criminals. The high status elephants were given better feed and also attendants. Elephant Jung Prasad was attended by two she-elephants, which used to help him (the elephant) while bathing. Mosquito nets and shoes were used for such elephants. Elephants like Jung Prasad and Bijuli Prasad were well decorated with ornaments and velvet cloths. Bijuli Prasad was a very smart and good fighter with the wild elephants so in the *Hatti-khedas* (operations to catch the wild elephants) the Bijuli Prasad was always kept in the front and Jung Prasad was in the rear to guard and help other elephants in emergency. Jang Prasad's death was very shocking news to Jang Bahadur, two days before the latter's death.

The hunting camp is a worth describing operation. Almost every year Jung Bahadur, in order to relax, used to go to the Tarai region for the big hunting operations. In the main camp, there used to be several layers of the tents spread. The outer most layer tents were occupied by the lower staff and security guards. Then the other line of tents by the high level staff; in this way there were many lines of tents spread in the camp, which was guarded by many security guard regiments. In the centre of the camp there was the tent of the Prime Minister, his wives and favourite concubines. Just outside the tent, there used to be tents of the most dignified officers. Generally the evening hours in the campus were spent in rejoicing by songs and dances of the staff and eating the roasted animals like wild boars and deer which were hunted in the day time. Jang's interest on hunting and hunting expeditions are well described by Padma Jung and Oldfield who had accompanied the Prime Minister in the hunting expeditions. Oliphant and capt, cavenagh were also taken to a hunting by Jang. Oldfield has described his personal observations of how Jang used to enjoy fights between the wild buflalo and tiger, between hunting dogs and leopard and cutting leopard with a sword etc. Jang was very clever in catching the wild elephants and rhinocerouses. Every year Jang Bahadur used to catch a large number of the wild elephants. He had about one thousand elephants in the *kattishars*, most of the elephants were used in the hunting expeditions. Jang Bahadur's prizes of the hunting expedition is as follows:

Arrangement of the hunting expedition was very hard task. The officers like lieurturant Khadge Singh and men of the hunting department used to have a very hard time in determining the movements and locate the tigers and other wild animals. Many export professional *Shikaris* were employed to ascertain the whereabouts of the wild beasts. They used to tie the goats and buffalo-calves as the baits to the wild animals. After getting the informations from those *Shikaris* who watched the wild animals having killed and eaten the bait from the top of the trees, the Shikar Camp Commander used to make necessary arrangements to encircle nearly a mile area of the forest with hundreds of elephants mounted with armed men Then the Prime Minister mounted on a very big and expert elephant waited for the game at a vantage point Meanwhile the encircled ring was gradually tightened and the encircled animal was scared by different ways. Sometimes many carnivorous animals were encircled. The Rana Prime Ministers sometimes enjoyed the various animals fighting within the encircled area. After enjoying a lot at the helpless condition of the animals, the hunting group used to slay the animals in a large number. The Ranas as others also took much pride in having killed a big number of tigers, rhinocerouses, deers, leopards and others.

After killing the animals they used to bring the skulls, skins and others to decorate their palace. Up to this time when we visit the Rana palaces we see their room floors decoreted with the skins of tigers, leopards, spotted deer etc., skulls of the stags, deer and other animals hung on the walls. Such huntings were not free from risk also. Many a times the Ranas were saved by their seccurity guards also. Prime Minister Juddha Shamsher once feel from his elephant while hunting the tigers. But the timely rescue from the part of his ADC, *Hazuria* Colonel Dal Bahadur Basnyet saved his life for which the latter war given *Bakshish* of one lakh rupees. Juddha also used to enjoy the fight of the different animals which were encircled by the elephants in the hunting expeditions. Dr. Iswari Prasad, obiographer of Juddha Shamsher, has written that during seven seasons (1933-40 A.D.) Juddha Shamsher bagged 433 tigers, 33 rhinos, 93 leopards, 22 bears, 20 crocodiles, one wild buffalo, three elephants, many wild dogs, hyenas, deer, any many others. The biggest tiger shot by him measured ten feet and nine inches. We have still some masterpieces of paintings and photos of hunting in the palaces of the Ranas. Their pride was in counting the numbers of the animals they had killed and bagged, as they had least sense of conservation of the faunas, the national property. Inspite of such mass massacre of the wild animals to entertain the Ranas, there was a large number of such animals alive, as almost all the low-land (Tarai) with tropical climate was thickly covered with dense forest, which have now been deforestated. Jang Bahadur died of cholera at Pathargatta in 1877 A.D. while in a hunting expedition. The time when the great earthquak took place in 1934 A.D. Prime Minister Juddha was also out of Kathmandu for the hunting. Juddha's hunting in 1934 A.D. can be compared with Nero's fiddling while Rome was burning. When the astrologers had forecasted the evil owen, Juddha should not have gone out for hunting.

The hunting of various wild animals, thus, was one of the most interesting entertainments among the Rana Prime Ministers and their favourite relatives which no other common mass could ever enjoy. Sometimes on their will the king was also taken along with them to enjoy the hunting expeditions. The hunting expeditions meant the relaxation and enjoyment of the Rana Prime Ministers and hard labour sometimes risk of the life of the employees and lower staff.

It was a traditional religious belief that if a man would kill and offer the warm blood from the palpitating heart of a rhino, sitting inside the opened stomach of the beast, the deceased ancestors would straight way go to heaven so the rulers and their favourities were very eager to kill the poor creature in large number. For this purpose the rhinos were shot and before they died, the stomaches of the fallen animals were opend in haste so as to make a room for the priest and the person offering blood. In this way many persons offered the blood in the name of the dead ancestors. It is said scores of rhinocerouses were killed for such purpose only.

What we observed is that no other rulers of Nepal enjoyed hunting so much as the Ranas. Besides the Tarai areas where they visited for big games, they had conserved forests in the Kathmandu Valley like Nagarjun, Gokarna, Godavari, Nagarkot and others with the wild animals. In those days there were very strict rules relating to the hunting of the wild animals. So the common mass was scared of being punished by the Ranas.

The Ranas had generously entertained the British royalties, Viceroys and other dignified personalities of the British government at times in order to please them and serve their personal interests. The Britishers also could have enjoyed the hunting expedition in British India, but the Ranas to please the Britishers invited them very often to hunt the wild animals of Nepal. The Ranas felt themselves very much graced when the Britishers came to Nepal to hunt the Nepalese animals which were not lacking in India and they felt much appraised when Nepal was described as the *Hunters' Paradise.* Even "The Morning Post" and "Times" newspapers of U.K. had described about hunting in Nepal.

Albert Edward, the Prince of Wales of Grcat Britain, was the second Britishers to visit Nepal for hunting. Jang Bahadur invited the Prince of Wales for a hunting expedition in 1876; and he himself supervised the royal hunting camp at Banabas. On February 16, 1876 the Prince of Wales, on entering Nepal, was cordially welcomed by Jang Bahadur and his officers. Jang Bahadur presented him two caged tigers, one baby elephant and others. Albert Edward enjoyed the hunting in Nepal for nearly two weeks *i.e.* February 19 to March 5, 1876.

In 1866 A.D. His Royal Highncss, Duke of Edinburg, second son of Queen victoria, came for a hunting on invitation to the Tarai of Nepal. He bagged two tigers measuring ten feet and six inches and ten feet and three inches respectively. He was the first British dignitary to visit Nepal for hunting.

During the days of Bir Shamsher, the grandson of Queen Victoria, England, His Royal Highness Prince Albert Victor, Duke of clarunce, had visited Nepal for hunting. Prime Minister Bir Shamsher had excurted His Royal Highness for hunting in the far western Tarai of Nepal in 1889-1890 winter. Similarly Duke of Caunaught had bagged three tigers in 1894. A.D.

King George V was the another British royaltly to visit Nepal for a hunting on Decembers 27, 1901 A.D. at the invitation of the Nepal Durbar *i.e.* Chandra Shamsher. In those days although the royal seal was used and important documents were signed by the king, they were all done at the instigation of the Rana Prime Minister. So when George V visited India Chandra found it the most suitable opportunity to please the British Emperor. So the invitation was extended to King George V to hunt in the Thori jungle of Nepal, which was agreed. George V and his entourage were accorded the most warm welcome by Chandra on behalf of King Tribhuvan, who was minor then. Several hundred well trained elephants were taken to the hunting campus from different *hattisars.*

Motorable roads were constructed in the forest and telephonic cables were laid for communications. Very extensive preparations were made befitting to the British regality George V and his royal entourage stayed for ten days during which they bagged thirty nine tigers, eighteen rhinocerouses, one bear and other animals. Being very much pleased. George V invested the order of G.C.V.O on Chandra. Besides the British royalties many others were also entertained. Oldfield himself had written that he had also accompained Jang Bahadur in the hunting expedition in 1851 A.D., Many others were also provided opportunity to enjoy the hunting in Nepal by the Ranas.

Gambling

Gambling was one of the chief recreations in Nepal right from rulers to ruled. Although Prithvi Narayan Shah had abolished the gambling in his kingdom, as already mentioned, after him it seems that the gambling was restored in the kingdom. There were different types of gambling like dice playing, *Satranja,* throwing the cowries etc. The most popular was the throwing of cowries and then the dice. During the days of Bhimsen Thapa the gambling seemed to have become quite rampant. Jang Bahadur had to face a big problem to tackle the most rampant gambling, which had become a regular feature of the royal recreation and amusement. Jang Bahadur himself was interested in gambling. On *Tihar*, gambling was declared for five days throughout the kingdom. On that occasion Prime Minister called his brothers, cousins and other dignified persons at his Durbar to play the *cowries*. The daily turn over in the game used to be several hundred thousand rupees. At that time several tents were pegged in the different centres of the localities where the common mass played freely. Some of the lucky fellows made fortune whereas many people used to lose a lot including their houses, lands and others.

Jang Bahadur made certain rules to stop the gamblers in staking their immovable properties; hence we have a chapter about the rules of the gambling in the Code of 1854 A.D. Only the cash could be betted henceafter. Jang had specified the days, and in certain cases the places also where gambling was allowed on certain day. Five days gambling was allowed during *Tihar*, two days on the *Janmastami* which was to be played at Panchayan Ghat, within Jang's Durbar compound where the temples of the Ranas' family God were constructed, two days at the commencement of the new year which was to be played at Tudikhel, and two days at a place known as Mrigasthali. Padma Jang wrote that Jang Bahadur had won a sum of Rs. 25000/- in gambling on May 18, 1860 A.D.

Regarding the rules and rugulations about the gambling we see many changes from time to time at the whim of the Rana Prime Ministers. The numbers of days and occasions were decided by the Prime Minister's will, which we will see later on. Jang Bahadur's sons and nephews were also much indulged in gambling. This sort of gambling sometimes led to the clashes not only among the common mass but also among the members of the ruling families. The clashes of the common people were watched and controlled by the policemen, but the clash among the members of ruling family led to bitter enmity. Such incidents we see when the sons of Jang Bahadur and Dhir Shamsher played the gambling. Jang's sons were rich enough; so they used to bet a huge amount as which Dhir Shamsher's sons could not venture to stake that much. This sort of innident further embittered the relations between the two groups of the consins. Many such other incidences must have taken places unrecorded.

Dev Shamsher is described to have taken much interest in gambling. He is being described as the greatest gambler among the Rana Prime Ministers. Except on the festival days the gambling was permitted even on the day of *Sindur Jatra* of the king and Rana Prime Minister. During his short administartion of only one hundred and fourteen days, he allowed gambing for the maximum number of days. It is said that he had observed *Sindur Jatra* for eight times at eight different places, although the tradition was to observe the *Sindur Jatra* only three times in three towns *i.e.* Kathmandu, Lalitpur and Bhaktapur. Every time there was the *Sindur Jatra*, the gambling was permitted. About the frequent permission of gambling, Dev Shamshere is said to have said that he had done so because he wished the people to be indulged in it so that they would not have time to think of politics. How far the statement is true has to be varified. It seems that Dev had permitted the gambling frequently because he, as was bred up in the most pompous way, was personally indulged in debauchery, gambling and vain glorious life. He did not care the impact of such frequent gambling on the poor common mass.

Later on also the Prime Ministers used to permit the public gambling on various occasions besides the traditional festival days. When the Trichandra Military Hospital was inaugurated, on September 9, 1926 A.D. Prime Minister Chandra permitted the public gambling for three days. Chandra Shamsher himself took interest in gambling. His son Keshar was also a great gambler. When the Ranas played the gambling in the Singh Durbar, many higher rank Ranas were invited. At that time the Ranas used to employ confidential civil servants, who were expert in calculation, to keep the record of the accounts of the bet. When the gambling would be over, those civil servants used to produce the whole account of the amount to be paid, because it was not possible to carry lakhs of rupees, as the coins only were in circulation at that time. Another interesting feature of the Ranas' gambling was that they did not need to put thousands of rupees in the gambling stop. Their way of putting the cash was to display the coins in virtical and horizental ways, one would mean in thousand and the other in hundred.

Sometimes King Tribhuvan was also invited to entertain himself in gambling by Chandra. It is said that while throwing cowries if king Tribhuvan would win the amount was sent to the king's treasury and whatever amount was lost by him was paid from the state treasury by the order of the Prime Minister. In those days some of the public were also given access to play in Singh Durbar. One such person was Dibya Dev Pant who is described to have been a veteran gambler. In throwing the cowries he was a matchless person. He used to take the *Choukadawu* and was never beaten in the cowrie play. It is said that he used to win lakhs of rupees which were carried in many horse driven carts. His ever-winning in the gambling and collection of lakhs of rupees aroused much gealousy in the minds of the Ranas. Chandra Shamsher, who never wished to see the people becoming a millionaire, could not tolerate it. Moreover some other Ranas were also humiliated by Pant while gambling. Pant was much provoked in the gambling by the Ranas. He also being provoked used to ask for huge amount to be put as a bet. Some of the Ranas although in big posts were not rich enough to bet a big amount; but being much provoked Pant used to abhor such meagre amount of bet which aroused fury among those Ranas like Bhima Shamsher, Juddha Shamsher, and others who were not so well enough. As such all the jealous Ranas wanted to know the secrecy of Pant's ever winning in the gambling. Espionage was employed to know the secrecy of Pant. It is reported that during the days of gambling, Pant's wife used sit down naked observing fast and recite certain *mantras* in front of an oil lamp. When the Ranas could not know the reality they made Pant almost naked and gamble; even then he won in the gambling. There was a superstituous feeling among the people that anyone keeping the umblical cord of a black kitten would win the gambling, so Pant was made naked to find out whether he had any such thing kept secretly in his body. No being satisfied with that only he was made to throw the cowries some times by the left hand and sometimes by the mouth also. Being undaunted by any of such things the Ranas made him throw the cowries by his mouth from the second floor of Singh Durbar to the court yard. Even then he won the gambling. It is a said after the incident *i.e.* after throwing the cowries by the mouth on the courtyard, he could not win in the gambling. Moreover the jealousy of the Ranas continued to work against him. He was charged on many fake reasons and exhorbitant fines were imposed on him, which made him so much fade up that he left Nepal for Benaras, where also he could not stay for long due to poverty. Atlast he came to Nepal and died a pauper.

Dambar Shamsher, one of the brothers of Bir Shamsher, was also a veteran gambler. Sometimes he bet more than he could afford. Such betting many a times led to the miserable life of the family members of Dambar Shamsher. His son Samar Shamsher was also a great gambler. Mohan Shamsher, Shankar Shamsher and Kishar Shamsher were also much interisted in gambling.

Prime Minister Juddha Shamsher also enjoyed gambling very much. That is why he introduced gambling on the day of *Bhotajatra* of Mat chhendra Nath at Jawalakhel, his residential area. Within the zoo there is still a house where Juddha Shamsher used to play gambling. Sometimes the gambling for common mass was permitted for a couple of days whereas it was enjoyed for five days or any number of days as the Prime Minister wished Balkrishna Sama has written that his father Samar Shamsher become a famous gambler as Juddha took interest in it. It was natural in an autocratic system that the sychophants used to indulge on those things in which the ruler was interested. Thus the favour of the ruler was won.

Juddha was so much interested in gambling that even in the *Skikar* (hunting) camp, the gambling was permitted. Balkrishana Sama has described that once Juddha Shamsher, on the request of Keshar Shamsher, who was a very curusing Rana and an addict to all sorts of vices like gambling, heine and women, permitted gambling in the *Shikar* camp in 1934 A.D. In that gambling for a few hours, Juddha won Rs.

18000/-, *Kanchha Rani Sahib* (young wife of Juddha) Rs. 1200/- *Mahila Guruju* Pt. Humraj Rs. 3400/-, Samar Shamsher Rs. 2100/-, and among the main losers *Bada Maharani* (chief wife of Juddha) lost Rs. 4001/-, *Mahila Maharani* Rs. 3000/-, Keshar Shamsher Rs. 17000/- and a few others.

Gambling was permitted on many other occasions like the offering of the medals ' to the Rana Prime Ministers by foreign dignitaries like those of England, France, China, Italy, Japan and others. Falls of Germany in the world wars were also the occasions for the permission of gambling. Later on during the Rana period gambling was permitted on different days like the full moon day of Bhaitra, *Bhota Jatra* and so on. In those days Tundikhel, the parade ground of Kathmandu, was the place permitted for gambling on the full moon day of Chaitra and Jawalakhel on the occasion of *Bhota Jatra* of Matchhendra Nath. Thus what we see about gambling is that on oertain occasion it was permitted throughout the kingdom and on other occasion on certain locality only. Since Juddha Shamsher had his house at Jamalakhel, so for his entertainment he had introduced the gambling at Jawalakhel.

In those days although in the name of entertainment the gambling was permitted, it had left many unhappy incidents after it mas over. In most cases those people in Kathmandu who had staked huge amount of the property and ruined used to commit suicide generally drowning themselves in the Ranipokhari, which was open and unfenced. Later on the Ranipokhari was fenced, inspite of it up to this time it is a notde place for committing suicide by the desparate people.

To prohibit the unhappy ineidents, many rules were made by the Rana administration. During the time of gambling loans were not transacted by the contending parties, and only people having the requisite money was permitted to take part in the gambling. If anyone would bet movable property like utensils, jewels, gold ornaments, cattle, kinds and even houses, they were dealt with severely and had to pay heavy fines. In those days when the gambling was to be andounced, some government employees playing special musical instruments used to take around the towns declaring the permissiod of the gambling. The main announcer used to declare that the people could play gambling but no one could bet ornaments, dresses, land, house etc. To close down the gambling also there used to be announcement. During the *Tihar* the government used to announce the cloce-down of the gambling for a few hours in the midday on the *Bhaipuja* day so that the people could observe the *Bhaipuja* in time. During the later Rana period, the gambling was permitted five days during the *Tihar* (*Deepavali*), one day on *Kojagrata Poornima* (full moon day immediately after *Dasin*), one day on the Chaitra full moon night, one day on the *Bhotajatra* and on other occasions when the Prime Minister wished.

Gambling was one of the most popular entertainments among the Nepalis, from the youngsters to the grown-ups. It in one way it was a source of entertainment on the other hand it was a curse to the people. Whenever the guardian of a family played gambling, the whole family passed the time in worsy. So after the down of democracy the gambling was officially prohibited.

Sports

Sports had been a favourite pastime in Nepal as elsewhere in the world. It provided recreation as well as physical exercise to the people. We have both indigenous and western sports. But due to the paucity of the materials we do not exactly know when did the various indigenous sports originate. Moreover some of the indigenous games were popular throughout the country whereas some limited only to certain locality or community. In those days games were very much ignored as it was considered that it would spoil the youngesters, whole main duty was only to read. No sense of the need of physical education and extra-curricular activities had developed. As such to think of national policy on sports was beyond imagination. Inspite of it the closure contact with the British had some positive impact on the slow growth of the popularity of the sports.

Now let us deal with some of the indigenous games which were popular in the modern Nepal.

Kusti (Wresiling)

It was a popular game right from the ancient time as we have already seen the existense of the *Mallayuddhagosthi* during the ancient time. During the modern period also the *Mallayuddha* (wrestling) was much admired by the rulers. The Shah Kings had taken personal interest in such activities. Later on Jang Bahadur had also keen interest in the wrestling. Padma Jung, son and biographer of Jang Bahadur, has written that Jang had taken much interest in organising the wrestling competition on the occasion of the annual *Pajani*; such competition was also held in the honour of the foreign dignitaries. Jang Bahadur held the competition of the wrestlers on every Tuesday. Padma Jang writes :

> "Of all manly sports, Jung Bahadur loved wrestling most, wrestling matches are still in Nepal as in many parts of India, quite a national function, writness the celebration of the great Nag Panchami festival in variably wresthing and boxing compatition. For people of even high position to discusd to the arena to learn the art of wrestling is not considered detrogatory. Perhaps one might try to illustrate thls fashion by a reference to the old Roman days, when the emperor himself fought like a common gladistor in the common amphitheatres of the imperial city. Keen was the ardour with which Jung Bahadur took to wrestling, and great in consequence was the skill he came to passess in that favourite sport. It has been ascertained that in wrestling contests he *never* lost a game, and gained considerable renown by successively

overthrowing the champions of his time, the celebrated professionale *pahabwans* of the day."

Wrestling seemed to be quite popular sport in those days do not only in Nepal but also in other parts of the world. When Jang Bahadur went to England, he and his followers visited Angelo's fencing rooms, where they witnessed some sposts. When a runowned British wrestler came to know that some of the Nepalese visitors were also expert in wrestling, he made a challange to the Nepalese also. At that Jang Bahadur signed Dhir Shamsher, his youngest brother, to wrestle with the British boaster in a combat. Withein a few minutes the English wrestler was thrown down flat on the ground, gasping for breath. It proves that the Nepalese were also good wrestlers, so Dhir Shamsher sould knock down the English wrestler.

Jang Bahadur's interest in wrestling had attracted some wrestlers from India also. Quoting Jang Bahadur's diary Padma Jang writes,

> "10th October (1860) there was a grand wrestling match at Thapathali. Six renowned athletis who had come from Baroda and the Punjab to challange the Nepalese Champions were, each and all of them, successfully overthrown by our men. The Maharaja rewarded the vanquished combatants with half the amount he gave to the victoer. In the evening there was a display of fire works in front of the palace."

Wrestling was patroniscd by not only Jang Bahadur but also other Rana Prime Ministers and Ranas.

Wrestling remained a popular game in Nepal quite later on also. The people used to take pride of their local wrestlers. Later on the Ranas of the younger generation and their *Chakariwalas* took interest in the wrestling, for their coaching the experts were invited from India. The wrestling was encouraged by the Rana youngsters. On the occasion of

Ghodejatra, wrestling competion was also held among the bicycle and horse racing. Dharma Bhakta Mathema had participated in the wrestling competition. His smartness in the competition had drawn the attraction of king Tribhuvan and the Ranas of the younger generation. Later on King Tribhuvan made Dharma Bhakta, who was haghed by the Ranas later on in 1940 A.D., his instructor of wrestling. General Narashamher, whose name stands apex in the sport activities in the history, also got coaching on wrestling from Dharma Bhakta. Thus wrestling sceens to be one of the sports given patronage by the royalty and the Rana youngesters. In the Tarai region also the wrestling was a favourite game among the mass. Generally *zamindars* (the landlords) in the Tarai area used to have a hoard of the wrestlers to collect the rent from the tillers,

Dandi Biyo

Dandi Biyo is a game played with two sticks; one a *dandi* almost a half metre long and *biyo* just a hand's span length. As a signal a piece of stick is erected in the playground. Players were divided into two groups in an equal number. One member of a group strikes the *biyo* and throws it towards the opposite team and if the *biyo* is thrown successfully at the stick erected, the striker loses it and the chance of striking the *biyo* goes to the opposite team. If the *biyo* can not touch the *dandi*, the striker goes to the spot where the *biyo* had fallen. He then tosses the *biyo* by the *dandi* a bit higher than the ground and continues on tossing it as many times as possible. If the tossing continues for many times it is considered as a very good marksmanship and the striker's main attempt is to carry the *biyo* as far as possible, when he fails the distance is counted. The striker's attempt is to toss more than two times so that the distance is counted by the *biyo*. In case of tossing once the distance is measured by the *dandi*.

This game was the common people's game. It was generally popular among the young boys throughout the country. These young boys play it everyday with much enthusiasm.

Khopi

Khopi is a game played by both youngsters and grown-up people with a few coins. The players fix certain small area where the small coins are thrown. The participants point out a certain coin placed among others, which the striker has to toss by the big and weighty coin without touching other coins. In case of success the striker with the whole amount and if he fails he has to pay certain amount as the fine. This game is played in turn among the participants. The striker is supposed to be a good marksman. It was a popular game among the people, but the policemen whenever they saw it used to collect all the coins and warned the youngsters to give up the habit of playing such game. So the people used to play secretly without being noticed by the policemen. It is still played in the country among the common mass.

Chhelo (Shotput)

The *Chhelo* was played with a stone or an iron ball of a definite size and weight depending on the decision of the players. This game is just like the shotput of the present athletic game. The players threw the ball as far as possible. The distance from where it was thrown and the place where the stone fell was measured. The winner was he who could throw at the longest distance. It was mainly the males' game determined by the strength of the player.

Gir

Gir is a famous and popular game among the youths of the hill area. A round wooden ball was striken with a weighty curved stick (just like hockey stick). The striker tried to reach it beyond the fixed boundary line. If the ball crossed the boundary, the player was supposed to have won the game. Winter was considered to be the most suitable time to play the game. Any number of the players could participate in the game, but it was generally by two opposite parties. Victory in the game depended upon the number of each party crossing the ball beyond the boundary line.

Jhinge Dau (Fly position)

Although Bimala Shrestha mentions it as an indoor game played by the females only in their biesure time, it is neither limited withing the doors nor to the females only. It is played by both sexes and within and without the house. No doubt it is one of the most dull games which requires neither intellectual or physical exercise. What requires in this game is simply patience to watch a fly sitting on a coin. The winner is he on whose coin the fly sits first. Such game is played generally in summer when the flies breed in a large number. The winner collects all the coins of the participants. This game was played into those days also specially among the common people having leisure.

Jor Bijor

This game of *Jor* (even number) and *Bijor* (uneven number) is also a dull game which depends merely on luck and guess work and demands no mental or physical taxation. Many persons play this game together in which they collect things like soyabean, maize or even marbles. On the mutual consent a person will first take a certain number of the objects that they have in his first and then asks the others to guess the number of the object in the first. If anyone's guess comes correct, he is declared victorious and the others have to pay the fixed amount to the victor. This game was and is popular specially among the ladies and teenagers of the common mass.

Kapardi

It mas and is a game of the young boys and the girls who were and are strong and skillfull enough to play. The game is still played, in which two groups of persons of equal number show their talent in defeating the opposite group. In this game one member of either side of the team, stopping his breath and speaking certain words, crossing the line marked in the centre, tries to touch as many persons of the opponent group as possible and comes back to his/her group crossing the central line. In case the person succeeds in crossing the line in one breath, all the persons of the rival group he/she had touched are suppose to leave the ground. The opponents' attempt is to catch hold of the person and not to let him/her cross the line. During that time if he/she cannot stop breathing he/she will lose and leave the ground as a loser. The game continues until all the members of a team are not out. The game was quite popular specially in the Tarai area. On certain occasions like fairs such games were played among various groups representing the villages. In some places the competition of such game was observed as a fair. People of different villages assembled and the old experts umpired the game. The winner group and village celebrated it most joyfully. It is a common people's game participated by a very large number of persons and an outdoor game. So it is said that the villagers used to encourage their youths to practise the *Kapardi* throughout the year. The big landlords also used to patronise such game and awarded attractive prize to the winner. But sometimes the competition used to had clashes among the villagers and many persons got injured. Enemity between the villages also took place.

Swing

We had and have three different types of swing which was and is enjoyed by all. Boys and grown up males also participated in the game. People of all ages of both sexes, youths enjoy it very much. The swinging game is not played on competition. It is simply an entertaining game which results into physical exercise. Generally the game is played throughout the country of Nepal specially during the days of *Dasain* and *Tihar*. All people, while swinging, tries to swing as high as possible. There is a religious belief that one should leave the ground at least for some moment during the period. The game was quite popular throughout the country. We had and still have different types of swing. One is called *Linge Ping* which is made of a thick and strong rope tied to the bamboos. Four or five bamboos are well erected having two or three feet of the buttom of the bamboos buried under the earth. The top of the bamboos are tied with a strong pole in the centre, around which the rope to swing is tied. This type of swing is the most popular one in the country. Another type is *Rott Ping* which is like a merry-go-round. The seats are attached to the circular type of *ping* and ranged from four to twelve. It is made to go round and round by either pulling the seats down or pushing from the centre, turn by turn. The *ping* was and is still used by the people in many parts of the country. The third type of swing is made by tying the rope around a strong branch of a tree.

Topi Lukaune (Can-hiding)

The game was and is very interesting one played by the youngesters of both sexes. The participants sit around and make a circle. One of the players holds a cap or handkerchief or a piece of a cloth, goes around the circle from behind the sitting participants and drops the object very carefully behind one of the players, who have to be very alert. If the player saw it, he/she instantly has to get up and chase the dropper to touch him/her till he/she (the dropper) reaches the vacant seat. If the dropper touched before he/she occupies the vacant seat, he/she is out. This sort of game was and is generally played by the young boys and girls. This sort of game is played among a sizeable number of the boys and girls. It was also a game played by the children of the common people.

Gatti Khelne (Play of pebbles)

Gatti Khel is exclusively meant for the girls of higher or lower class. We still see the girls and even grown up females collecting fine and smooth pebbles in the bank of rivers. The game is played in different ways with different rules. The pebbles are spread on the ground and picked up by the players according to various rules and techniques.

Lukamari Khel (Hide and seek)

This game was one of the popular games played among the boys and girls of young age. One of the players was made to find out the others who were hidden either in the dark places of the houses or somewhere within the limited area. After all the players had hidden in different places, one of them gave the permission to find the hidden persons. He or she who was traced out first was again to search out the others. It was one of the interesting games played by the youngsters in Nepal.

In this way we had and still have many indigenous games like *Tela kasa*, *Kanakana Picha*, *Ghwain Kasa* (all games played by youngsters) and many others, quite popular and interesting also. Some of them are regional, some belonged to certain community and some were played throughout the country. Most of which have become unpopular now due to the knowledge of many new western games as well as the present boys and girls have very little time to play such games. Some of the games were played only by the girls; others by the boys and some by both the boys and girls. Some were played by the grown-ups only. In this ways since the days yore we had many types of games which were enherited from generation to generation. Most of these games were maintained by the common people.

We have mentioned many times that the establishment of the British Residency had brought about many changes in different walks of life. The presence of the Britishers in Kathmandu had also brought about certain innovations in the recreation side.

Cinema

Cinema when introduced in India became the most sought-for-form of the recreation in Nepal also. Those Nepalese who could not go to India had heard of the cinema shows told by those people who had frequented India along with the Ranas or visited India for business or purpose or pilgrimage. We did not have it for the public shows as an entertainment. The members of royal family, Ranas and their attendants who frequented India had enjoyed it. The royalties and the Ranas imported costly cinema to graph apparatus from England and other European countries and installed them in their palaces. According to Bimala Shreatha, Jang Bahadur was the first Rana Prime Minister who brought these costly apparatus together with the English films.

Dev Shamsher was the first Rana Prime Minister who had arranged the exhibition of the films to the common mass at Tundikhel, Kathmandu. It was really an amazing thing for the mass to witness such films. But such activity did not last long as the liberal Prime Minister was exiled by his reactionary brother Chandra. For many years there was no exhibition of the cinema to the common people. Only those who visited India either as the attendants of the Ranas or business purpose or on pilgrimage had an opportunity to see the cinemas. Their description to their family members, neighbours and friends aroused much curiosity. Visit to India prior to the introduction of Nepal Government Railway (NGR) by Chandra was very difficult task. It was quite risky of either being looted by the highway robbers or infected by the malaria disease. One had to walk a long way off. Later on after the NGR started working it became easier to go to India. There was also a necessity of getting *Rahadani* (permission) from the government to visit India. So the visit to India in those days was more difficult than visiting any part of the world at present. The students who got permission and stipend from the government for higher studies in India and abroad also enjoyed the opportunity. The description of the cinemas of those highly priviledged people (because they had the golden opportunity to visit outside world) to their friends, members of the family and others aroused enthusiasm and also a surprise because they could not even guess how the life size actors and actresses performed their actings on the screen. It was just like tell-tale to the common mass, as it was beyond their reach.

Later on the Rana Prime Ministers and other higher Ranas imported the 16 mm film projectors and enjoyed the films. They had their own stages in their palaces, where the cinemas were exhibited for their family members, relatives, employees and others. In those days the cinema shows were the most attractive source of entertainment to the privileged group of the people. Hindi and English films were imported and shown. Later on some rich persons among the common mass also started having film-projectors. They exhibited the shows in their *chowks* (court-yards) to the public by charging some amount. The people of Tarai specially near to India like those of Birgunj, Biratnagar and others enjoyed better opportunity to visit Indian towns near to their towns and see the movies. Later on, the Ranas also felt the necessity of having only public cinema hall in Kathmandu. So far they had restricted it on the ground that such shows might spoil the people and also awaken the public politically, because the then Indian film-producers were producing many films which aroused nationalism. India was struggling for independence. The Ranas after the independence of India, also realised the necessity to loosening the tight administrative system of Nepal. At last in Baikash 2006 B.S. 1949 A.D. a public cinema hall was inaugurated, which became famous as Jana Sewa Cinema Hall. The first film exhibited was *Ram Vivaha*. The common mass was so mueh attracted to the movie that there used to be always a huge rush of cine-goers. The religious minded old folks even offered coins the see the Gods and Goddesses in the movies.

Western games

In the field of sports also we see gradual introduction of the western games in Nepal, for which the British Residency people must be credited. The Residency people played some of their games to pass their idle time in their camp, as they were neither allowed to mix up with the local people nor to move around without the permission of the Nepalese authorities. Wright has written that up to Jang Bahadur's time there was a strict restriction to the Residency people. To quote him." There is a guard of Nepalese soldiers on the road leading to the Residency and no Gorkha can enter the limits of the Residency, without permission from Sir Jung Bahadur, and without being accompanied by the Vavil." These foreigners brought many things to play so as they could entertain themselves. Initially indoor games like billiard, careem board and others were brought. With the rise of Ranarchy, the Rana youngsters started getting closure with the Britishers. The sons and nephews of Jang Bahadur used to visit the Residency to play the western games very often, might be after Jang Bahadur, because wright comtemporay to Jang, has written. "Attempts have been made at various times by their tutors (Englishmen and Indians) to get the young men to play at cricket and other games, but such amusements are throught aegrading. They played the billiard mostly. Western games gained popularity among the higher circle and then among the common mass.

Football

Football game, unknown to the Nepalese before the present century, gained popularity even among the common mass soon after its introduction. In its initial stage it did not become the common people's game. Some of the higher class people, who had seen the tournaments in India and were enthusiast in the game, took the initiation. Football games were played privately in the big compounds of the well-off Ranas and courtiers. It is said that football matches were unofficially arranged by Narayan Narsingh (one of the Ranas) and Chandra Jang Thapa (a very powerful officer). Later on different football teams were organised by the enthusiast Ranas. Nara Shamsher organised Jawalakhel Football Club (JFC), Basant Shamsher's team was Mahabir Team and Sharada Shamsher's KSU (Kathmandu Sports Union ?). Besides these many other teams appeared like Thamel Team, Thapathali Team patronised by Drona Shamsher, Nepal Vidyarthi Khel Mandal (Students' team) and so on. The first formal football match was held in 1936 A.D. in which JFC led by Nara Shamsher became first and Mahabir Team second. When the football teams were patronised by the powerful Rana youths like Nara Shamsher, Sharada Shamsher and Basant Shamsher (all of them were in the roll of succession, hence called *Rola-walas* and grandsons of the Rana Prime Ministers), the football game became quite popular and nobody could say anything against it. King Tribhuvan also took interests and had his own team also. But it does not seem that his team participated in the tournament.

All the interested top Ranas had a football ground in their compound, where their own employees and others were allowed to practise the game. Nutritious diet was given to the plapers by them. The football ground for the matches were the Sano Tundikhel (present stadium), Chhauni ground, Lagankhel in Lalitpur. The famous players during 1930s were Nazar Man, Gopal Das Vaidya, Shyam Raj Dhoj Joshi, Bhim Bahadur Pandey, Manindra Raj and others. In 1948 King Tribhuvan granted a running shield for the knock-out football match, which is still running; and following it Rana Prime Minister also awarded another shield for league match, but this shield disappeared, might be after the fall of the Ranas. the shield also disappeared. From among the common mass a team called New Road Team was organised in 1935. The team was organised by the enthusiast youths of the New Road area. It gained the public support at the time of match and other time. In the league or knock-out matches the NRT represented the people. The role of NRT in bringing political consciousness can not be ignored.

In 1948 the league and knock-out tournaments were played in which a new team called *Naresh Eghar* (Naresh Eleven) patronised by Nara Shamsher came out first. By that time JFC disappeared and *Naresh Eghar* continued for many years later on also. Nara Shamsher's contribution in the development in football can not be one of minimised. He took so much interest in it that he wanted to be the football players of the Mohan Bagan Team, one of the most famous teams of India. It is said that after his much request, he was given the membership and also allowed to enter the football ground as a player of the team for a while. It was a matter of great pride to him.

During the time the young boys belonging to the family of privileged classes who frequented India used to play the ball whereas those of the common mass played the *Bhogate* (a big citrus fruit) as a ball or a bail made of cloth filled with husk. One thing which we must not forget about the sports is that during those days no guardians were in favour of their children playing any game, because it was considered that indulgence in sport meant wastage of time. The young boys' main duty was to read. One who would indulge in sport was considered as spoilt. Inspite of such restriction the games gained it popularity among the mass. Football became more and more popular among the common people. Its contribution to arouse mass against the Ranas indirectly cannot be ignored. The common mass took side of the teams belonging to the people like Nepal *Vidyarthi Khel Mandle* and New Road Team against the teams patronised by the Ranas. It was only in the football ground where all the players including the Ranas were treated as equals. People cheered those courageous players who could knock down the Rana players in the ground Inspite of such feeling the Rana youngsters cherished the game.

Hockey

This game was also played by the British Residency people in the initial stage. In those days these players played the game at the Lainchaur ground near the British Legation. Later on, the Ranas took keen interest in the game also; Nar Shamsher, Vijaya Shamsher, Rishikesh Shah, Krishna Bahadur Verma and others took interest in the game in 1939 A.D. They had learnt the game in India. The first Hokey match was held in 1942 in which Nara Shamsher's team won and got the Tribhuvan Cup. The game thus started in Nepal, but it could not gain much popularity among the mass.

Cricket

Cricket game was championed by Madan Shamsher in Nepal. It was also initiated by the British Residency people at first even during the days of Jang Bahadur. In 1936 A.D. the first cricket match was held inside Madan Shamsher's camp. Later on the Nepali cricketeers played informal matches in the British Legation. As the game was initiated by Madan Shamsher, after his death his wife established Madan Shield for the cricket tournament in Nepal.

Badminton

Badminton, although originated in Poona, was very much popularised by an Englishman first in England, and then in the world in the 19th century. The game was also introduced in Nepal by the Britishers and the Ranas. The first match of the game was held in 1933-34 A.D. But the tournament could not be completed by the great earthquake of 1934 A.D. But the game continued as an indoor game among the well-off people only. In 1950 Nepal Badminton Association was formed.

Thus many western games were introduced during the Ranas period; among the football game became most popular among the common who enjoyed it a lot. In those days a large number of people assembled to witness a football game.

As a whole we find that the Nepalese had their own way of entertaining among themselves right from the ancient time. Since the people were very much religious minded, they had many fairs and festivals had had also entertained them lot. The fairs and festivals were the main occasions among the poor people to rejoice and eat delicious food. Besides these occasions the people had many others ways of rejoicing themselves. The poor section of the people enjoyed in their own way whereas the richer and privileged ones had their own. Some of the methods of rejoicing proved very harmful and even fatal, for example, gambling. Almost every year after the big gambling, many persons, having lost their property, committed suicide. Some types of the entertainment were either local, seasonal or communal. Whatsoever nature of a source of entertainment might be, they had contributed in making the people happy and relaxed after long time's labour. These means of entertainment also changed according to the change in social outlook. At present meny of those games have become a past memory. The new western types of entertainment got more priority in compare to the age old tradition bound games. Inspite of all these things the Nepalese had many active sources of entertainment among themselves as a part and parcel of their life.

9

Education

Ideals of Education

Education makes a man sober, cultured and polite. The value of education is very much understood by the people of the ancient time also. So they had written that education makes a man sober. Whenever difference between an educated and uneducated person was sought, it was always assumed that an educated person was an enlightened one who had overcome the darkness caused by the ignorance and illiteracy. From the ancient time emphasis was very much laid down on the education. So the ancient scholars had expressed that a king was worshiped only within his kingdom whereas a scholar was honoured everywhere. With that sort of idea the Hindu society had developed in this part of the world. From the ancient time the society had laid much emphasis on education. We have many stories which tell us how the renowned rulers used to pay respect to the learned scholars. In those days those renowned scholars lived a very austere and simple life without any worldly lust and greed. As such they were highly respected. The kings used to feel themselves highly honoured and blessed when such scholars resided in their kingdoms. On crucial condition their advice was sought. Those scholars in those days were called *Rishi* or *Maharshi* who dwelt in the forest area where a large number of pupils stayed with their

Guru (*Rishi* or *Maharshi*) for training. Even the princes had to stay along with other ordinary pupils doing all sorts of manual works. In those days also education did not only mean mastering over the theoritical knowledge but also the practical education. The *Rishis* oe *Maharshis* used to teach many things like archery, horse-riding, wrestling and other professional aspects. Ancient scholars had many subjects to import in the minds of their pupils in India. In those days the highly esteemed scholarly works were the four *Vedas* and four *upavedas*, namely, *Rigveda, Samaveda, Yajurveda* and *Atharvaveda* and *Dhanur veda* (archery), *Silpa Veda* (skill development), *Gandharva Veda* (music), *Ayurveda* (medicine) respectively. Besides these *Vedas* these were many other subjects. *Smritis* were compiled at different times by different scholars which prescribed many rules and regulations to maintain law and order in the society. To be a scholar one had to master himself in all those subjects and then he was called "*Shastrashastraparangata.*" One who could control his worldly desires and mastered himself on the *Shastras* was called *Rishi* and *Maharshi*. In those days the society had also paid sincere respect to scholars and the latter also gave the proper guidenee to the former. So the Hindu ideals mention that the *Guru*, father and mother should be treated as God.

The Hindu ideals continued on having strong influence in the Nepalese society for a long time. With the advent of the Muslims in India, there was a change in the educational system. The Muslim in Vaders destroyed the famous educational institutions like Nalanda, Taxila, and many others. Many ancient scholarly works were set to fire. With the establishment of the Islamic rule, the Muslim educational system got the priority. Governmental facilities were provided to the Muslim educational system. That fromed to be a great blow to the flourishing traditional Hindu, Buddhist and Jainist educational system of India. Inspite of it the indeginous educational system was anyhow lingering. If the Hindus gave priority to the studies of *vedas*, the Muslims to the *Qarana*. But Varanasi continued to attract the Hindu scholars,

With the advent of the British power the educational system of India also uuderwent a drastic change. Activities of Christain missionaries, interest of the people to attain the western education and the Company government's policy to impose their education made the western education more and more poular. Macaulay's Minute, the Magna Carta of the English education in India, was a deathblow to the oriental educational system. The British policy of encouraging their education in India by providing better job opportunity to the people with the western education made the occidental education more and more popular. In a short span of time the western education became the most-sought-for-education in India. Almost all the youths, giving up their traditional education, took the western education for their better future and the well-to-do families sent their youngsters to England for better education. The obvious impact was that the traditional system of education which forbade the low caste people from education was gradually given up atleast in the urban area. The cast-bar in the education system was totally ignored and rather the low caste people were encouraged in getting the western education. The very objective of the education was changed. Ignoring the oriental approach the western education aimed at westernising the educated youths who, in course of time, started thinking and behaving like the westerners. That sort of change in India had its impact in Nepal also. During the carly half of nineteenth century the necessity of having western education was also felt by the ruling class. Later on the western type of school organised by the government was established in Nepal, although admission to the school was limited only to the higher class of the society. The introduction of the western education did not attract the mass participation in initial phase due to administrative and socio-economic reasons. But it had its impact in the society. The ideal of the education now became to be acquainted with the western knowledge and westernisation in thinking and outlook. Those having western education got the white coloured job. Education was more or less attached with the job. Conservatism in the society was challanged by the rapid growth of education. Idealism and austirity were replaced by materialism and Dophistication. Orientalism gave way to Occidentalism. We started evaluating our traditional social values from the western points of view.

In this background we are to deal with the history of education in Nepal. Since the beginning of the historic period in Nepal, we had followed the Hinduism as our social ideal. Hence it is natural that our ancestors followed the Hindu rules and regulations. But the Hindu rules stood in the way to the universal education, because the lower caste people were not allowed to read and even listen the *Vedas* recited. Manu's law of pouring down the red hot iron on the ears of the lower caste people who deliberately listeaed the *Vedas* recited or cutting the tongues of those who read them stood as the greatest hurdle in the education to the Sudras. Education was the right and privilege of the high caste people *i.e.* the Brahmins and Kshetriyas and Vaisyas to some extent. The Brahmins were the privileged people who were entitled to read and explain the *Vedas* and other Hindu texts. It was they who were the only authorised people to teach the other groups of the society to read and write the texts. Kshetriyas used to learn the various *Shastras* which would help them in running the administration.

Education during the Lichchhavi period

During the Lichchhavi period it seems that the educational system was well developed. The Brahmins must have been the mainly educated persons. To think of the inscriptions sue to the paucity of materials we do not exactly know as to what sort of education was adopted prior to the Lichchhavi period. Thus must have been some sort of education by then also and their contents the Brahmins had wide varieties of the knowledge on the various subjects. They had mastered themselves in the Hindu Holy texts. Their mastery in writing on the eulogies of the kings and hymns are revealed by the inscriptions. Unfortunately we do not have detailed account of the educational system of the then Common mass. The kings, royalties and the courtiers seem to have gained knowledge about the various *Shastras*. Royalties had given patronage to the scholars, as in India during the Gupta period. We have evidences of many scholars getting the royal patronage under the Gupta Kings the result of which was the Hindu renaissance in India during the period. Similarly, the Lichchhavi kings had also taken initiation to that end. Almost all the scribes of the Lichchhavi inscriptions were the well versed Sanskrit scholars. The Lichchhavi kings themselves were well versed in Sanskrit and learned. Manadev I was also much dedicated in the learnings, Amsuvarma had written the *Sabdavidya* as Huien Tsang has described. The book has not yet been found in Nepal. But the account of it made by Huien Tsang is an evidence of its importance. Its fame was widely spread that is why the Chinese traveller who had come only to the western Tarai of Nepal also mentioned it. It was a classical work on Sanskrit grammer. Jayadev II seems to be a very successful poet. Five stanzas of the famous Pashupati inscription were written by the king. It shows that the Tichchhavi kings had also taken interest in composing poems. Anuparam, a courtier, was also a well read person as his inscription stands as an evidence of it. Out of two hundred and five inscriptions of the period, except a few ones, all of them are classical examples of the highly developed Sanskrit literature of the time. Had not the educational system been well organised and developed such works could not have been achieved. Among the scribes of the Lichchhavi inscriptions only one person named Buddhakirti can be cited. On the epigraphic evidence Buddhakirti was the composer of the famous Pashupati inscription. During the period Sanskrit was the state language and Gupta script was in use, whereas there seamed that the people had their local language *i.e.* Kirati language, as is evidenced by the Lichchhavi inscriptions. Local dialect was totally ignored.

Subjects studied

The subjects preferred for the studies in those days were astrology astronomy, mathmetics, old Sanskrit literature, history, and others among the Hindus. The scholarly Brahmins must be the teachers who taught the education to the people. We have also evidences of *Brahmangosthi* and *Taittiriyasakhagosthi* and others. *Brahmangosthi*, although a trust of Brahmins, must be an organisation to faciliate the Brahmins who were to teach the Hindu Holy texts and performed rituals accordingly. *Taittiriyasakhagosthi* was a trust to study and work on *Vedas*. The scholars dedicated to the studies of the *Vedas* were provided facilities by the trust. In this way the rulers had encouraged the education.

Besides the studies of the Hindu Holy texts among the Hindus, studies of the Buddhist literature was also quite popular among the Buddhists. Devpatan inscription has clearly mentioned that fiascoes based on Jataka stories were made in a monastry, constructed by a female. It is an example of the studies of the Jatakas. In those days there were a large member of Buddhists whom the rulers had also show great concern. Right from Vrishadev, the Lichchhavi kings had constructed different monastries, which prove the existance of a large bulk of the Buddhist subjects. The rulers had to take steps to keep the Buddhist subjects well satisfied. The *Vihars* were the centres of the Buddhist learning. They also mastered themselves in their Holy texts, mathemetics, astrology, astronomy, and other subjects. Nepal, as a centre of Buddhist learning, had already developed in those days. Scholars visited Nepal for the purpose in those days also. For both the sects *i.e.* Hindus and Buddhists, study of the grammer was very important so that they could write in a correct way. As the grammer was a very important subject to study, king Amsuvarma also took interest in writing a book on the subject.

One pertinent question is whether the common mass was dedicated to the learning or not. We have already seen that there was no democratisation of education. Moreover it was also a tradition that the higher strata people only felt necessity of the studies. The people of the lowest ebb in the social structure might not have felt it necessary to study. Whether their economy permitted them to studies is also a pertinent question. These people were meant for manual labour, as such neither did take interest or could afford to learning. The rulers and courtiers were well read persons. The businessmen might have also read for the transaction of their business; the rest might not have taken interest in the studies.

Vocational education

In those days vocational education seems to have been well developed, for which the rulers had also encouraged. The people, following many occupations for their livelihood, had maintained their skill of their professions. We can observe that there were many skilled carpentars, masons, architects, musicians, sculptors and others. These professional people inherited their skill from generation to generation, as such they became more and more perfect in their profession, We have the high appraisal about the Kailashkut Bhawan from the Chinese travellers, which is an evidence of the perfection of the then architecture and sculpture. Goldsmithery. ironsmithery etc. were also well developed. The pillars of the palace were also decorated with various precious stones The goldsmiths, ironsmith and others had continued their profession in perfection from generation to generation. Similarly coppersmiths had shown their skill in the construction of the temples, palaces and also in minting the coins. The roof of the Kailashkut Bhawan was made of copper plates and there were four images of crocodiles from whose mouths the water poured down during the rainy days.

The sculptors of the Lichchhavi period must be appreciated. The images of the Lichchhavi period are the masterpeices of the stonecraft. Those images available up to this time give us an idea of the skill of the then sculptors. Those sculptors had maintained their skill very meticulously.

We have reference of *Archagosthi* which was granted four *manikas* (of paddy) by King Shivadeva I and Amsuvarma. This *gosthi* meant a trust for the making the images. It seems that there were guild-like-organisations which trained the youths on the skill and also produced the objects. Such organisations must have been bestowed facilities and other grants by the rulers.

Mallayuddhagosthi was another trust which organised the wrestling as well as trained the youths to learn the skill of wrestling. *Mallayuddha* (wrestling) seems to be very popular in those days as there are frequent references to it. Lele inscription has mentioned twice while consecrating the grant; in one place it is mentioned that sixty eight *manikas* (quantity of crops) were granted to it and in the other three *manikas* were given. Thus *Mallayuddhagosthi* was granted much favour. Wrestling was an art and also skill the then society adhered.

Learning on the medical science was also a popular and necessary one in the society. Lele inscription has mentioned the grant of two hundred *manikas*, the highest consecration, to the *Arogyashala*, a dispensary. It is quite probable that the *Arogyashala* was a dispensary which supplied medicine and also treated the patients. There must have been many physicians who had studied *Charaka's* and *Sasruta's* books on medicine. In those days *Ayurveda* was studied by the medical practitioners. Medical persons seemed to have occupied a very high position in the society.

Besides the above mentioned vocational education, there were many others like shoe-making, handicrafts, potteries, oil-pressing, musical instrument playing etc. The vocational education made the people skilled in certain occupation through which they earned their livelihood and also name and fame. It is the vocational education which made the then Nepalese society very much developed and self dependent. Nepalese woollen blanks, iron goods, musks and others were famous in the then Indian market.

Female education

When we talk of the female education in ancient Nepal we feel the paucity of materials in dealing with the subject. There are no records which mention the type of education available to the then Nepalese women. But while dealing with the subject minutely the then Nepalese females were trained in various aspects. If we consider educated meaning mastering over the higher learning only a few people can be considered to have been educated. But learning does not mean that only, it means knowledge of skill through which a person could contribute to one's own society and nation. Such skilled person is the wealth of a nation. In this regard Nepal was rich with her skilled persons in the days yore also. Taking it into account, the Nepalese females were also well educated. The females of those days also seemed to have been fully aware of the importance of higher learning as well as the importance of skills in many things.

The very first inscription available in the Kathmandu Valley mentions that an unidentified woman had constructed a monastry with fiascoes based on the *Kinnar Jataka*. It is also referred that let her not huve rebirth as a female. This account shows that the female was an enlightened one who had fully realised the miserable condition of a woman in the then society. She wished that she would be reborn as a male. That woman was well enlightened and had nlso knowledge of the *Kinnara Jataka*. Similarly the queens of Manadev also seemed to be well enlightened. Vijayavati, the daughter of Mandev I, is described as "*Prekhyata Vivtdhakala Vichakshyanatwat*" (famous as well versed in different arts). She must have been trained in different skills, like singing songs, playing musical instruments, painting and others. In those days the females of the royalties, courtiers and affluent society were trained in reading, writing, arithmetics, painting, playing musical instruments, cooking, singing songs, dances etc. Moreover the females listened to the religious texts being explained. The females among the common mass might not be so well educated. They must have learnt the necessary skills for domestic life like knitting, weaving, sewing, cooking food, and others.

Educational institutions

Although we do not have direct mention to the educational institutes in those days, the scattered references of various organisations give us some hint of the organisations which must have played importance role to impart education to the then people. It will be improper for us to expect the modern type of educational institutes in those days. In those days as already mentioned there used to be the *Rishis* or *Maharshis* in an isolated forest areas where the students were taughtand trained. Such *Rishi ashramas* were generally meant for the *Brahmacharya* who had to lead an austere life dedicating to the learning on various aspects. In this contest we have certain references to *ashramas* like *Bharatashram* and *Gautama-shrama* in the Lichchhavi inscriptions. Both of them seemed to have located in the Kathmandu Valley. *Gopalaraj Vamsavali* has also mentioned that many *rishis* like Gautam had visited (the Kathmandu Valley and stayed here). This account is varified by the reference of the existence of *Gautama-shrama* up to eight century. Both the *ashramas* were popular in those days as they were mentioned to denote the demarcation line of some areas. These *ashramas* must have been the centres of learning in those days. Dhanavajra Vajracharya is of opinion that there must have been many such learning centres. Bagvati, which was, later on, called Bagmati, a name of the river, was named in Sanskrit language even before the rise of the Lichchhavis. The term Bagmati is related to the knowledge and learning and there must have been many centres of learning besides the river Bagmati. These centres must be the institutions where the youths got the training and aspired the knowledge during the Lichchhavi period.

Besides these centres, the priests (Brahmins) must have given the education to the young boys in their own houses. The scholarly Brahmins themselves were the main persons who educated the youths belonging to Kshetriya and Vaisya castes. These scholars were highly respected by the then people and also by the rulers. As already mentioned king Shivadev I and Amsuvarma had granted lands to the *Brahmingosthis*; those *Gosthis* were the organisations for the welfare of the members (Brahmins) and the Brahmins' duty was to educate the mass. So the rulers had granted the land for their maintenance.

Centres of learning among the Buddhists were the *Vihars.* We have the references of so many vihars like Manvihar constructed by Manadev I, Sriraj Vihar by Amsu Varma I, Gun Vihar, Kharjurika Vihar, Madhyam Vihar, and others. These *Vihars* were the religious shrines as well as the centres of learning among the Buddhists. The *Vihars* used to collect lots of religious texts which were recited and explained. The youths used to reside in the *Vihars* for learning. We have references of *Aryabhikshu Sangha* and *Aryabhikshuni Sangha.* Both *Bhikshus* and *Bhikshunis* dedicated their life in higher studies and ascetic life. The Buddhists were well trained and educated by the *Bhikshus* and *Bhikshunis.* During the days of Anuparam the Buddhists were looked down upon as is evidenced by the content of the then inscription, but Amsuvarma had encouraged the Buddhists who appraised him as an ornament of the monastries Many lands were granted to the Buddhists monastries. Thus the Buddhists had a sigh of relief and Buddhism developed. Along with that Buddhist learning must have developed a lot.

Centres for training the vocational education must be the workshops of the different skilled people in those days.

The metal workers used to have their workshops in their own houses, where their own youngsters and others worked as apprentices in the initial stage. The blacksmiths, goldsmiths, shoe-makers, tailors and the others used to train their own male children in their own workshops howsoever small they were. We have the account of the fame of the Nepalese woollen blankets and metallic utensils in the Indian market. It was an evidence of the developed skill of the Nepalese in the production of those things. We can also surmise that the vocational education continued to be hereditary in general for which there were no formal training centres aided by the government directly. But the attitude and patronage of the rulers and rich men helped a lot in the retention, growth and development of the vocational education.

During early medieval period the people of Nepal seemed to be highly skilled in the technical knowledge. These people continued on constructing building temples, drinking water sports etc. The architecture of Nepal got its fame far rnd wide. The Lama of Sakspa monastry wished to construct pagoda style temple, so he made a request to Nepal to send a group of Nepalese architects for the construction of the temples, monastry and icons. To comply with the request Nepal sent a group of about eighty architects under the leadership of Aruiko.

The vocational education further developed during the medieval period. It was specially due to the reform of Jayasthiti Malla (1380-95 A.D.). He had reorganised the society on the basis of the professional activities. The people, who had taken certain occupation for their livelihood, were granted the legal sanction; and they were to continue the occupations uninterfered. Royal sanction and recognition of the professional caste helped the growth of the specialisation of the work and division of labour also. When the different occupational castes developed, there was the further growth of the skilled man power. On the other hand these skilled man power had not to face the affects of the competition. People felt themselves secured in their job and livelihood. Jayasthiti Malla's reform had sincerely helped the development of the vocational education; thus every person was found busy in his own profession, which made every person of the Newar society specialised in one skill. Thus everyone in the then society became the real wealth of nation.

Moreover Jayasthiti Malla's regulation also emphasised that no one should either give up his own occupation nor take other's occupation. Such regulation made the people assured of their occupation. In those days when the people had their own guarranteed occupation their attempt was to attain perfection in the skill. We see almost all the castes among the Newars being assigned with one occupation, *viz. Tamrakar* (coppersmith), *Chitrakar* (painter), *Bhandel* (cook), *Vaidya* (physician), *Joshi* (astrologer), *Charmakara* and *Matangi* (workers in leather), *Dhobi* (washerman), *Mali* (gardener). *Vyanjanakar* (cooks), *Suvarnakar* (goldsmith), *Naplta* or *Nau* (barber), etc. In this way the professional caste system helped in the self dependence as well as rich development of the society. It had importance from the educational point of view also. The different occupational caste people trained their own youngesters in their particular profession, as its consequence the people of the Kathmandu Valley became more self dependent and every member of the family became skilled man power. Thus every house became the school for the vocational teaching and every senior person in the family became the sincere teacher of his youngsters.

Retention of their ancestoral profession was considered their pride and duty. Thus we see the growth of the vocational education during the medieval period. To cite example we have the *Chitrakars, Dakarmis, Sikarmis, Lohakarmis, Kumhales, Suvarnakarmis* or *Lukarmis, Marikarmis*, and others. Moreover there was also a tendency of developing skills in their own caste groups for example, the Jyapus, who are skilled in playing the musical instruments, farming, cooking etc. Let us now see the impact of Jayasthiti's reform in the development of skill. We see many temples, palaces and others in the Kathmandu Valley. To see the architectural designs of those buildings we must agree that the then people had a high class engineering skill. These people had got the training by their own experience which they had gained through generations. The glaring example of the engineering skills of those days can be found in the building of the towns, roads, huge buildings, drinking water spouts, drainage system etc. Masonary skill was well developed. Those masons trained in their own houses by their elders constructed such fine building. *Jayasthiti Malla's reform made Kathmandu Valley richest in arte, architecture and sculpture in Nepal.*

The medieval people had developed aesthetic sense in the vocational training also. To give an example of bricks making also we find that bricks used in the construction of the temples and palaces are one of the finest products of the most skilled man power. We have many masterpieces of the terracotta figurines. The most classical example of the finest terracotta art is the Mahabauddha temple of Lalitpur. It is the worthiest example of the highly developed skill of the terracotta art. Similarly the example of the stone carving can be taken into consideration. Krishna Mandir of Lalitpur is one of the finest stone carving the people of Nepal can taken pride of. To look at that we can uisualise that the then *Lohakarmis* (stone sculptors) were very much skilled in their profession. The *Lohakarmis* were locally trained in their own houses. Similarly the wood-carving skill can be seen in almost all the temples and the palaces. The images carved on the wood are very lively and artistic. To see all these crafts we can say that the then people had well organised and systematic vocational training system. The carpenters also had such a developed skill that the wooden buildings they had constructed did not fall even in the great earthquake of 1934 A.D.

Although Kathmandu Valley surpassed the then other states of Nepal in art, architecture and suclpture, other dates outside the Kathmandu Valley had also skilled technicians, who had constructed buildings temples and others. One important aspect is that when the rulers took imitation such technicians were inspired and contributed a lot. The khasiya Malla kings had given patronage and exempted taxes to the scholars of both sects-Hinduism and Buddhism and also the technicians. They had constructed temples, monastrices and palaces. One classical example of the architecture and sculpture is the Kankre Vihar of Surkit a Prithvi Malla's pellar with inscription is and their well known contribution of the period. Had not the technical education much developed in those days such works would not have been achieved.

Later on after the emergence of *Baisi* and *Chaubisi* states the rulers of the principalities had also encouraged the local techancians. Goldsmiths, ironsmiths, masous carpenters and many other technicians continuing the profession from generation tu generation. Mining industry flourished and the local needs were fulfilled by the local mines. Hamilton had written that most of the *Baisis* and *Chaubisis* were almost self dependent. There were skilled weavers, miners, masous and others. Sudarsan Shahi had constructed a fine palace for his residence at Sinja. It took years to complete the building. Had Jumla not tne skilled technicians, such palace could not have been constructed.

Similiarly in other principalities the technical skills was retained under the patronage of the rulers and the people. There were particular caste groups with assigned jobs like the Damais, Kami Sarki and others. The Damais used to work as Tailors and also play musical instruments on occasions like rituals and religious festivals. Kamis were the miners and ironsmiths. Sarkis were and are still the shoe-makers. These people continued the profession from generation to generation. The technical know-how was inturited in the family since centuries But in the technical know-how the Newar community of the Kathmandu Valley was richest at compared to any other Community of Nepal.

Modern Period

The traditional vocational training continued even during the modern period in Nepal as already mentioned the family was main training centre. Senior person in the family was the main trainer in the professi onal education right from the priesthood to the masonary. In this respect the Kathmandu Valley surpassed the other areas in Nepal. That is also one of the reasons why Kathmandu Valley had the best examples to show their development in art, architecture, sculpture etc. to the world.

With the rise of British power in India there was the gradual introduction of western technical knowledge. Many organised training centres were opened where the people were trained on both technical as well as theoritical side. Highly developed and scientific training was given in the government owned and private institutions. Persons trained in such institutions were found fully equipped with wider horizon of knowledge based on the scientific background. The had traditional professional training gave way to the new vocational training which the highly advanced western people led developed. Highly developed and sophicated industrialisation of the west had its impact in British India and other parts of the world. Further the quick inventions of new tools and machineries affected the traditional cottage industries of the world. Moreover the oriental traditional technology could not cope with the western technique. British colonial policy in India not only affected the Indians but also the Nepalese. There was also a gradual tendency to copy the occidental technical knowledge as we see in the theoritical knowledge. Cheaper, standard and better manufactured goods were overflowed to India. The free-trade policy of Britishers helped a lot to enrich the industrialists of Great Britain at the cost of Indians and indirectly the Nepalese also. Availability of cheaper, better and standard daily necessary British goods affected the local traditional productions which direcly affected many of the traditional skills: The local weavers, metal-workers and many others lost their business. The oriental skill training gradually became obsolute and could not become profitable. Those very skilled workers could not find their profession profitable. They gradually took another profession. The western industrialisation had not only told to our economy but in fact it had its fatal impact in our traditional skill training also.

At such a time when there was a question of the very future and existence of the indigenous technology, the zeal of the then rulers also could have contributed a lot in the maintenance and protection of the local technology. But those very person with the reins of power in their first took little interest in protecting the indigenous skills and technology. Those expert sculptors skilled in wood carving, stone carving, and other technologists gradually found their profession unprofitable. Formerly when the rulers constructed very artful buildings, temples and others, those persons with skills of wood carving, stone carving, etc. had enough opportunity to show their skill and found their job quite profitable. At that time people took much interest in gaining the knowledge of such skills. The indigenous technology was quite admired. But after coming power, the Ranas took more pride in coyping the western way of life. Big western type of palaces were constructed which were well furnished with the western objects.

Local fine artistic wood carving, metal works, stone carving and others had to give way to the western curies, The Rana palaces were adorned with the western goods. Those poor skilled man power of the country gradually lost their job and had to seek new jobs. Thus that aspect of vocational training which was run traditionally was gradually ignored.

To replace old system a new training system was introduced in different institutions organised in public and private sector for the vocational education from the second quarter of the century. In this respect we see the gradual introduction of some vocational educational centres specially from the time of Juddha Shamsher, which we will refer here.

Lalitkala Pathasala

To train the youths in fine arts a rchool called *Lalitkala Pathasala* was established in Kathmandu on Chaitra 31, 1991 B.S. We have seen the painting, art and architecture, sculpture etc. being trained by the senior members of the painter's family to their juniors and thus the profession was continued in the family for many generations. But now a government school was established where the youths of different castes and creed were trained in fine arts. Those enthusiast youths were trained on the scientific theories and the different school of thoughts of the subject. Although the school had very limited impact on the subject, its importance can not be ignored. Now the fine arts did not become the monopoly of the *Chitrakar* caste only. People of any caste, willing to learn the skill, could take up the profession. Moreover a permanent government organised school was set up for the scientific and better training to the youths of country. The *Lalitkala Pathasala* has become a campus now.

Gharelu Udyog Bibhag

We have already seen that the skill of the cottage industry was imported to the youths from generation to generation in a traditional way.

We had and still have many districts which did not have skilled carpenters and masons. Moreover the cottage industry which had supplemented the economy of the people had almost completely succumbed to due to the supply of machine-made-products imported from the foreign countries.

As a relief to the poor agriculturists of Nepal it was felt dire necessity to revive the cottage industries. Keeping it in mind the their Maharaj Juddha Shamsher a true nationalist, emphasising on the need of the technical education, expressed his attitude in these words.

> "My knowledge of living nations of today and the experiences I have gathered during my travels in foreign

> countries have convinced me that no nation can ever proper without the development of commerce and industries and it is here that we are backward. The greatest need of our country today is not education in its general sense, but technical and industrial education which will increase the material wealth of our country by enabling us to start factories and workshops of our own and there by opening up new avenues of employment for many of our poorer brethren."

Juddha Shamsher was not only a man of words but also action. So in persuance of his policy a technical school was opened in 1939 A.D. on an experimental basis to impart training on carding, spinning weaving and dying. Response to it was quite encouraging. A large number of people joined the training. The traditional system of technical education had to be modernised. 80 a technical school was opened in 1940 A.D. and a there months course was prescribed. Students from different villages and communities here selected for training and stipends were awarded to the descriving students. For technical school the *Ghaelru Udyog Bibhag* was established. The subjects taught were cotton and woolen hand spinning and weaving, new designs and technique in weaving, wearing Dhaka cloths and dyeing yarn cloth etc.

Ishwari Prasad writes,

> "It was the Maharaja's desire to train each and Therefore, schools here started in many parts of Nepal to import regular instruction in weaving and spinning on on a more scientific basis. The villages were provided with better spinning wheels and other materials on easy in statement system. The undispased surplus output was purchased by Government. Besides the technical schools a Sub-overseer school was also established to provide scientific vocation training. A large number of students were annually sent to India for specialised studies in arts, commerce, science, technology, medicine, enginee-

ring, metallurgy, veterinary and various crafts and industries.

The training centres gone training on many basic skills nurssary for the country. The main intention was to universalise the knowledge of the skill to all the enthusicast youths irrespective of caste. Moreover in 1941 A.D. Juddha Shamsher established the Juddha Research Laboratories to undertake research of many aspects. *Nepal Vastrakala Prachar Sanstha* was set up to supply cotton years to the weavers at cost price. In order to encourage the industries and technical education three industrial exhibitions were held in Kathmandu the first in winter 1934-35, the second in 1939-40 and third in 1944 A.D.

Krishi Parishad

It was established to train and acquaint the cultivators scientific and better knowledge of the cultivation of land. Well trained agriculturists were employed to train the cultivators on the better cultivation. It does not mean that the farmers were unskilled in the farming but the scientific knowledge had to be given to them. *Krishi Pradarshani* (agricultural exhibition) was organised for the first time in the history of Nepal, in which the skilled people could exhibit their skill. It provided an opportunity to encourage the local skilled manpower.

Besides the establishment of many training institutes on the technical knowledge, many youths of Nepal were sent to foreign countries to be educated on the technical education. Such persons were sent to Japan and India on scholarship. These persons came back with the qualification on engineering, agriculture and medicine. Dr. Ratna Das Vaidya was the first L.M.P. doctor in Nepal. The *Arogyashalas*, traditional health centres, gave way to the modern medical science. People were sent to India for the training on compoundary also. Similarly persons got training on sericulture, ceramics, textile industries, and many other subjects. But one thing we must not forget *i.e.* the western technical knowledge was meant for the urbanised people and elite groups, whereas the lower grade people, howsoever difficult it was, sustained their technical know-how for the common mass. Those very skilled man power of thedays yore whom we called the "Wealth of nation" were very much ignored. They were reduced from "riches to rags"; even then the socio-cultural heritage maintained them; and those people, although turned to rags, lingered on their profession with pride. It must be mentioned here that the hereditary traditional technical know-how is maintained with much hardship in the urban area by the strong traditional belief whereas in the hilly region the necessity and compulsion made it survive for such a long time. Age long traditional technical know-how had contributed a lot not only to earn livelihood for the common mass but also to enrich the cultural heritage and retain the technical education in Nepal. The traditional education made the people competent to stand on their feet.

Female education

In a traditional society it is very hard to find any drastic change in any aspect of social life. Changes could have occurred had there been some impact due to major changes in any aspect. Although we have seen the waves of immigrations of the people either from the north or south. But those very migrated people had more concern about the safety of their life and keeping their traditional feelings intact. Moreover another hurdle in the promotion of the female education was the traditional strong feeling of having one's daughter married in an early age. Generally girls were married before they were adolscent. We have the examples of early marriage. Rajalladevi was married with Jayasthiti Malla while she was quite young. Similarly, later on, also the young princesses were married. It was the first duty of the parents to have their daughters married before they (girls) attained puberty. The parents hardly thought of giving education to their daughters. Such a situation continued even up to the Rana period. Education was not felt necessary for the females whose main duty was to limit themselves within the four walls of the house and perform the domestic duties. Generally the girls were trained in the cooking, knitting, weaving and other activities necessary for the domestic purpose. The females actively participated in the religions activities, as such they took much interest in hearing the religions texts recited and narrated. In such field they seemed to have been well acquainted. The females of the higher class, specially the royalties, seemed to have been educuted in every aspect even after marriage through the special teachers. Those queens like Devaladevi, Gangarani, Lalamati Dayavati, Chandraprabhabati (Gorkha) seemed to have enough knowledge in running the administration. They must have been well acquainted with the *Dharmashastras* according to which the administration was run. In this way we have very scanty informations about the female education during the medieval period.

With the dawn of modern age we have a few evidences of the female education atleast among the royalties and nobilities. Prithvi Narayan Shah was also trained by his step-mother Chandraprabhabati when he was a minor. Chandraprabhabati seemed to have much knowledge of running the administration for which knowledge of *Dharmashastras* was needed. Some of the elite families used to educate the females. Pranamanjari, the third wife of Pt. Prem Nidhi Pant, a renowned Sanskrit scholar of the 18th century Nepal, can be cited an example. She was well read and could also write well. In memory of her deceased son Sudarsan, she wrote *Sudarsan Tika* in 1723 A.D. She had also translatedthe Sanskrit text *Prayaschit Pradeep* into Nepali. She is also credited to have written *Tripurasundari Paddhati* in Sanskrit. She is credited to have been the first female writer in the history of Nepali literaturers.

Hira Gayeneni should be referred here as a composer of two songs in appraisal of Prime Minister Mathbar Singh Thapa (1843-45 A.D.). Actually she could neither read or write but belonged to a caste in which singing songs was the main profession for livelihood. She had sing two songs which Henry Lawrence, the then British Resident to Nepal, had collected, in his collections. No doubt, in those days there were many such female singers in Nepal unrecorded. But Hira's songs, as had impressed the British Resident, had come to light. Nepal was rich with many singers like Hira.

Bhakti Kumari, the wife of Padma Jung, who was assassinated in the coup of 1885 A.D., was also an educated female. She had witnessed the most harrible and songine scene of her husband's murder and was very shocked. She passed the rest of her life in hearing the *Puranas*, *Mahabherat*, *Ramayan* etc. narrated by the Brahmins. She herself was an educated lady. Being impressed by the Holy texts, she wrote many hymns which were lithographed in 1904 A.D. The title of the work was *Bhakti Lahari* the major portion of which is in Braj language and minor in Nepali. Later on we find the females of the royalties being given education and they had also shown their educational calibre. Lalitatripurasundari, the last queen of Rana Bahadur Shah, was well educated. She had written a book named *Raj Dharama* which is still preserved in the Madan Puraskar Library. Bhimsen Thapa, the then de-facto ruler (1806-1837 A.D.), seems to have employed the scholars to teach the feemales of the royalties. *Lilitatripurasundari could* write the book because of the Bhimsen Thapa's encouragement. She was the second Lady to contribute for the enrichment of the Nepali literature. Although the females were given education through the tutors it was not yet been realised that the females must be educated. They were given education just to make them feel competent to read and write. Up to the nineteeth century there was no organised institution to educate the girls, which was considered unnecessary.

With the dawn of the present century we find a change in attitude regarding the female education in Nepal. That sort of change could be had only through the liberal attitude of the rulers in a country like Nepal where everything was under the grip of the Rana Prime Minister, whose attitude not only brought changes in political field but also in social and economic aspects. Under such circumstance any change in the social life can be expected only under the sweet will of the ruler. Being impressed by the development in Japan Dev Shamsher (1901 A.D.) wished a change in the country. He had realised that the development of the country could be aspired only through the educational development. It is said that one hundred and fifty primary schools were established in Nepal. Schools for the girls were also opened. It is mentioned in the *Nizamati Kitab Khana Register* dated 1958 V.S that four girls schools were established in the Kathmandu Valley. They were *Kathmandu Janana Pathsala*, *Patan Janana Pathsala*, *Bhaktapur Janana Pathsala* and *Tripureswor Janana Pathsale.* Three teachers *viz.* Pt. Ram Bhakti Pant, Pt. Bhuvan Nath Panday and Pt. Shesh Kaman Rhanal with the salary of Rs. 180/- each per annum were employed in the *Kathmandu Janana Pathsala*; similarly *Patan Janana Pathsala* had two teachers named Pt. Jit Ram and Pt. Amber Raj Tiwari who got Rs. 96/- and Rs. 180/- per annum respectively. *Bhaktcpur Janana Pathsala* had only one teacher named Pt. Sridhar who got Rs. 120/- per annum. *Tripuraswos Janana Pathsala* had also one teacher named Pt. Tirtha Raj Timisina who was given salary of Rs. 120/- per annum. The *pandits* were supposed to teach the simple reading, writing and arithmetics. Many guardains came forward willingly to send their young daughters to the schools. But the schools were not allowed to run smoothly as the reactionary group of the Ranas did not wish any change which would bring about consciousness among the mass. So the liberal Prime Minister Dev was driven out from the power and once more conservative and autocratic government was revived Consequently the girls schools were closed. Once more there was a set-back in the female education in Nepal.

But the females who had gone to India got an opportunity to read the western education. One lady named Durga Devi wrote Acharya Dixit many books. Her first work entitled *Anusuya Sita Sambad* came out in 1908 A.D. which was a substantial contribution on behalf of the Nepalese women. Her next book was *Bhabhi Kartavya* came out in 1913 A.D. Her books dealt with the moral lesson of a woman and the husband was considered as the God's creature on earth. Although she could not be considered as a progressive woman, her contributions can be treated as the foremost work of the Nepalese women. She was educated in India where she was much influenced by the radical ideas of India, yet she thought of bringing about evolutionary change in the minds of Nepalese women folk. Her appeal to eradicate the feeling of *Kala Akshyak Bhainsa Barabar* (black letters were like the black buffaloes) had its gradual impact in the minds of the Nepalese society. Magazines in Nepali language like *Sharada*, *Gorkh Sansar*, *Tarun Gorkha* and *Udaya* were very much responsible for creating a degree of interest in the uplift of women and also revaling the sad plight of the women. Similarly the magazine *Chandra*, published from Benaras, contained poems and articles written by the Nepalese and encouraged the females to write articles and poems The then female writers here Sukeshi Devi, Sachet Pathika, Naveena Devi Alochak Pathika and others.

In 1914 A.D. Sukeshi Devi, a Nepali woman, wrote a long poem under the title "Nari Shikchya" (Female education). *Mahila Guruju* Jaya raj Pandey's wife was a well read female and also a good conversant in many languages like Sanskrit, Marathi, Bengali, Urdu etc. She had written many articles under different captions and published in many magazines. In those days most of the educated females had their education in India. The females of the higher class residing in the border of India also got their education in India. The women folk of the royalties and Ranas recieved very little education through the tutors. It is said that special attention was given in the selection of the tutors for the girls. Generally very simple and not good looping persons were selected as the tutors so that the girls might not be attracted towards those tutors. Moreover some maid-servants used to sit along with the girl-students while the teacher taught them. King Tribhuvan wanted from the Rana Prime Minister Chandra posting a lady teacher to teach the *Maharanis* and the young princesses, which was complied with.

Melawa Devi, born in Gurung Community in 1907 A.D., entered in the palace of Chandra Shamsher at the age of seven. She was a renowned *Talime* and singer. She had written a drama entitled *Ekadasbi Mahima* which was also staged. Might be she was the first lady whose songs became so famous.

Yogmaya was another poetess of 1974 B.S. who had composed poems. As illiterate she was she could neither read nor write. But she had quality of composing poems verbally and had led a group of dedicated followers. She and her followers had led a movement of *Bhajan* in eastern Nepal. The oral poems of Yogmaya were collected by her follower Prem Narayan and published in the book form entitled *Sarbartha Yogbani* in 2012 B.S.

In 1976 B.S. Bhagvati Kumari was another poetess who had contributed hymns called *Bhakti Tilak* to Gorkhapatra Press, Naxal. Puskar Lohani, appreciating her work, writes "Her poem, beginning in a romantic dialogue between husband and wife, ends in a philosophical way." She was writing poems up to her death in 2028 B.S. (1961 A.D.). Her unpublished poems were later on compiled and published by her son on 20th Chaitra 2029 B.S.

We have sporadic references of the females who were educated right from the ancient time in Nepal. Except a few most of the educated females who have come to lime light were from the elite group of the society.

Dibya Kumari Koirala, wife of Krishna Prasad Koirala and mother of Bisweswor Prasad Koirala was also an educated lady of the time. She wished a change on the condition of the females of Nepal. As such she published article called "Stre Shikshyako Avashyakata" (Need of the Female education) in Gorakha Sansar, a weekly, in 1983 Marga. Being the wife of social reform and politician she had appealed for the promotion of female education in Nepal. We have a reference of another female nemed Lavanyamayi Devi who had written a forceful article entitled "Kasto Theyo ke Ra ke Bhayo" which was quite analytical about the position of women in Nepal. That article was published in *Gorakha Sansar*.

Ambalika Devi upadhyaya, wife of Ambika Pd. Upadhyaya, who had written the first book on the history of Nepal in Nepali language, had written a novel called *Rajput Ramani* in 1989 B.S.

Chandrakanta Malla, sister martyr Shukraraj Shastri, was educated in India, she had contributed a lot in the upliftment of the position of women and female education. Being a daughter of Madhav Raj Joshi, the first Arya Samajirt of Nepal Chandrakanta had the opportunity of getting Western education in India during the period of her father's exile, she had written a book entitled *Grihalaxmi* in 1992 B.S. She had opened a girls, school also in Kathmandu to train the girls knithing, weaving and general education also. She had impressed Juddha Shamsher also.

The growth of female education in India had its gradual impact in the Nepalese society. In 1928 four females named Vidyadevi Udasani, Dharma Devi Udasani, Vishnumati Malini and Radha Devi Malini, with the scholarship of six hundred rupees per annum, went to Allahabad for the course of nurse training. They were the first lady nurses in Nepal. Moreover the Rana families started feeling necessity of training their young girls to read and write the English and also Hindi, because the knowledge of the subjects was essential for their marriage with the Rajput princes of India. So tutors were invited from India to train the Rana young girls the English and Hindi languages and also the foreign etiquettes.

It is very interesting to note that there were some *Kanya Pathasalas* (schools) in the Kathmandu Valley in 1926 A D. as is evident by the official documents available in the National Archives, Kathmandu. The salary of the teachers employed in the *Kanya Pathasalas* of Kathmandu, Lalitpur and Bhaktapur is mentioned in the documents of *Nizamati Kitabakhana*, preserved in National Archives, Kathmandu. The salary amounted rupees two hundred and four per annum. It is commented that actually there did not exist any girl school up to 1933 A.D. But the fact is that there existed only one pre-primany *Kanya Pathasala* in Kathmandu.

In 1932 A.D. Juddha Shamsher gave permission to Chandra Kanta Malla to establish a girl's school. The students were trained on embroidery, needle works, weaving etc. Teachers of the schools were Chandra Kanta Mall (sister of Sukraraj Shastri), Laxmi Kumari Thakuri, Pt. Surya Nath and Pt. Lilanath, who taught the simple reading, writing, arithmtics and embroidery, needle works, weaving etc. Chandra Kanta, trained in India, had radical feeling about the status of women in Nepal. She wished to make the girls competent to stand on their own feet. Her school gave the basic education to the girls and was watched suspicionsly by the government. Up to that time the girls having played active role in the social activities and joining schools were not so much appreciated. Moreover Chandra Kanta, being the daughter of Madhav Raj Joshi and sister of Sukraraj Shastri and an Arya Samajist, was suspected. Hence the school could not run smoothly. Meanwhile the well-off and big shots started educating their daughters within their houses tutors were employed to teach the Western education, as up to that time there was no provision for the admission of the girls in the high school. Formerly the girls were taught the reading, writing and simple arithmetics, so that they could simply read and write. But now some of the families started educating their daughters with an objective of giving higher western education. Thus we see a departure in the tradition of the female education in Nepal. Lekha Rajya Laxmi Rana was the first girl to pass the S.L.C. examination. She passed in first division. This event gave stimulus to the females of Nepal. Four girls named Angur Baba Joshi, Shahana Devi Pradhan, Bhuban Rajya Laxmi Devi Shah and Sadhana Devi Pradhan passed the S.L.C. examination in 2004

B.S. (1948 A.D.). In 2005 B.S. (1949 A.D.) Shanti Shah, Madhuri Shah, Chiniya Devi and Brinda Malla got through the S.L.C. examination. In 2006 B.S. (1950 A.D.) Tara Devi, Shashikala Sharma, Shadhana Khatri and Padma Devi Shah passed the S.L.C. examination.

Later on in 1947 A.D. (Ashad 20, 2004 B.S.) the first recognised girls' high school called Padma Kanya School was established by the initiation of Prime Minister Padma Shamsher. This school provided an opportunity to the girls to get education formally in a institutionalised basis. Many guardians got their young girls admitted in the school. In the same year (2004 B.S.) Kanya Mandir School was established at the initiation of some intellectuals. In was a publics chool. Meanwhile Shantinikinya Public School was established in 2002 B.S., which started on a co-education basis, a revoluntary step in those days Wiswaniketan School and Sitaram School were established on the co-education basis in 2003 B.S. Much enthusiasm was shown but by a very minor section of the society. The main problem faced by the school was the higher percentage of the droppers in the higher classes. In those days the guardians' main concern was to get their daughters married in time. Education was secondary concern of the guardians. Moreover there was a strong feeling that if the girls would get higher education, they would be indocile and also uncontrolable for the domestic affairs. Girls of about fourteen or fifteen were married, if they were not married at that age, it was very difficult to get bridegrooms. The female education was accepted with much reluctance in the urban areas only; otherwise the female education was almost ignored up to dawn of democracy in Nepal.

Education during the medieval period

Rich varieties of the literary works in the form of dramas, poems, hymns and many others like those of astrology, astronomy, veterinary science, religious ideals etc. are an evidence of the well developed educational system of the medieval Nepal. Vaidya has written "Richer a country in literature, the better is the condition of a country in every aspect." Before we go in details about the growth and development of the education of the medieval Nepal, it will be very apt here to deal with the question as to why Nepal became rich in the literary works which signified highly developed educational system of the country. Many factors are responsible for the it. During the medieval period Northern India was ravaged many times by the iconoclast Muslim invaders. Staunch Hindus and Buddhists were exposed badly to the merciless military activities of the invaders. As such many Hindu and Buddhist scholars took asylum in Nepal. Those very scholars contributed a lot by writing various scholarly works, and Nepal could retain the scholarly activities for centuries. No less important was the attitude of the rulers who had given patronage to the scholars, had invited them from India and were themselves much inclined to the writing of the poems, dramas, hymns and others.

During the medieval period the learning centres were *Vihars* for the Buddhists and the priests for the Hindus. We did not have the educational institutions as we have at present. But the scholars, under the patronage of the royal family, seemed to have been quite active. They had given education to the princes, princesses and also the nobilities. The whole administrative system was based on Kautilya's *Arthashastrya*, *Manusmriti*, and many other texts. The code of Jayasthiti Malla was based on the *Smritis*, as such the administrators were supposed to know those ancient texts. Even the ministers had employed the learned persons to translate the ancient Hindu texts for their children, for example, *Naradasmriti* was translated into the then Newari language for the son of a minister during the reign of Jayasthiti Malla. Similarly, many other ancient Hindu texts, *Ramayan*, *Mahabharat* and others were translated in the local languages for the benifit of the people. What it seems is that the education was the concern of the higher class of the society, whereas the common was least bothered about it.

The kings of the Karnali Malla dynasty, *Baisi* and *Chaubisi* states, Senas of the East and Malla's learned persons. Royal edicts of the Karnali Mallas had clearly mentioned the release of the various taxes to the scholars and religious people of both sects-the Hindus and Buddhists. The kings themselves were the learned persons. Many of the inscriptions mention that the Malla Kings of the Kathmandu Valley were well versed in *Shastrashastra* and *Sangeeta* ; among them Pratap Malla, Siddhinarshina Malla, Parthivendra Malla, and others were the scholarly kings. Mallas of the Kathmandu Valley had much inclination towards the development of the literature, as its results we have piles and piles of the manusscripts in the National Archives,, Kathmandu. Pratap Malla had taken the title of *Kavirai* with pride and had also composed many poems and hymns. His inscription at Hanumandhoka consisting of fifteen scripts is an evidence of his knowledge of those scripts. The visits of the Christain missionaries had made him acquainted with the Latin, French and English words also. Among the Malla kings, who had written books on various themes were, Jagajyoter Malla Ranjit Malla, Jayaprakash Malla and others. Many other books were written by other scholars. Greatest contribution of the Malla kings was the promotion of the cultural heritage of the country. Vedas were well read and religious rituals were performed on the vedic ways. *Vidyapithas* (learning centres) were consecrated lands for their smooth running.

After the emergence of the modern period, the early Shah kings like Prithvi Narayan Shah, Pratap Simha Shah, Rana Bahadur Shah, Girbanyuddha Vikram Shah and others had hardly any time to devote on the educational affect. They were busy either in the military activities or on the conspiratorial politics of Nepal. Among them Pratap Simha Shah had given interest to the learning. But after the political stability was restored due to the emergence of a strong person like Bhimsen Thapa, there was a tendency towards the encouragement of the learning. Bhimsen Thapa had many of the old Hindu texts translated in Nepal, as the Nepali language had now become the official language. There were many scholars like Lalitballabh who wrote "*Bhaktavijaya Kavya*," *Prithvindravarnodya* etc. Shaktiballabha who wrote "*Jaya-ratnakar Natak*" and others, Subananda, Banibilas, Pt. Sundarananda and others. Those were the renowned scholars of the time, who works are of much importance. What we see during the first half of the 19th century was that there was the continuation of the learning of the traditional education in one hand and need of the knowledge of the Persian, Tibetan and English languages. The correspondence with the British India and native states of India was done in the Persian language before the introduction of the English language. But the introduction of the western education and rise of the British power in India made Nepal and Nepalese learn the western education. Knowledge of the English language was found necessary in the country after the establishment of the British Residency in Nepal in 1816 A.D. Knowledge of the Chinese and Tibet languages was also found essential for the closure contact with Tibet and China. The existence of the Nepalese *Vakeel* at Lhasa demanded the knowledge of Tibetan language. But the education of the different foreign language was given to a few number of the selected persons, whereas the traditional education continued to be the concern of the major number of the population.

Bhimsen Thapa showed interest in the western education. Some learned persons were invited from Bengal to train the royal family members and his own family members. The Bengali teachers were employed to train a selected number of persons. Moreover there was a growing interest to know of what was going on the world. Newspapers of India and England were also subscribed for the king. Thus we see the gradual inclination towards the western education, but yet no school was established to impart education. Up to that time the

Nepalese society had not felt the necessity of having the public educational system which we do have now. The scholarly people and priests of both sects were training the youths. Where Lamaism prevailed, that is in the northern area, one of the male issues of a family was dedicated to learning. To the whole life that person passed the life of an ascetic and devoted to learning. That sort of system prevailed during the medieval period. Such a person resided in the *Gumba* (monastery) and dressed himself as an ascetic. It was a matter of great honour and pride to have a *Lama* in the family. But in the Kathmandu Valley, youths of both sexes of Buddhist community specially could join the *Vihars* for a certain time, study the Buddhist literature and return to the domestic life. Thus the *Gumbas* and *Vihars* were the centres of the learning since the days yore and are still playing the same role.

Western education

We have already mentioned that there was some sort of inclination towards the western education in Nepal during the first half of the nineteenth century. That trend was further pushed ahead by Jang Bahadur after his visit to Europe. But he also did not establish any formal school for the common mass, as such Danial Wright, the contemporary British Resident Surgeon, had rightly mentioned :

> "*The subject of school and colleges in Nepal may be treated as briefly as that of snakes in Ireland. There are none.* Sir Jung and some of the wealthier class have tutors, either Europeans or Bengali Babus, to teach their children English, but there is no public provision for education of any sort. Every man teaches his own children, or employs the family priest or Pandit for the purpose. The lower classes are simply without education of any kind whatever."

Durbar Hig School

On the basis of the records available at our disposal it could be said that the beginning of English education of Nepal in a modest way began after the return of Jung Bahadur from the tour of foreign countries in 1853. Earlier there were Sanskrit schools conducted by the Brahmin priests and subsequently with the advent of Muslim rule in India. Persian language was introduced and continued to be used in the transactions of the rules. Thus before the advent of the influence of English company in the Kathmandu Valley, Persion language was taught in the schools and *pathsalas* by highly paid imported *Mullahs.* This system was not stopped by Jung Bahadur. Rather he introduced the teaching of English in the Durbar School by appointing English speaking men.

It was believed that such an initiation was essential for sustaining and perpetuating the ascendency of his family. Thus as soon as Jung Bahadur returned from abroad and he set up a small English class under the tutorship of canning. On the ground floor of the Thapathali Durbar, Canning used to give lessons in English, Mathmatics and History of Jung Bahadur's sons, brothers and nephews and this was the first step in the direction of establishing modern education of the western type. But the arrangements for public education at the end of Jung's rule (1877) were so inadequate and deplorable that it could be termed as mainly a beginning in the diffusion of knowledge. Wright had obsesved that :

> "The subjects of schools and colleges in Nepal may be treated briefly as that of snakes of ireland. There are none. Sir Jung Bahadur Rana (1846-77) and some of the weather class have tutors, either Europeans or Bengali Babus (Indians) to teach their children English, but there is no provision for public education of any sort. Every man teaches his own children or employs the family priest or pandit for this purpose. The lower classes are simply without education of any kind whatsoever."

This state of affairs continued till Bir Shumshere.

Thus the Ranas modestly supported the ancient Sanskrit education but they wers favourably inclined towards English education which they imparted to their own children as well as member of effluent society. The official Ranas also liked the new system which was "a fatal death-blow to the decaying traditional institutions of the country." However, the Durbar School, established in or about 1889 was not opened to the common people and it was exclusively meant for the children of the Ranas. It could be known that the first Nepali who went to Calcutta to appear at the entrance Examination was Chandra Shamshere Rana in 1884. But the number of students appearing at subsequent examination could not be available.

The Durbar School originally had few teachers, out of whom 80% hailed from Calcutta. They were all English teachers imported from Calcutta and they were highly paid. For nearly ten years the number of students of Durbar School could be counted on fingers. London wrote that the school consisted of children of Jung Bahadur's family, children of Commander-in-chief and top officials of the state. The discipline was various and the training was somewhat on the pattern of English school. The school was attached to the university of Calcutta but it was in 1933 that S.L.C. Examination of the kingdom could held under its completed management. However. the Durbar School was first centre of English education of the country which in beginning had ten teachers and one headmaster. They were all Indians and subsequently Englishmen were also appointed as teachers in the school. However, the Durbar High School was an aristocratic pattern and education here was costly. Indiscriminate admission was the order of the day.

Rani Pokhari Sanskrit Pathsala

After Jung Bahadur's death, his brother Rancddip Singh's reign began which was marked by the development of Sanskrit education. He enconveyed the opening of Sanskrit School which imparted religious education to the Brahmans as far as possible. Many Pathsalas were converted into this Sanskrit School. Durbar High School and Rani

Pokhari Pathasala were the only institutions of Nepal. This Rani Pokhari Pathasalas had also arranged to teach Sanskrit particularly Vyakarna Kabya, astrology etc. to the all students irrespective of their attitudes and distinctions of castes.

The assassination of Ranoddip Singh, the rise of Dhir Shumsher's sons and the beginning of Bir Shumsher's primiership was a landmark in the development of Sanskritised education. Durbar School and Tindhara Paksala were established simulataneously and teachers were appointed to teach Sanskrit and English at the same time. It could be known that ten teachers with distinctive specialisations in various subjects were appointed for the purpose. The Head Pandit was Bishnu Hari who was well versed in subjects like veda, Vyakarna Kabya, Astrology, Jurisprudence.

However, during the primiership of Bir Shumshere, the families of the Ranas and their close relations were affected by western education, The middle class people of the hilly areas and only Brahmans of Kathmandu Valley had remained aloof from it and depended solely an Sanskrit education for their enlightment. In other words, the Ranas received english education in the Durbar High School and other people particularly belonging to the middle class consoled themselves with Sanskrit learning imparted at Rani Pokhari Sanskrit Pathsala and Tindhara Paksala. Thus it could be said that the education was imported chiefly through the medium of Sanskrit language throughout the nineteenth century and nothing remarkable could happen except making available few more facilities for the Sanskrit studies. There were a few learned scholars here and there, who imparted in their own way and received encouragement from the officialdom.

Sylvain Levi, who came to Nepal about the close of last century (1898), had given a pitiable picture of the educational condition. He wrote that :

> "The great discrepancies in the epigraphy, which no other document can fill up, prevent the study of the

> history of the institutions in the middle age. The inscriptions take new life with the dynasty of the numerous Mallas, it is true, for the more recent period, but "stuffed with stilted literature and almost bare of facts. The Sanskrit is only a school language, useful for the construction of centres or imitations, the real and positive notes are expressed in the indigenous language, the Nevari, and the study of the epigraphy in Newari still remains to be created. It is necessary to reach the Gorkha period to discover useful documents."

Such a deplorable state of affairs continued during the whole period of our study.

The people of this hill locked country were the lovers of Sanskrit. The traditional education was no doubt Sanskrit and from Benares, the centre of Sanskritised education, they drew inspiration off and on. The Brahmins sent their wards to Benaras to learn the religious scriptures which were written in Sanskrit. Such pupils learnt at the feet of great Pundits but they lived a very miserable life at Benaras. Still they required the religious knowledge of the scriptures and got by heart the sacred literatures. On their return to their homeland they devoted their time in diffonsing the knowledge they had learnt. The Brahmans were not the only scholars who :

> "Annoted and embroidered the secred texts which guided man's action towards the highest stage of being. They taught the young and counselled the aged to ascend to the experience of absorption into the sacred."

They played a significant role in the uplift of Sanskrit education. The centre of the educational development were the Bhasa Pathsalas which were managed and run by the Brahman Pundits returning from Benaras. The Pandits passed 'Madhyama Examination' from Benaras and they took keen interest in the traditional system of education than the modern education brought by the Ranas from abroad. They commanded great respect in the society. All religious rites were performed by them. Even at the court of Ranas their status was supreme. In religious matters their verdicts were accepted by the people and the Ranas without any opposition. They were regarded as the monololist of all knowledge, sacred or otherwise. The position of the Raj Guru had been well described by Tucci who remarked that:

> "A person of great importance and authority during the rule of Ranas was the Raj-Guru, the spiritural director and state controller supreme moderator of the moral, social and religious life of Nepal."

Ranoddip Singh had opened Durbar School which was exclusively meant for the members of Rana family and Bhardars. Bir Shumsher subsequently opened the school to the common people. A new building was constructed at the site of Rani Pokhari and the English school was kept in the upper floor of this building where as the sanskrit Pathsala was situated in the ground floor. Later on the Sanskrit Pathsalas was shifted in another new building. At this time, there was vast difference in the payscale of the teachers of Sanskrit and English School. If the english teachers received two, three or four hundred rupees, the Sanskrit teachers, received a pallry sum of thirty of thirty-five rupees per month and the Head Pandit got forty-five rupees only. The discrepancy in pay scale of the Sanskrit teachers led one to believe in the fact that sanskrit was meant for the Brahmans and common people and english was meant for the wealthy persons. By and by the teaching and learning of Sanskrit felt into disuse.

Prime Minister who in his own way intended to bring changes in society by opening Bhasa Pathsalas modelled on the western pattern. To help in this massive task, he selected Jaya Prithivi Bahadur Singh, a relative of the Ranas. He was educated in the missionery schools at Culcutta and had developed a strong nationalistic attitude. He made provisions to allot one teacher to any community having fifty children of school age. Two teachers were provided if the number of pupils crossed the mark. The curriculum contents were reading, writing, arithmatic, history and geography, Text books and others reading materials were given free of charge.

Dev Shumsher was first man who opened Bhasa Pathsalas in the various places of the country in 1901 and introduced the Nepali language. He was the first Rana statesman to realise the miserable condition of the country and he regarded the western educational system not only as a means of enlightment but also as a means of pulling the country in the map of the other advanced countries of the west. He adopted the policy of expanding the facilities of public education and planned to establish one Bhasa Pathsala (primary) in each village. But, he was not able to survive long with his liberal policy and his brothers conspired against him and soon exiled their liberal brother.

It is remarkable that 150 schools were actually opened before Deva Shumsher was exiled by his brother. There is a difference of opinion as to how many schools Deva Shumsher had opened during the short period of his rule. The contemporary historians give a very exaggerated number but the Report of the National Educational Planning Commission refered to the opening of 57 primary pathsalas. Kamal Dixit has written that :

> "Plan was made by Deva to open about three hundreds schools (pathasalas within three years on the basis of population percentage of the district of Nepal. And 37 (?) pathsalas were actually opened before was exiled. According to Dr. Regmi, Deva Shumsher had opened a network of Primary Schools all over the Kathmandu Valley and his scheme", envisaged one school for one village at the other end and at the top a first grade college as a step towards the establishment of a University."

The entire network of primary schools ranging no less than 300 institutions had been spread by Deva Shumsher throughout Nepal. Though Chandra Shumsher exiled Deva Shumsher and withdrew the entire network of primary schools spread by the latter, yet at this time the traditional beginning of Bhasa Pathsalas was an important event, a historical contribution in the publication of 'Gorkha Patra' by Deva was another important event of his period.

Dev Shumsher's actons were sudden, surprising and sincere. He was a nationalist and his attitude seemed to be democratic. Before introducing these reforms Dev should have strengthened his own foothold in the administration by re-organising the army and by appointing his trust worthy men in the key positions of the civil service. But Dev was an idealist and not a practical politician. He lost himself in his ideal thoughts and neglected the most important organs of the state like the intelligence department and the armed forces. On the other hand, the conspirations successfully overthrew him and the power went into the hands of gun men.

After the exile of Dev in *Dhankuta* Chandra Shumsher came to power. He closed the entire primary schools opened by Deva except a few. He opened new schools in his name. The report of National Educational Planning Commission observed that cut of the schools set up by Deva, only eight or ten had been opened during the time of Chandra Shumsher. The reform of Deva were kicked and the opening of new pathsalas had also been abandoned. Two pathsalas and two old teachers were retained by Chandra. Later he gave new appointments to some of the teachers of old schools established by Deva. But Chandra did not stop the publication of 'Gorkha Patra' due to the action of Deva Shumsher who distributed free of charge the daily newspaper to the king of England and the English Ambassador stationed at Kathmandu. Subsequently many free primary schools had been started in different parts of the kingdom by Chandra for the spread of education among the mass.

The long primiership of Chandra Shumsher (1901-1929) was eventful in the educational history of Nepal. He was the first Rana who passed entrance examination from the Calcutta University. He had received English education and he also had the credit of passing the Bachelor Examination from the same University. But he never tolerated that any other man should attain name and fame in the field of learning. He also did not like people engaged in cultivation of arts and crafts. The attitudes of Chandra Shumsher and his conservative lief-tenants in this respects had been explained by Landon in the following words :

"One or two schools were indeed founded in Kathmandu but they did not at first meet with much appreciation from the Nepalese. In fact, the first beginning of education were looked upon with something of the misturust with which the medieval church of Rome heard of the activity of scientist within her fold. We have seen that the Present Maharaj (Chandra) began a new reign by sending some of the sons of the aristocracy to Japan (for technical education) in 1902. In permitting the spread of knowledge he (Chandra) foundo pposed to him the traditional obscurantism or at least the jealous exclusiveness of a religion which had its roots deep not only in the minds but in the hearts of his countrymen."

To check the progress of liberal and popular education, Chandra Shumsher, in 1902, planned to send some of the sons of aristocracy to Japan for technical education. The Ranas feared the introduction of liberal education was revealed by another statement of Landon in which he explained Chandra Shumsher measure of sending source of the sons of the aristecracy to Japan to technical education. Landon said :

"It was thought that the advantage of moderns cience could be enjoyed by Nepal without the corresponding danger of the introduction of men imbued with western Principles of democracy."

The feeling of Ranas towards the educated people could be best gauged by the following remarks of Tucher who said :

> "In India many of his young men had been encourage to seek their education. Many were returning, charged with new battles. Young men in a hurry. An autocrat at the head of an olgarchy can in the end only maintain his and his colleagues station by forthsight, even harsh, methods against those who would encroach on their privileges or change the order of things. In the end there is no room for toleration."

With regard to the Ranas' attitude towards education, Chandra Bikram Budhathahi remarks :

> "The object was to exclude the possibility of installing into young minds the knowledge how the democratic countries of the world had envolved the system of self governing institutions. But a study in an institution also possessed the inherit merit of lending the people to revolution. But it is significant that the Ranas who regarded to western education with contempt sent their own sons to India to study in the different Indian Universities privilege of receiving western education was confined to the Ranas and the aristocratic houses on whom the Ranas reposed their confidence."

Shrestha Pathsala & Nizamati Pass

The Prime Minister Chandra Shumshre had established the vivil service examination, called Nizamati Pass in 1904 for appointment to jobs under the Government Immediately soon after Shrestha Pathsalas having different courses in law and mathematics were established. This pathsalas prepared the recruits on job-oriented courses, and it was found subsequently that all the young government officers had received training in this institution. There was an overwhelming number of Kaziz, Sardars, Mir Subba, Khardars, Ditthas, Mukhiya, Naib Ditthas, Bahidars, writers, Naib writers, the Bhardars, Rakamis in the pre-1950 stratification of the civil service who were mostly the products of Shrestha Pathsalas. In this connection Pradhan wrote :

> "One must get through this (the civil service examination called Nizamati pass) examination to apply for a job in the Government during the Rana Regime because free competition was not known. It was not important whether a person was qualified for the job or not. The ability to please the people in key positions in the govt. counted as the qualification for appointment in the Govt. service... The person who entered the civil Administration rose to the post of kazi, the highest post in administration open to the non-ruling population of the country."

Thus the recruits of the Nepal civil service went through the courses of the Shrestha Pathsalas and a few of them had previously obtained degrees of Matriculation and Intermediate Examinations. But there had been still a marked difference. Dr. Regmi had remarked :

> "Ranas are averse of giving employment to educated men who have been showing dislike for education. And thus a host of youngmen who should have ordinarily found their way to educational institutions waitsupon the Ranas for his good grace. In all matters affecting oppointments in or dismissal from services the Ranas act as high handedly as possible and as though it were dispensing purely private business and favours. There is no public service commission to consider the facts of merits. Day in and day out there is a peculiar congregation of youngmen at evern door of the Rana and the latter makes his choice of the nominess from those who have put up to their credit the meanest king of flattery. Thus result is the greatest impediment to the efficiency of administration."

Education outside Kathmandu Valley during Rana period

The development of education outside Kathmandu Valley was more or less meagre. In those times there were no primary pathsalas in the villages. The children of wealthy and priests or Brahmins or their own guardians. The system importing education was still primitive. The pubils wrote on slate made of wood and wrote on it by pencils and the dust of red soil. For writing purposes the leaves of Sal and Mango were used in some of the villages. Even the official documents and note sheets were written by pencil like pointed bambook stricks. It was a very common among the villages and even in urban areas of Nepal and people wrote through the bamboo pen. The paper was not available, and the imported or indigenious paper could be seen in the palaces of the Ranas and highest dignataries of the kingdom. A few people could afford to possess a new and indigenous type of paper, called *Pahadi Kagaj*. This *Pahadi Kagaj* was used by all the well-to-do people as well as the officers of the government.

Education in Nepal was always related to religious institutions where the religious Texts, like Ramayan, Mahabharat, Krishna-charitra, Kedarkalpa, Jaiminibharat and other Sanskrit books were taught and studied. The slokas of the sacred texts were memorised and recited before the public Even the beginners were asked to follow the preceptors, in this respect education was on the pattern of the traditional institution like Brahman ashram and Gurukul. The institution called Rani Pokhari Sanskrit Pathsala was something like a Gurukul where Sanskrit was the medium of education. There was also a Sanskrit Vidyalaya in Dingla in the eastern side of Nepal, and it was established by Brahmachari Khadananda Adhikari in 1877. It was older than the Rani Pokhari Sanskrit Pathsala. Later. this institution was amalgamated into Khadanan Sanskrit Secondary School, the only of its kind in the eastern hilly part of the kingdom. It was a contemporary of the Motihari Sanskrit Pathsalas situated in the Mahattari district of the Terai.

Matihani Sanskrit Secondary School was only one in the Terai region which provided facilities of free board and lodging to the students. Later this school was converted into a secondary school in whose premises was situated the Sanskrit Mahavidayalaya. Hanuman Nagar Pathsala was also founded during the time of Chandra Shumsher and arrangements for board and lodging had also been made for the students. All the teachers were well-versed in maithili language and the teaching was therefore imported in maithili. Most of students also hailed from Mithila but the Brahmin and others students faced acute difficulties of language taught through the medium of Nepali language.

At the time of Bir Shumsher, Sanskrit Vidhalaya was opened in 1897 in Ridi Bazar of Gulmi district. Likewise, Bharse Sanskrit Vidhalaya was established in 1930. It was conversed into Middle School in 1951 and subsequently into a High School in 1961. Chandra Shumshere also opened a few Bhasa Pathasalas on the outskirts of the capital. Bhasa Pathsalas were also established at Khalanga, Mugu of Jumla District and Rukum and Rolpa districts. In the districts where the population of the Lamas was thick, education was imparted through the Buddhist Gumbas.

In Achham district and the hilly districts, the first Bhasa Pathsala was opened in 1924. The new system of education did not touch or affect the people of these places and so the old pattern was followed. Only Sanskrit Pathsalas and Bhasa Pathsalas were established in the outskirts of the capital. The female education at all these places was practically nil. The first female to pass the S.L.C. Examination from the Karnali Anchal was in the year 1970.

Higher Education-Tri-Chandra College

Higher education in Nepal began with the opening of Tri-Chandra College in 1919. Prior to this there were only two medical graduates and two engineering graduates in Nepal and both of whom had received the degrees from India. The early Ranas were hostile towards diffusing knowledge in the kingdom, but Chandra Shumsher was compelled to open a centre of higher education due to various factors. In the course of coversation with George V while on visit to India in 1912, Chandra Shumsher admitted that one of the result of keeping the Nepali people in ignorance was that there were no revalutionaries like Tilak and Gokhele in Nepal. This made it clear that the Ranas did not like to educate the people for the simple reason liberal like their counterparts in India, they might have to fare waves of resentment against their autocratic rule.

In spite of their determined opposition to popular education, forces operating in and outside the country compelled the Ranas to relax their anti educational policy. During the 1st world war (1914-18) the British Governor-general of India declared that recruits for the British Indian Army should hence at least some knowledge of reading and writing. This declaration compelled Chandra Shumsher to make provision for the education of those people who were likely to join the British Indian Army. The policy of Chandra was to appease the British in India. One of his ways to please the British government was to send Gorkhas soldiers to the British army. As a result, a few schools came into existence, especially in the hilly regions. He also established Tri-Chandra College.

During the war of 1914 and after many European most of foreigners visiting India preferred to visit Nepal also. Thus Chandra Shumsher "was put to a difficult position as to how the inward degrevation and exploitation be covered and veiled." Consequent by, he made a show of reforms in the social, economic and educational life of the people. Chandra Shumsher, after inaugurating the Tri-Chandra College which was Nepal's first modern college was reported to have said: "This is the beginning of our end". His motive behind the establishment of the college was to make the Nepali students aware of the Indian National Movement, which among other things dewanted the establishment of complete freedom for the Indians.

The establishment of a college at Kathmandu was consequently hailed with great delight by those who were eager for higher studies. The college was named Tribhuvan Chandra College. The college was orginally started as a second grade arts college providing two years course of studies with the provision for the teaching of six subjects. The subjects comprised Mathematics, Logic, History and three other languages. The first principal of the college was Batu Krishna Maitra, M.A. B.L. The college was originally affiliated to the university of Calcutta but after the opening of Patna University it was attached to Patna University for the purposes of examination and degrees. After two years of the opening of the college, more teachers were employed in the college to teach different subjects. Among them was Nepal Chandra Benerji, whose initial scale of pay was Rs. 1250/-per annum. Hari Prasan whose intial payscale was Rs. 1610 per annum. Sudhir Kumar Raychaudhari whose initial payscale was Rs. 1610/-per annum. They were all appointed as teachers of Tribhuvan Chandra College in 1920. The results of the College at the University examinations showed nearly hundred per cent success. But education in the college was not free.

> "Occasions for meeting of students among themselves on any matter even educational was taboo. No body dared indulging in any discussion with any class feelow test it might be taken to be a political discussion and everyone suspiciously felt that even walls have ears."

The college was up-graded to the B.A. standard in 1924 and its name was changed to Tri-Chandra College. However, in the matter of education, the Durbar High School and Tri-Chandra College could not provide education to the general masses. Among the general drawbacks, it had been pointed out that the old Ghakari system was still prevalent and under this system the common or even the talented people had to perform Chakari at the court of the Ranas for securing jobs under the autocratic government students also visited tbe Ranas' palace for getting admission into the colleges. Even scholarships were granted by the Ranas to those who performed Chakari at Rana's palace. The education at based on the aristocratic and it was very costly affair. The gates of these government owned schools and college were open to those who could run to the doors of the aristoera tic Ranas and performed Chakari at their palaces.

Tutors

In the institutions based on Gurukul system, the teachers were chiefly Brahmans who taught different subjects. In the 'Ashram of Guru' nearly fifty pupils were admitted and they belonged to different castes excepting the sudras. Vajracharyas and Shakyas (the Newar Buddhis priests) acted as tutors in the bahals (quadrangles) but in the Varnashram system of Hindu education, the tutors were mainly Brahmans, the Newar Brahmans, the Joshis, Archaryas, the Maithili and the Parbatia Brahmans. Such practices continued for a long time and it was only in 1768, when a few Christian missionaries founded schools in Nepal. The moment the Ranas captured power the old system was given up and education became exculsive luxury of the elite. The few wealthy people imported British or Indian Pundits to teach their own children on the pattern of western methods. Jung Bahadur, provided education to his brothers, sons and nephews by appointing a English teacher, Mr. Canning. Similarly the Commander-in-Chief Dhir Shumsher found occasion to give to his children education of high order by appointing highly paid English tutors. Among the Ranas Prime Minister Chandra Shumsher received a good education at the hands of English tutors and about spoken that "Chandra Shumsher not only trained and disciplined the Nepalese military, but he himself was able to writelike an expert of Sword." The Ranas did not send their children to the Durbar High School. The preferred to appoint English teachers for their words who received education in the palaces.

Bir Shumsher had appointed many such teachers to teach his sons in the palace. Such English tutors received a very good salary for the job. Maharaja Chandra Shumsher also did not send his sons to the newly opened schools. He appointed many teachers of different subjects and special arrangements was made for the teacher's board and lodging in the palace. Bhim Shumsher and Padma both did not admit their children to schools. Rather like other Maharajas they gave education to their children under the tutorship of English, Indian and Nepali teachers. Some of the relations of the Ranas' families got their children admitted into the Durbar High Schools, but they had tutors in their own houses where they were taught from morning to evening. Only B and C class Ranas preferred to send their wards to the schools where other Bhardar's children were admitted for education. When king Tribhuvan was aged five years, Guru Hemraj Pandit was appointed to teach him. When the king grew up, he demanded that a lady teacher, preferably English lady, should be appointed for giving western education to the members of the royal family. An English lady was therefore, appointed by the Prime Minister to teach the king as well as other members of the royal family. Later a Bengali tutor was also appointed by king Tribhuvan himself. But when the said teacher gave lessons of political science to the king, he was immediately dismissed by the Prime Minister. The net result was that the people of the kingdom remained completely drinched in poverty and ignorance. But it also must be emphasized that, in the course of is long history, Nepal was never under any colonial rule at any time and was thus able to maintain complete independence. In this respect American writer Rose has written :

> "Jang Bahadur and Chandra Shamsher deserve recognition as two of the great nationalist herors of Nepal. Whether they were acting in the interest of the nation or the Rana family or both, as is most likely is incidental from the broader historical perspective. The fact is that they deviced policies suitable to the period in which they

lived and implemented those policies with considerable sophistication and skill. In the process they made possible the emergence of Nepal as an independent state after the demise of the British Raj in India."

Scholarship

The reign of Bir Shamsher witnessed the establishment of many Sanskrit Pathsalas and Durbar High School at Kathmandu. Subsequently the opening of Bhasa Pathsalas during Dev's reign produced some salutary improvement in the field of education and literature. But no attempt was made to introduce the system of scholarship till the advent f Chandra Shumsher who was a supporter as well as advocator of English or western education. He sent a number of students to foreign countries for receiving technical education. All of them received government scholarship. Six of his own relations were sent to Japan at the expense of the government. Some students were sent to Patna to receive education in the Engineering Goll get they received scholarship of rupees sixty to seventy rupees per month still they completed their education. The students of Overseer were given scholarship of the value of rupees seven hundred twenty per annum to study it Patna. Some students went to Calcutta for Medical education. According the Nizamati of 1987 V.S. (1930), the following students had gone to India for education :

Scholarship on a very modest scale were distributed to the students of schools and Pathsalas o. Nepal. During Chandra Shumsher's reign, two students from each district of Nepal had been sent by the Government to India for the study of Ayurvedic medicines. At that time Jaipur in India was the best centre of Ayurvedic education and since the reign of Jung Bahadur as the Government was interested in the development of Ayurvedic, it granted scholarship to much students who wished to study it in India Chandra Shumsher had himself stated that the Ayurvedic system of medicine should not be neglected and for the proper development of Ayurvedic edu-

Place	Course	Name of students	for year	Scholarship in a year
1	2	3	4	5
Patna	Civil Engineer	Nar Bahadur	4	840/-
Patna	Overseer	Luxman Thapa		720/-
Shivapur	Engineer	Pirja Thapa		666/-
Calcutta	M.B.	Gyan Bahadur	6	840/-
Calcutta	M.B.	Lalit Kumar (Combwell Medical School)		
Calcutta	L.A B.	Bhakta Bahadur Shrestha	4	720/-
Calcutta	L.A.B.	(?) Ananda Shrestha 1984-1988 V.S. (1927-1931)	4	720/-

(*Contd.*)

1	2	3	4	5
Calcutta (Combwell Medical School)	Compounder	Brahma Prasad Upadhaya (1985-1987 B S) (1928-1930).	2	360/-
Calcutta Cambell Medical School	Compounder	Hari Prasad	2	360/-
Calcutta Medical School	M.B.	Shankar Lal Shrestha		440/-
Calcutta Medical School	L.A.B.	Bhawani Bhakta		720/-
Calcutta	B.L.	Hiranya Bahadur Bista		840/-
Calcutta	B.L.	Tilak Shumsher Thapa		840/-
Allahabad	B.L.	Gunjaman		847/-
Darbhanga	L.M.P.	Dwarika Prasad		847/-

Calcutta	B.Com.	Narendra Bahadur Shah	2	840/-
Calcutta	B.A.	Prachanda Man Pradhan	2	840/-
Calcutta	I.A.	Najar Man Pradhan	1	720/-
Calcutta	I.A.	Brahmadev Panta	2½	720/-
Calcutta	I.A.	Prasana Dev Panta	1	727/-
Calcutta	I.A.	Yosana Dev Panta		247/-

cation he sent students to India to receive specialised training in it. His plan was to send such trained people to the interior of the hilly and terai regions so they could serve the oiling humanity Kaiser Jung Thapa, after completing his studies at Calcutta Medical College, received a special training in Ayurvedic at Dehradun and he was made in charge of it. The Engineering Department was also placed under the charge of a chief Engineer. A Bangalee, who build Bir's palatial Durbar after the model of the Government House at Calcutta. But later on several Nepalese came out successful in the Engineering Examinations of the Universities of Patna, Poona and Roorkee and they were subsequently made in charge of the Engineering Department of the Government. A contemporary writer, Suresh Chandra Das Gupta, observed :

> "Five Nepalese students have passed the M.A. Examination of Calcutta University in various branches including English, Economics, History, Sanskrit etc. and three others have passed the M.B. Examination from the Calcutta Medical College in the regular course and several qualified themselves as Engineers from Roorkee and Sibpur. There are numerious students today in various parts of India studying law, science, electricity, painting and special Military Training etc. at Govt. expense. Six students, sent by His highness the Present Maharaj returned from Japan after completing their studies in Engineering, Mining, Agriculture, Explosiveness and Ammunitions and began the work in their respective departments."

This tradition continued till the other day.

Mass Education

During the Rana Regime, mass educations was almost unknown in Nepal. However, a certain section of the population, by virtue of their birth or their status in the society, has monopolised the education they could get. There were a few Sanskrit Primary Schools but the curriculum was designed to train in the arts of priesthood. Thus the common people were barred even from the Sanskrit education because the priesthood was the monopoly of the Brahmin class only. Other people were deprived of the opportunity of practicing priesthood, because their vocational was chiefly attached to the Brahman caste only. The non secular base of this Sanskrit education became the reason to exclude them ass of the people from the opportunity of education.

Soldiers were the first common people to get mass education in the country. They were also the first source of public contact with the outside world. Indirectly there soldiers were instrumental in compelling the masses to know about the political, social, economic and educational development of the country. Another unpelling factor was the initiative of the Terai dwellers who brought teacher from India and quietly started giving education to their children at their homes. Most of the participants were the people of the kayastha caste. In many cases families co-operated but the teachers also went from home to home on each sturday to cellect pupils and materials for the schools. These schools, played a prominent role in educating the people of the Terai. The isolationism imposed on Nepal by the Ranarchy for nearly a century before 1951, had kept the people unaware of events of the modern world and un-prepared to take a place in international field. After the end of Rana rule, a change was brought in every aspects of Nepal's life. In politics, a great number of patterns of behaviour had continued into the post revolutionary period, but it was in this aspect of the culture that the break through to a modern outlook first occured. It is more accurate to quote that :

> "Prior to 1951, it was in the area of government that the culture did not satisfy the Nepalese under classes, so that the change was forced by their unrest. And once begun, development could not be limited to Govt. economics become immediately involved in the overthrew of the wealthy eligarchy, then education was introduced as a tool for change and Pandona's box was wide open,"

Department of Education

Prime Minister Ranoddip Singh, who shifted Durbar School from his palace to the present site, appointed the Commander-in-Chief, Dhir Shumsher, to look after the educational institutions of the kingdom and this was the beginning of the Department of Education. At this time, this school was opened only not for the Sat Bhai and Satra Bhai of Rana family but for the others too-like the children of Bhardars, Guru purohit and the children of other wealthy families. The Director of education was first general in the Rana's army. After the Dictatorship of Dhir Shumsher, Kedar nar Singh became the second Director but he did nothing significant to merit any recognition. When Deva was the Prime Minister. Chandra Shumsher was the third Director of Education who faced a lot of difficulties in implementing his reluctant policy. During his period Deva had established a network of primary and language schools through out the country. He was convinced that a suitable educational system was the primary need of the kingdom. But Chandra Shumsher as a Director of Education felt that the diffusion of knowledge and literacy would ultimately lead to the decline of the rule of the Ranas. For various other reasons also he dethroned Deva and became the Prime Minister of the kingdom. He wanted to demolist the educational institutions set up by Deva and so he appointed an inefficient Rana, Bahadur Shah, as Director of Education, who, according to the expectation of Chandra Shumsher, remained least interested in education. He had neither the capacity nor ability to manage the department of education. However, in spite of his disinclination, Chandra Shumsher did not close the schools opened by Deva. He tolerated them so long as they retained the school in his name. Above all, the religious minded people also made a strong plean for the establishment of Sanskrit Schools. As a result, quite a few pathasalas were established in the different parts of the country. A separate directorate of Sanskrit Education was established with Pandit Hemraj as the first director General Mrigendra Shumsher became the subsequent director of education. These directors remained in office as long as the Rana Prime Minister remained pleased with their work. During the period of Chandra Shumsher, there were 150 Pathsalas, one English High Schools and one English College (Tri-Chandra College).

Statistics of Schools

In those days there was no custom of taking population census and so statistics about individual profiles were lacking. Therefore, it was difficult to trace the age and address of the people who were educated or uneducated as well as to tabulate the numbers of schools, Teachers and students.

By 1950 (2007 V.S.), when the Rana oligarchy was overthrown, there were two colleges (one college), 22 High Schools, 203 middle schools and 265 primary schools. Another source says that in 1950-51 A.D. there were only 310 primary schools with 8,551 students, 11 Secondary Schools with 1650 students and two Colleges (one Sanskrit and one Trichandra College) with 250 students. However, Trailoky Nath Uprety given a statistic of schools existing at end of 1950 A.D. as followed :

"There were 310 primary and middle schools, 11 high schools, 40 religious schools, 2 technical schools, 1 teacher training centre, a few centres of adult education, and two colleges. There were 265 primary schools and the number of students was 7950 and there was one civil medical school. Jeremg Bernstein wrote that by 1951 there were 310 primary and middle schools, two colleges, one normal school and one special technical school was estimated by Reeds that in 1950 the total number of college graduates through out the entire kingdom of Nepal was less than 300. A very small number of people had studied in a few private secular schools in Nepal or in Indian schools and colleges. One of the most remarkable figure in Nepalese education who Father Nrshall Moran whose Jeruit school of Patna was crowded by several Nepalese including members of Rana family. In the reign of king Tribhuvan, he founded a private elementary school which was situated outside capital."

Library

Some of the Ranas were generally interested in the collection of valuable and rare books in their palaces. For example, the Prime Minister Bir Shumsher was very found of books and he established a big library called the Bir Library or the Durbar Library, which was the first modern Library in Nepal. His successors made many additions of books in it. Another library named Pustak Chitai Tahabil was established in 1869 V.S. (1812) during the reign of Gribhan Yuddha. Since then the work of organising and managing the Libraries had been in progress but all of them lacked proper condition and preservation of old and new books. They had not been based on the western system of Library service. However, as a matter of policy the Ranas disliked the diffusion of knowledge either among the ruling family or the common people. They did not loke the contact of the king or the people with the books and so the libraries were kept quite at a distance. After the establishment of Durbar High School, the books of the Narayanhiti Durbar and Thapathali Durbar were shifted to the upper portion of the Durbar High School.

It was not a surprising matter that those books were lost and damage due to the lack of proper maintenance and preservation. The Prime Minister, Bir Shumsher had constructed a new building for the Library and immediately the books were transferred from the Durbar High School to the new building Kamal Prakash Malla had observed :

"In Nepal a losting monument to their (Brahmin) scholarly accomplishment is great library of 24,000 manuscripts, originally collected in 1885 by Maharaja

Bir Shumsher J.B. Rana. The library is a monument, not only to the achievement of traditional Nepalese-scholarship, but also to the limitations of the tradition."

P. Nildev Panta, who had been venerated as Guru even by the great scholars of Kashi, was entrusted with the responsibility of managing the new liberary. But the Rana rulers subsequently showed disinterestedness towards the progress of the library.

Another great scholar, Hara Prasad Shastri had begun the compilation of ancient manuscripts and book of Nepal during the reign of Bir Shumsher and the process of compilation of such book including the ancient Indian books was continued under the patronage of the Asiatic Society of Calcutta. The Durbar Library had become the centre of many intellectual activity and consequently the new building situated near the Ghanta Ghar, built by Maharaja Bir Shumsher was visited by great many scholars of Nepal and India. The new Library was also known as Sarkari Pustakkhana Subsequently Hara Prasad Shastri made valuable contributions by publishing a catalogue of books preserved in this library. The rare books and manuscripts were divided by him into many parts according to chronology. Later, Henry Pandit published the collections under three categories and those publications received praise from the scholars of Nepal and abroad. Though Henry was a supporter of the Rana rulers, still his work in the library had merited credit and praise from all shades of people. Soon many foreign scholars visited the library and among them a French Scholar, Levi prepared the list of Tibete-Chinese books with the help of Hemraj and Siddhi Harsha Vajracharya.

After the death of Chandra Shumsher in 1929, the Prime Minister Bhim Shumsher made many additions including his rare Tantrick books to the library. The library was converted into Nepal National Archives. Indicating Bir Library, Shukraraj Shastri had written that if anybody wanted to read books of his own choice, he had to obtain precious permission of the authorities. That task itself was so irritating a job that the casual reader preferred to remain outside the gate of the building admiring the architectural beauty of the structure of the building itself. No one looked after the maintenance of the books which remained locked and untouched for years in the almirah. Hardly any one was benefitted by the books of the library. Supporting to the observation of Shastri, Dr. Regmi added there are no libraries for the public, no reading rooms, though each Rana maintains a grand collection of books merely for purpose of exhibits to be shown to some distinguished visitors from Europe and India. There are no newspapers worth the name the whole kingdom has only one paper. But this also stands very much below when compared to the worst paper in India, The library is a closed institution.

Some papers from India allowed entry into the library but the reading of Newspaper was looked upon with disfavour. In fact many people had been punished for reading Indian newspapers. Baburam Pandit paid a fine of Rs. 30/- (1930) for reading a Hindi News weakly in a shop. During the reign of Chandra Shumsher, Kuwalraj was Bada Guruju from 1952 V S. to 1970 V.S. (1895-1913). Chandra Shumsher did not like him as he was well versed in English when he entered the Chakari of Chandra Shumsher. he used to read the English books kept in the racks of the palace. It was Chandra's habit to underline interesting portions of book in red and Kuwalraj by remaining in the service of the Prime Minister had occasions to read those books Kuwalraj was once charged for reading the books of Chandra Shumsher and the situation became so intolerable that Kuwalraj was compelled to leave Nepal for good. He spent the rest of life in Bombay.

It would be interesting to note that the Kesar Library was established by Kesar Shumsher, a son of Prime Minister, Chandra Shumsher, who was in the habit of collecting books on various subjects, a number of foreign newspapers were added by him to this library. Particularly, he devoted his time in adding more and more English books to this library. After his death, his wife, Rani Krishna Chandra handed it over to the Nepal Government in 1969 and the liberary was Christened as Keser Library to perpetuate his memory. Another library was established by the Raj Guru Hamraj Sharma who as a past of hobby collected numerous books on different subjects. In organising this library he received active help from scholars like Motiram Bhatta and Rahul Sanskrityan who regarded the Rajguru as a 'Dictionary of Nepal.' This Library was named Bharati Bhawan and subsequently it was converted into a National Library in 1955. It was bought by the Nepal Government at the cost of three lakhs rupees. The materials were located in a few small rooms of the secretariat Building. At the beginning the library was open to the few intellectuals close to the Ranas, but in 1962 it was opened to all the people outside the valley, Pandit Pustakalaya was the only institution which was owned by the family of Parajuli Pandits of Pokhera in Kaski district since the time of the king Bichitre Birya of Kaski.

10

Conclusion

The study of the social history has revealed the chara-cteristics one is very much tradition bound and the other being uniformity in diversity is since the days long. We keenly observed that Nepal has many groups of peoples of various culture and religious feelings. All these communities assembled together to form the Nepalese society. It can not be mentioned that any group is superior to other group. Each group has its own identity when we observe it keenly. But the attempt to bring uniformity in the society has contributed a lot to bring social harmony and unity. Age long attempt in this respect has brought about positive impact in the society in which the various rulers had very tactfully blended the different cultural groups into one strong and uniform Nepalese society. Contributions of the far-sighted rulers like Jayasthiti Malla and Prithvi Narayan Shah in blending the Nepalese society in one unified society must be taken into consideration. Attempts of many of other rulers to bring about unity and consolidation in the society cannot be ignored. Hence various types of rules and regulations befitting to various groups were also made; but priority to bring unity was the main objective of the various rules. To cite an example we had many beafea ting communities but due to the implementation of the law pro hibiting the cow-slaughter and discouragement and looking down upon the beef-eaters gradually brought an end to cowslaughter

We have also observed that the traditional Hindu system had taken so much deep root in the Nepalese society that those very non-Hindu autochthonous communities later on, took pride in calling themselves Hindus. Nepal, having Hindu rulers since long, became a staunch Hindu kingdom. The Hinduism flourished undisturbed in Nepal for centuries. Hinduisation was so much encouraged that as already mentioned many of the non-Hindu communities later on took Brahminism as their religion and Brahmins became the priests of such communities. Hinduism has contributed in keeping the society intact, well disciplined and united in one hand while on the other hand it is responsible to a large extent to keep the society constant and at a standstill. As the laws and social rules and regulations were very much based on the Hindu traditional Shastras which had prescribed very strict rules and regulations, the Nepalese society was well organised, disciplined and unified. Every member of the society had to abide by the rules and regulations prescribed by the law according to has social status. In that way Hinduism has contributed much in keeping the Nepalese society intact.

On the other hand the religious feeling was so much deep rooted that on change could take place in the society which was indire need. There was a standstill and a hell in the society. Stability in the Nepalese civilization is the most fascinating of its qualitys to the European historians whose working life is spent in dealing with revolution, social conflict, nationalist warfases and cultural changes and at times destruction. No doubt many scholars, artists and literate exercised much influence and power not only in the society but also in the Nepalese government. One of the reasons of the stability in the Nepalese society was the domination of the religion in every walk of life. Although there had been so many scholars and artists in Nepal, the Nepalese society did not have any dynamism. We have seen the introduction of the western education in Nepal from the 19th century, yet no expected change could take place in the society. Such thing we find in the Chinese society also. To cite an example, printing was first invented in China in the Tang period many centuries before Europe witnessed the invention of printing press, but its influence on Chinese society was far, far less than might have been expected. Once printing was established in the west in created conditions for a possible cultural explosion. Thus once a person had mastered the elements of reading, he could attack with confidence almost every branch of knowledge he had read. Thus printing in the west not only intensified the possibilities of ideological clashes between contending social groups, but also encouraged upward social stability; self-taught man, was the common phenomenon in the west. Printing in the west led to the renaissance, reformation and revolution. But in Nepul inspite of presence of many men of betters no change could take place, as the whole system was bent arrogantly to maintain status-que in the society. No body could think of challange but only a modest attempt to bring about any change was considered as a sin, vice and crime. It was taken even as a sedition, for example the case of Sukra Raj Shastra. The then vested interest group was very much determined to maintain the status quo most fealously. They had taken much benefit out of that. Society thus became static, dull and traditional. Inspite of many revolutionary changes in British India, Nepalese society stood still due the interest of the rulers and their supporters.

In the stable Nepalese society we have seen that the people were so much suppressed in every walk of life; for example, in the social structure, position of women, dress and ornaments, sorial entertainments, construction of the buildings and habitational sites, food and drink, family system etc.

Social structure of the Nepalese society was based on the Hindu Dharmashastra *i.e.* Brahman, Kshetriya, Vaisya and Sudra; Brahmans occupying the apex position and Sudras the lowest. No change in the system could ever be expected in the Nepalese society. The rulers had supported the system so much that all the rules and regulations were framed to safeguard the system called *Aryamaryada* right from the ancient time. At times the social structure was amended; that too was aimed at the interest of the vested interest group. That very group of the people which was once considered lower grade was elevated in the social strata. Such thing also depended either upon the political system of the country or the persons in power. The Mallas in the prime of their power claimed themselves as the Rajputs behaving the people as inferior. Once they were defeated they were reduced to the Newar community. Similarly the Kunwars who were considered just as the Kshetriyas later on became the Ranas and thus Rajputs. Any group of persons was elevated or degraded at the will of the ruling family; in that way there was much flexibility in the society. But in totality the social structure of Nepal was retained static on the principle of the Hindu Shastras, which were interpreted to suit the will of the ruling family by the Rajguru, Rajpurohit and others who were dependents to the rulers.

Position of women was in way better throughout the ages. As we have already seen the wish of a female of the Lichchhavi period that let her not have a rebirth as a female denotes the miserable condition of the female in the patriarchal Nepalese society. The subordinate position of the female was so much deeply rooted as a system that even when the females played a very active role in the political scene of Nepal, they could take on step to uplift their position. It was considered that the females were born to be dominated by male whether as a father, a husband or a son. Females were treated as the tools for the sexual entertainment of the males. The males could have as many wives as they wished whereas a female, on the mere suspicion of having any sort of relation with a male other than the husband was most inhumanly treated. Lucky were those females of some of communities where divorce was permitted or those females belonging to the community where polyandry was in vogue. Ours in such a society in which the widower was bethrothed before the tears dried up in the eyes of children of the deceased female, whereas on the otherhand the females were compelled to observe *Sati* or passed the most miserable widow-hood, ignored by everyone. They very religious prescriptions regarding the females were most inconsistant and self-contradictory. In one hand it is expected that the god would be pleased where the females were well treated, on the other hand females should also remain quite do cite to the husband Any sort of weakness in the female's character was never pardoned. Under such circumstance the females became just a means of sexual injoyment and child-bearing machine in the Nepalese society.

Regarding the dress and ornaments also the religious prescription was the main guide line as to which dress and ornaments interpreters of the Holy texts, gave the permission as which dress and ornaments the people could use right from the Lichchhavi period. The people, however rich they were, should not use gold ornaments on their legs. Common people of lower social strate had to be satisfied with the silver ornaments. Rama Shah had further unphasised that the golden anklets could be used by the people other than the royal family members only after getting the permission. Similarly Jayasthiti Malla's regulation mentioned that the Sudras could wear on only the sleeveless dress and no cap should be used. Such rules with some modifications were rigorously implemented inspite of many political changes. Any sort of change and innovation in such aspects were meant for the persons in power. Any attempt to bring about any change in such thing by the common mass was liable to be punished. The privileged group of persons kept jealous eyes on these things to safeguard their special priviliges. The changes that we have witnessed in the pages of history were brought about by the big shots not by the common mass howsoever elite they were.

Similarly the style, architecture, size and type of the houses also made the status of the house-owner clear. The location of the houses also denotes the social status of the house-owner. Moreover the altitude and interest of the ruling family and the well-off persons were mach responsible for the design and decoration of a house. Up to the rise of the Ranas the palaces and other houses were constructed in the traditional way, as its result many skilled persons like wood-workers, stone-workers and others got employment. The traditional skill got the patronage. But later on the Ranas in copy of the western style started constructing palatial buildings furnished with western artistic goods. The policy of the Ranas not only affected the traditional age long heritage but also the economic life of the people. The highly skilled manpower of the country *i.e.* wealth of nation were reduced to pauper and had to remain without any job.

Food and drink also underwent a major change among the affluent group of the society. The food culture, a major measuring rod of the richness of the culture of a community was also much affected. Those who drank the foreign liquor were considered the high shot and those consumers of local beverage were look down upon. To think of the food culture the Newars of the Kathmandu Valley had maintained their heritage with all their might.

Education, which was considered and cherished as the means to enlighten the people, was also taken as a measuring rod for employment. During the Rana period neither the traditional education could flourish nor whole hearted support was given to the western education. The highly educated persons were much suspected. Teachers and students reading political science and history were watched. One thing we must keep in mind is that how did the Ranaism and western education went side by side. Ranaism stood for family autocracy; and it flourished in a stagnant society; whereas the western education aimed at producing the enlightened mass with the liberal altitude. But the closure contact with the British compelled the Ranas to introduce the western education in an institutionalised way. The farsighted Ranas had realised that with the growth of western education in Nepal they would have to face their fall. So they were not much enthusiastic for the fast growth of it. Only a limited group of persons were given an opportunity to have the western education. Although the educated youths, belonging to the family of their own docile employees, were given scholarship to have further studies in India, the Ranas left no stone unturned to have watchful eyes on the activities of those persons. Espionage was employed. Western education was not a welcome introduction but a compulsion in Nepal.

We have observed that Hinduism has played a dominate role in shaping and smooth running of the social life in Nepal through ages. But the Hinduism was also adjusted in a befitting in Nepal. Many aboriginal communities were also adjusted into its fold its result many modifications were made. Apparently we have Hindus who eat buffalo-meat also in one hand and others abhor it. Similarly we do not discriminate. On the basis of religion. The main concern among the Nepalese was one should be religious minded.

We have also observed the gradual change in the society through ages, but the speed of change was so slow and negligible that one is bound to say that the Nepalese society in totality hardly underwent any change. Some changes found in the urban area *i.e.* Kathmandu which constituted a negligible percentage of the entire population cannot be taken as a change in the society. The vast people remained as ignorant, uneducated, tradition bound ete. as was wished by the vested interest group *i.e.* the rulers. Stagnancy in society meant the perpetuity of their exploitation and rule. In the name of religion and maintenance of law and order, no change was aspired. Nepalese society remained still up to the down of democracy.

Selected Bibliography

UNPUBLISHED SOURCES

Documents and Papers at

National Archives of India New Delhi

Kausi Tosa Khana, Kathmandu

Lagat Phant, Kathmandu

Ministry of Foreign Affairs, Kathmandu

National Archives of Nepal, Kathmandu.

Interviews

Prof. Madhav Raj Pande, Kirtipur Campus

Sri Dhana Bajra Vajracharya, Research Centre for Nepal and Asian Studies

Sri Guna Dov Bhattarai, Tri Chandra Campus

Sri Govind Prashad Gorkhali, Central Office (T.U.)

Late Sri Gopal Dass Vaidya, Kausi Tosa Khana.

Sri Netra Bahadur Basnyat, Ex-Registrar, T.V.

Theses and Dissertations

Joshi, Shankar Lall "Amsuvarma and His Times," Tribhuvan University.

Pande, Madhav Raj "Historical Study of Nepali Society and Culture" Jabalpur University.

Rijal, Ghana Shyam "History of Education in Nepal 1850-1950," Tribhuvan University.

Shrestha, Bimala "Social Life in Nepal : Continuity and Change" Patna University.

Vaidya, Tulasi Ram "Prithvi Narayan Shah and His Times," Allahabad University. (Recently published is book form)

PUBLISHED SOURCES

Books

(South Asian Languages : Nepali unless otherwise mentioned)

Dixit, Kamal (ed.), *Buigal*, Lalitpur : Jagadamba Prakashan, 2018 B.S. *Kalo Akshyar*, Kathmandu : Sajha Prakashan, 2036 B.S.

Joshi, Hari Ram *Nepal Ko Prachin Abhilekh*, Kathmandu : Royal Nepal Academy, 2031 B.S.

Khanal, Mohan *Prithvi Patra Sangraha*, Lalitpur : Bhola Nath Poudel, 2028 B.S.

Manandhar, Thakur Lall *Pulangu Me*, Kathmandu : the Author, n.d. (Newari).

Nath, Narahari *Gorkhaliharu Ko Sainik Itihas*, Kathmandu : Annapurna Press, 1954.

Nath, Narahari *Gorkha Vamsavali*, Varanasi : Arya Bir Sangh, 2013 B.S.

Nath, Narahari *Itihas Prakash Ma Sandhi Patra Sangraha*, Kathmandu : Dang Spiritual Conference, 2022 B.S.

Nath, Narahari and Babu Ram Acharya *Sri Panch Bada Maharaja Prithvi Narayan Shah Ko Dibya Upadesh*, Kathmandu : Sri Bagiswor Press, 1953.

Nepali, Chittaranjan *General Bhimsen Thpa Ra Tatkilin Nepal*, Kathmandu : Jore Ganesh Press, 2014 B.S.

Nepali, Chittaranjan *Shree Panch Rana Bahadur Shah*, Kathmandu : Shree Mati Mary Rajbhandari, 2020 B.S.

Pandey, Beni Bilash *Prasastri Ratnavali*, Translated by Naya Nath Poudel, Kathmandu : Department of Archaeology, 2022 B.S.

Pant, Naya Raj and others, *Shree Panch Prithvi Narayan Shah Ko Upadesh*, Lalitpur : Jagadamba Prakashan, n.d.

Pokharel. Bal Krishna *Pancha Saya Barsa*, Kathmandu : Sajha Prakashan, 2031 B.S.

Pradhan, Pratap Chandra *Ek Vyakti Anek Abhivyakti*, Kathmandu : Kumardhar Sharma 'Jnani', 2041 B.S.

Rajvamsi Shankar Man *Bhaktapur Silalek Suchi*, Kathmandu : Department of Archaeology, 2027 B.S.

Rajvamshi, Shankar Man *Kantipur Silalekh Suchi*, Kathmandu Department of Archaeology, 2027 B.S.

Rana, Hemanta and Dhana Bajra Vajracharya, *Tistung Chitlang Bhek Ko Aitihasik Samagri*, Kathmandu : Institute of Nepal and Asian Studies, 2029 B.S.

Regmi, Jagadish *Lichhavi Sanskriti*, Kathmandu : Ratna Pustak Bhandar, 2026 B.S.

Sakya Hem Raj and Tulasi Ram Vaidya *Medieval Nepal*, Kathmandu : T.R. Vaidya, 1970.

Shama, Balkrishna *Mero Kavita Ko Aradhana*, Kathmandu : Sajha Prakashana, 2029 B.S.

Sharma, Kunu *Kirtipatakha*, Translated by Narahari Nath, Kathmandu : Jagadamba Prakashan, 2018 B.S.

Tewari, Ramji and others *Abhilekh Sangraha*, Vols. I-XII, Kathmandu : Samsodhan Mandal, 2017-2020 B.S.

Tewari, Ramji and others *Aitihasik Patra Sangraha*, Part II, Kathmandu : Nepal Samskritik Parishad, 2021 B.S.

Tuladhar, S. *Malla Shah Kaalaya Me*, Kathmandu : Man Dass Sugat Dass 2013 B.S. (Newari).

Vaidya, Tulasi Ram *Prithvi Narayan Shah Ranjit Malla Kalik Kagaj Patra*, Kathmandu : Nepal Adhyan Sansthan, 2028 B.S.

Vaidya, Tulasi Ram and Dhana Bajra Vajracharya *Gorkha Ko Aitihasik Samagri*, Kathmandu : Nepal Adhyan Sansthan, 2029 B.S.

Vajracharya, Dhana Bajra and Gyan Mani Nepal *Aitihasik Patra Sangraha*, Part I, Kathmandu : Nepal Samskritik Parishad, 2014 B.S.

Vajracharya, Dhana Bajra *Lichhavi Kalaka Abhilekh*, Kathmandu : INAS, 2030 B.S.

Vajracharya, Dhana Bajra *Itihas Samsodhan Ko Praman Prameya*, Lalitpur : Jagadamba Prakashan, 2019 B.S.

Vajracharya, Dhana Bajra *Panchali Sashan Vyavastha*, Kathmandu : Nepal Ka Aishiyali Anusandhan Kendra, 2035 B.S.

Vajracharya, Dhana Bajra (ed.) *Tri Ratna Saundarya Gatha*, Kathmandu : Nepal Samskritik Parishad, 2019 B.S.

Vajracharya, Dhana Bajra and Gyan Mani Nepal *Jaya Ratnakar Natak*, Kathmandu : Nepal Samskritik Parishad, 2014 B.S.

Vajracharya, Dhana Bajra and Tek Bahadur Shrestha *Shah Kalka Abhilekh*, Kathmandu : CNAS, 2036 B.S.

Vidyalankar, Satyaketu *Prachin Bharat Ka Itihas*, Moussauri, Sarswati Sadan, 1960 A.D.

Books

(Western Language : English unless otherwise mentioned)

Anderson, Mary *The Festivals of Nepal*, Calcutta : Rupa and Co., 1977.

Beal, Samuel *Travels of Hiouen Thsang*, Vol. III, Calcutta : Susil Gupta, 1958.

Dawson, Raymond *Imperial China*, England : Penguin Books, 1972.

Dutta, K.K. *Studies in the History of Bengal Subah*, 1740-70, Vol. I, Calcutta : University of Calcutta, 1936.

Fillipo De Fillippi (ed.) *An Account of Tibet : The Travels of Ippoli Desideri of Pistoia S.J.*, 1712-27, London : George Routledge and Sons Ltd., 1932.

Habib, Irfan *The Agrarian System of Mughal India*, Bombay Asia Publishing House, 1963.

Hamilton, Francis *An Account of the Kingdom of Nepal*, Edinburg : Constable, 1819

Hasrat, B.J. *History of Nepal* Hosiarpur : V.V. Research Institute Book Agency, 1970.

Hodgson, B.H. *Essays on the Language, Literature, and Religion of Nepal and Tibet*, London : Trubner, 1874.

Hooker, J.D.*Himalyan Journal*, London : Ward and Lock Co., 1905.

Jha, Hit Narayan *The Lichchhavis*, Varanasi : Chaukhamba Sanskrit Series Office, 1170.

Kirkpatrick, William *An Account of the Kingdom of Nepaul*, London : W. Miller. 1811.

Landon, Perceval *Nepal*, Vols. London : Constable, 1928.

Levi, Sylvain *Le Nepal*, 3 Vols, Paris : Annals du Musee Guimet tome, 1905-6. (French).

Luniya, B.N. *Evolution of Indian Culture*, Agra : Laxmi Narayan Agrawal, 1986.

Nepali, Gopal Singh *The Newars*, Bombay : United Asia Publications, 1965.

Northey, W. Brook and C.J. Morries, *The Gurkhas*, Delhi : Cosmo Publications (Reprint), 1974.

Oldfield H.A. *Sketches from Nepal*, 2 Vols. Delhi : Cosmo Publications (Reprint), 1974.

Petech, Luciano *Medieaval History of Nepal*, 750-1480, Rome : INESO, 1958.

Petech, Luciano *I Missionari Italiani Tibet E Nel Nepal*. Vol. II, Parts 1-7, La Liberia Dello Stato, Rome, 1953 (Italian).

Rana, Padma Jang *Life of Maharaja Sir Jang Bahadur of Nepal*, Allahabad : Pioneer Press; 1909. Kathmandu : Ratna Pustak Bhandar, 1980 A.D. (Reprint)

Rana, Pramode Shamsher *Rana Nepal : An Insider's View*, Kathmandu : Mrs. R. Rana, 1978.

Regmi, Dilli Raman *Medieval Nepal*, Vols, I-IV, Calcutta : K.L. Mukopadhyaya, 1965-66.

Regmi, Dili Raman *Modern Nepal*, Calcutta : K.L. Mukhopadhyaya, 1961.

Regmi, M.C. *Land Tenure and Taxation in Nepal*, 4 Vols, Berkeley : University of California, 1963-68.

Regmi, M.C. *A Study in Nepali Economic History*, New Delhi : Manjusri Publishing House, 1978.

Regmi, M.C. *The State and Economic Surplus*, Varanasi : Nath Publishing House, 1984.

Regmi, M.C. *Thatched Huts and Stucco Palaces*, New Delhi : Vikas Publishing House Pvt. Ltd., 1979.

Tod, J. *Annals and Antiquities of Rajasthan*, London : 1914.

Tuker, Francis, *Gorkha*, London : Constable, 1957.

Vaidya, Tulasi Ram and Tri Ratna Manandhar *Crime and Punishment in Nepal*, Kathmandu : Bini and Purna; 1985.

Vajracharya, Dhana Bajra and Kamal P. Malla *The Gopal Rajvamsavali*, Franz Steiner Verlag Wiesbaden GMBH, 1985.

Wright, Daniel *History of Nepal*, Calcutta : Susil Gupta Ltd. (Second Edition), 1958.

Journals and Periodicals

Ancient Nepal, Department of Archaeology. (English/Nepali)

Nepal Economist, Devi Chandra Shrestha. (English/Nepali)

Nepalese Culture, NEHCA Instruction Commtttee (T.U.). (English/Nepali)

Nepali, Madan Puraskar Guthi. (Nepali)

Prajya, Royal Nepal Academy. (Nepali)

Purnima, Samsodhan Mandal. (Nepali)

Rolamba, Joshi Research Institute. (English/Nepali)

Voice of History, History Instruction Committee (now Central Department of History), T.U. (English/Nepali).

